Fenton Glass
The Second Twenty-Five Years

by william heacock

Historical Data by
Dr. Eugene C. Murdock
Professor of History, Marietta College

Dedication

To Frank & Elizabeth Fenton

© Copyright 1995
The Glass Press, Inc.
dba Antique Publications
Post Office Box 553 • Marietta, Ohio 45750-0553

ALL RIGHTS RESERVED

PB ISBN #0-915410-29-X

HB ISBN #0-915410-30-3

TABLE OF CONTENTS

I	TITLE PAGE, DEDICATION, FOREWORD, ETC.	Pages 1-6
II	HISTORY OF FENTON ART GLASS COMPANY (1931-1955)	Pages 7-24
III	FENTON GLASS IN COLOR	Pages 25-80
IV	FENTON GLASS CATALOGUE REPRINTS	Pages 81-135
V	MISCELLANEOUS FENTON GLASS	Pages 136-144
VI	CONCLUSION OF FENTON HISTORY	Pages 145-150
VII	INDEX	Pages 151-152

INTRODUCTION

This second volume covers the production of the Fenton Art Glass Company during their second quarter-century. My earlier book on the subject covered Fenton glass made from 1907 to 1932. Actually the Fenton brothers first went into business for themselves as glass decorators in 1905. Thus we will be offering here an overlap of the years 1930 to 1932, making it possible to present in this second volume a number of transitional pieces made around 1930, with production continued into the later years. The decision was also made to limit the time frame on this book to 1955, which the company considers to be its Golden Anniversary.

Many hours of research and work went into this book. The records available on the second 25 years were considerably more complete than the first. I had a wealth of catalogues, early ads and inventory records at my disposal, much of which is shared with you here. Unfortunately, we couldn't include everything. I had to be selective with the catalogue reprints. The glass we photographed was only a representation of many other shapes and colors available. We are trying to represent a production span of a full quarter-century within the pages of this book, which is no simple task.

As much care as possible has been taken to provide accurate dates of production on each of the items illustrated. The catalogues after 1938 were dated, but the earlier catalogues and salesmen's brochures had to be dated from existing inventory records from their respective period. However, every reader should bear in mind two simple facts when considering the dates offered by this reference. Many items appeared in the line for several years. The dates we generally offer are when the lines first appeared in the inventory. In the case of an especially long production life, special notation has been made. Remember, the dates provided are for the exact item illustrated. Another color or a different shape in the same pattern may have been produced at a different time.

I have made no attempt to list all colors made in each of the Fenton lines, since this has proven to be virtually impossible when researching hand-made glassware. Rare and unlisted colors are always surfacing, which would make any list of colors susceptible to many misleading omissions.

The measurements provided with each color illustration were taken at the time of photography and may differ slightly from the measurements listed on the catalogue pages. A vase can measure 10½" actual size, but the catalogue will refer to the same vase as an 11" vase. Again, we are talking about handmade glassware and size will vary occasionally.

It is much too soon to consider such a venture at this time, but with the rapidly increasing popularity of Fenton glass, new and old, a volume featuring their third quarter-century (1955-1980) could someday become a reality. Until that day, the true testament of the quality of recent Fenton products is that the collectible value has increased in such a short period of time. I consider it an honor to have been involved in these two volumes, and to have had my name associated with the proud Fenton name.

ACKNOWLEDGEMENTS

The vast majority of the glass pictured in this book came from the collection of the Fenton Art Glass Museum, Williamstown, W. Va. However, several members of the Fenton family brought in items from their personal collections to fill in some of the voids. I am naturally grateful to all of them for their efforts.

My thanks also must be extended to the Welker family for sharing many unusual pieces from their collection, and to Frank Wallenhaupt for mailing a number of rarities to me at the last minute. Other collectors who shared items from their collection include Pat and Sharon Hagans, Otis and Ferrill Jean Rice and Vicki Harmon.

Most of the items pictured in this book had to be located in vaults and unpacked from storage boxes. Through the totally unselfish help provided by Helen Warner, this job was drastically minimized. Helen was always there when I needed her to find glass to finish a shot, and was my source of instant information whenever I needed a quick answer. I will be eternally grateful. Helen is Frank Fenton's secretary and is also second Vice-President of the Fenton Art Glass Collectors of America.

A very special thank you to Dr. Eugene Murdock for taking the time to update his text on the Fenton history, and for sharing his expertise with all readers of this book. His incredible attention to detail makes the Fenton company history an enjoyable reading experience.

Finally, and definitely foremost, I want to thank the man who is entirely responsible for this book. He acquired most of the glass illustrated, accumulated and preserved all the catalogues, and shared an infinite amount of research information. I am speaking of course about Frank M. Fenton, who spent hours and hours with me during preparation of this book, acting as my own personal editor, advisor and often as co-writer. These two Fenton books are a testament to this living giant of the glass world, and it has been perhaps the most informative and humble experience of my life to have worked so closely with him. The words "thank you" seem so insignificant when I say them. I think he knows how much I mean them.

MAJOR FENTON LINES

Listed below are the major Fenton patterns, colors or special color treatments produced during their second quarter century. Also listed are the primary years of production and where the best illustration of the line can be found in this book. Many items remained in the line for several years, with certain years including more extensive production than others. Also please consider the fact that Fenton produced glassware for other firms in its colors at times other than those listed. For example, ROSE CREST, in the Fenton line in 1946, was made as early as 1944 for the L.G. Wright Glass Company from Wright's molds.

PATTERN OR COLOR	Y.O.P.	ILLUSTRATION	SPECIAL NOTES
AQUA CREST	1940-42, 48-53	Page 47	Milk glass with blue edge
AZURE BLUE	1932	F1, Fig. 408	See page 86 for a number of items
BLACK ROSE	1953-54	Page 48	Peach Blow with a black edge
BLUE OVERLAY	1943-53	Page 41	Cased glass blue over milk; color re-introduced in 1961, called Powder Blue
BLUE PASTEL	1954	Page 58	Solid opaque pale blue—not cased
BLUE RIDGE	1939	Page 53	F.O. with dark blue edge
CHINESE YELLOW	1924-25, 1932-33	Page 29	Solid opaque yellow, not cased
COIN DOT	1947-64	Page 55	L.G. Wright variant has perpendicular dots
CRYSTAL CREST	1942	Fig. 332	Milk glass with double ring of crystal and white
DAISY AND BUTTON (No. 1900)	1937-39	Page 60	Reissued in 1953 in milk glass and pastel opaque colors
DIAMOND LACE (#1948)	1948-64	Page 46	Made first in F.O. and B.O.; later made in milk glass
EBONY	1922-35	Page 28	Some black glass made in early 50's
EMERALD CREST	1949-55	Page 47	Called "Green Crest" in 1949
FLAME (ORANGE)	1924-26	Page 26	Variegated red-orange to yellow-orange
GEORGIAN #1611	1931-39	Page 82	Inventory lists crystal, jade, ruby, royal blue, amber, green, rose, topaz, black
GOLD CREST	1943-45	Page 49	Re-introduced in 1963-64
GOLD OVERLAY	1949	Page 59	Transparent amber over milk—cased glass
GREEN OVERLAY	1949-53	Fig. 230	Do not confuse for cased IVY
GREEN PASTEL	1954-55	Page 58	Pale opaque green—not cased
HONEYSUCKLE OPAL.	1948-49	Page 57	Made in COIN DOT pattern
HOBNAIL			
Cranberry opal.	1940-79	Page 44	Not made in pressed items
Green opal.	1939-40, 1960-61	Page 43	Do not confuse for Lime opal.
Blue opal.	1939-54, 59-64,	Page 45	Limited production in 1978-79
French opal.	1939-64	Page 46	
Lime opal.	1952-54	Page 43	Cased French opal. over green
Milk glass	1950-present	Page 121	
Peach Blow	1952-56	Page 78	Made in 12 items, primarily 1952
Topaz opal.	1941-43, 1959-62	Page 46	
HISTORIC AMERICA	1937	Page 136-137	Made in crystal only
IVORY CREST	1940-41	Page 49	Collected as custard glass
IVY	1949-52	Page 42	Cased dark green over white
JADE GREEN	1924-37	Page 29	Re-introduced in 1980
LILAC	1955-56	Fig. 465	Limited items made
LINCOLN INN #1700	1928-39	Page 42	Inventory lists ruby, jade, royal blue, rose, green and black
MANDARIN RED	1932-35	Page 26	Similar to the Venetian red color made in the mid-1920's
MILK GLASS	1933-Present	Page 50	By 1955 this was the major color in the Fenton line

PATTERN OR COLOR	Y.O.P.	ILLUSTRATION	SPECIAL NOTES
MING	1935-37	Page 33	Made in crystal, green and rose
MONGOLIAN GREEN	1934-35	Page 27	
MULBERRY	1942	Page 36	Cased glass combining cranberry and light blue
PEACH BLOW	1939, 1952-56	Page 48	Re-issued in Hobnail only
PEACH CREST	1940-69	Page 48	Lengthy production
PEKIN BLUE	1932-33	Page 41	Re-issued in 1980, called PEKING BLUE
PERIWINKLE BLUE	1935	Page 27	A beautiful deep blue slag made for only one year
PERSIAN PEARL	1911-27, 1933	F1, Fig. 127	Also known as white carnival; see this book, page 86 for items
PLYMOUTH #1620	1933-39	Page 30	Inventory lists crystal, amber, ruby, French opal. and S. green (?)
POINSETTIA (Satin)	1939	Page 37	Scarce in color
POLKA DOT	1955-56	Page 55	Made in cranberry only
PRISCILLA #1890	1950-52	Page 118	See Figures 490-491; made in crystal, green and blue
ROSE CREST	1944-47	Page 49	Made for Weil Freeman in 1944-45; in Fenton line only one year
ROSE PASTEL	1954-57	Page 51	A pale pink opaque similar to "Crown Tuscan"
ROSE OVERLAY	1943-48	Page 51	A pale pink cased glass— rose over milk
ROYAL BLUE	1931-39	Page 32	A deep cobalt blue
RUBY OVERLAY	1942-48, 1951-53, 1955-74	Page 52	Sometimes called cranberry by collectors
SAN TOY (Satin)	1936	Page 39	Scarce in color
SHEFFIELD #1800	1936-38	Page 30	Inventory lists ruby, crystal, amber, rose and blue
SILVER CREST	1943-Present	Page 49	Milk glass with crystal edge
SILVERTONE (Satin)	1937-38	Page 37	Scarce in color
SNOW CREST	1950-54	Page 60	Made in ruby overlay, amber and green SPIRAL OPTIC with milk edge
TURQUOISE	1955-58	Page 58	A pale blue-green opaque
VELVATONE (Satin)	1938-39	Page 39	Known only in crystal satin
WISTARIA (Satin)	1937	Page 38	Scarce in color

DOUBLE NAME CONFUSION

Collectors of pattern glass are painfully aware of the confusion which abounds when a single pattern carries more than one name by which to identify it. Rather than have this occur with this book I have listed below a number of Fenton lines and the names which Fenton assigned to them. Also listed are the names of the corresponding Victorian patterns from which their designs were copied. In most cases the Fenton versions should not be considered REPRODUCTIONS, since the molds and general shapes were different from the earlier variants. These are merely copies of the design, not reproductions from original molds.

FENTON NAME	VICTORIAN NAME
BLOCK AND STAR	HOBB'S BLOCK
COIN DOT	POLKA DOT
DIAMOND LACE	HOBNAIL-IN-SQUARE or VESTA
DIAMOND OPTIC (Non-opalescent)	DIAMOND QUILT
DIAMOND OPTIC (Opalescent)	BUBBLE LATTICE
DOT OPTIC	COINSPOT
POLKA DOT	BABY COINSPOT
RIB OPTIC (Non-opalescent)	OPTIC
RIB OPTIC (Opalescent)	OPALESCENT STRIPE
RING (Opalescent)	BLOWN SPIRAL
SPIRAL OPTIC (Non-opalescent)	SWIRL
SPIRAL OPTIC (Opalescent)	OPALESCENT SWIRL
SWIRLED FEATHER	FLOWN TWIST
WIDE RIB	WIDE STRIPE

Chapter Five
DEPRESSION YEARS

Continuation of Murdock's Fenton history from Book 1, page 138.

It should surprise no one to learn that the Great Depression was the most critical period in Fenton history. The decline, begun in the late 1920's, gathered momentum in the next few years and lasted until 1939. From 1931 through 1938 five deficits were recorded, and in the other three years, the margin of gain was so narrow as to be inconsequential. Money was borrowed from every conceivable source, dividend payments were suspended, insurance policies were mortgaged, and wages and salaries were slashed. With orders falling off substantially—although the plant never closed for lack of business—it was necessary to divide up the available work among all employees. In some of the worst months a man might consider himself fortunate to get six turns a week.

* * * *

Financially, 1931, 1932, and 1933 were the worst years in company history, with continuing, sizable deficits. In the middle years of the decade, business was in a marginal condition with profits at about one per cent of sales. 1938 saw a large deficit as the nationwide "recession" hit hard at the glass industry, but business improved greatly in 1939 and got steadily better in the World War II years. Sales dropped to an all-time low in 1933 at the depths of the Depression, and it is easy to see why FAGCO almost closed its doors. However, by cutting expenses to the core, neglecting needed plant improvements, and slicing wages of salaried and non-union employees the crisis was overcome. The Archives contain a document of January, 1933, illustrating the trend: "Effective Monday, January 23, 1933," it read, "ten percent reduction in wages will apply to every employee in every department except members of AFGWU."

A study of expenses during the Depression reveals that, as usual, labor costs bulked the largest. Although in the early 1930's factory labor constituted about 40 per cent of the total cost, a new wage system, adopted in 1937, increased the figure. Consequently in 1939 and 1940 factory labor expenses ran close to 50 per cent of the total. Fuel costs remained fairly constant irrespective of the ups and downs of business, while raw materials reflected more closely the curves of profit and loss. Office payroll was cut drastically in 1933 and remained down until 1939. Salesmen and manufacturer's representatives did relatively well compared to factory and office personnel, although sales were off and their commissions down. There was some truth to Frank L. and Robert C. Fenton's oft-stated remark that "the only people [in the glass trade] who made money during the Depression were the salesmen."

Despite the difficult times in the thirties, FAGCO did not hesitate to introduce new lines and experiment with new colors. At the beginning of the decade large quantities of the #1611 Georgian tableware were produced in both plain colors of pink, light blue, light green, crystal, and amber, as well as in black, jade green, ruby, and royal blue. In addition, the #1700 Lincoln Inn line was made in the same colors, the most popular of which was jade green.

Designs for two covered candy jars, circa 1930, which unfortunately never made the Fenton line, perhaps due to the economic setbacks. The sketches shown above, and on the next two pages, appear to be the work of Frank L. Fenton, discovered in one of his old design scrapbooks.

As the decade—and the Depression—progressed, a variety of new colors and an occasional new line appeared. Among these colors were Mandarin Red, Pekin Blue, Moonstone, and Chinese Yellow in 1932, Mongolian Green (1934), and Periwinkle Blue (1935), as the emphasis shifted to opaque colors. The Georgian and Lincoln Inn lines were continued in 1932 and 1933 in some of the newer colors, while in the latter year the #1620 Plymouth pattern came out in crystal, amber, ruby, green, and French opalescent.

In addition to the tableware and novelty pieces, and some milk glass, the company introduced—in 1933—mixing bowls in Chinese Yellow, jade green, Moonstone, and Pekin Blue. Orange juice reamer bowls, accompanied by a reamer jug to accommodate the reamer in squeezing the juice, proved popular. That same year the company made paper vases (see volume 1, page 113), sterilizers, cream jars, and barber bottles in Moonstone, produced ivy balls in opalescent, royal blue, black, light green, amber, rose, and ruby, and even sold a black razor blade sharpener. Ming crystal and Ming rose patterns were added in 1935.

* * * *

Several changes in the makeup of the Board of Directors, mentioned in volume one, took place in the 1930's. Beeson, who had been first vice-president since the company moved to Williamstown, died on November 7, 1931, at the age of 70, and was succeeded by Charles H. Fenton. The office of second vice-president, which Howells had filled since 1926 was discontinued in 1934, and while he remained on the board until 1942, he held no office. Frank L. Fenton,

Sketch for 8" Swan bowl, never actually produced.

of course, was president, treasurer, and general manager throughout the decade, while Robert continued as secretary. With the death of Charles Fenton in 1936, Robert assumed the post of vice-president and was also named sales manager when that office was created in 1940. The other position held by Charles, assistant general manager, remained unfilled following his demise until Frank M. Fenton, Frank's oldest son, was elevated to it in January, 1942. Whatever the changes, effective control of the company remained in the hands of Frank L. and Robert Fenton.

The Depression compelled the Fenton company, for the first time since the early Williamstown days, to borrow money. The *Minutes* actually record only five such instances, but those who recall business affairs in the 1930's are convinced that a number of other loans were negotiated which are not mentioned in the *Minutes*. The first recorded occasion was in 1930, as the bite of hard times began to sink in. On August 5 the directors authorized the president to borrow $10,000 from the Northwestern Mutual Life Insurance Company of Milwaukee, the loan to be secured by the policy carried by FAGCO with that company on Frank L.'s life. In March, 1933, a contract was signed with the Manufacturers' Finance Corporation of Baltimore, by which Fentons transferred certain "accounts receivable" to that company as security against a loan of an unspecified amount.

The records are silent as to any loans from 1934 through 1937, although certainly some money was borrowed in that period. The recession year of 1938 witnessed the other three loans noted in the *Minutes*. FAGCO borrowed $6,000 in March from the Farmers and Mechanics Bank of Williamstown, which incidentally Frank L. Fenton had helped organize in 1919 and of which he was still president. In August, $10,000 more was obtained from the Peoples Banking and Trust Company of Marietta, and the following month, company insurance policies on the lives of Robert Fenton Sr. and Robert Fenton Jr. were mortgaged to Equitable Life and Traveler's Insurance for $2,000 and $1,800 respectively.

As for the product during these years, ruby, crystal, and the various satin finished decorations predominated by 1936, with Mandarin Red and other opaque colors disappearing. The Georgian pattern was still popular and the Sheffield pattern—in crystal, ruby, and a

Original sketch for Dancing Ladies covered urn (lamp), produced in 1933.

very light delicate Mermaid Blue—entered the line. Ming was still being produced in the satin colors and the San Toy and other satin finished treatments were also being made. The Georgian and Sheffield lines continued to do well in 1937. The Lincoln Inn line, made primarily in crystal, also sold well. The Plymouth pattern was made in both crystal and ruby. New to the line that year were the Wisteria and Silvertone patterns in the satin finished treatments. The #1900 Daisy and Button line also appeared. Hats, slippers, fan trays, ashtrays, puff boxes, vanity sets, bowls, and two-lite candelabra in this pattern were produced in substantial quantities.

* * * *

Despite these new lines, it would be no exaggeration to say that Fenton's survival during the Depression was largely due to two new accounts. In the mid-thirties, A. F. Dormeyer of Chicago became the largest single customer with its orders for opaque glass mixing bowls. Then at the end of the decade Allen B. Wrisley Company, perfume manufacturers also of Chicago, broke all previous customer records with its call for hobnail perfume bottles. While Wrisley's business was tremendous and got the company out of the financial depths, Dormeyer's business was also very important, coming as it did when other accounts were either declining or disappearing.

The Dormeyer connection grew out of negotiations between Martin M. Simpson, FAGCO's veteran Chicago representative, and a Dormeyer official named Schultz. The company, which manufactured small electrical appliances, was in serious financial trouble and needed someone to supply it with bowls for electric mixers. The former supplier had refused to sell any more bowls to Dormeyer because it had been unable to pay for previous bowls. Consequently, any arrangement FAGCO might make with the firm would carry some risk. Both sides needed the business, however, and although Fenton was compelled to borrow funds in anticipation of Dormeyer payments, the company eventually came through and the relationship proved a profitable one. In fact, the mixer business grew to such proportions in several years' time that Dormeyer was able to interest a machine glass manufacturer in furnishing it with bowls and Fenton lost out as supplier.

Dormeyer is first listed in the *Financial Records* in 1933 when the account was worth only $4,548. By 1934, however, it had jumped to $14,581, and the company was now third among FAGCO's customers. The following year the business more than doubled, rising to $31,000 and for the remainder of the decade it averaged between $30,000 and $40,000. From 1935 until 1939 when Wrisley entered the picture, Dormeyer was by far Fenton's number one customer.

But loss of the bowl business did not signal an end to FAGCO's dealings with Dormeyer. In the later thirties the Chicago firm began to manufacture orange juice reamers and bowls, but was unable to make white glass reamers to match machine-made bowls. Dormeyers approached Fenton and explained that while they could give it no more bowl business they would contract for the reamers if FAGCO could produce reamers similar in color to the machine-made bowls. With a sample of the machine product to guide them Fenton technicians went to work and soon developed a kind of off-white glass which matched the bowl. Hence the reamer account picked up the slack left by the loss of the mixing bowls and helped the company stay alive in the last stages of the Depression. As Frank M. Fenton put it, "We helped them when they needed it and they helped us when we needed it."

While Dormeyer kept Fentons alive, Wrisley infused it with new economic blood. Not only did Wrisley mark a sharp upturn in Fenton fortunes, but it also was responsible for the company's entry into the hobnail field on a large scale, although FAGCO had made a hobnail lamp fount in 1935. L. G. Wright

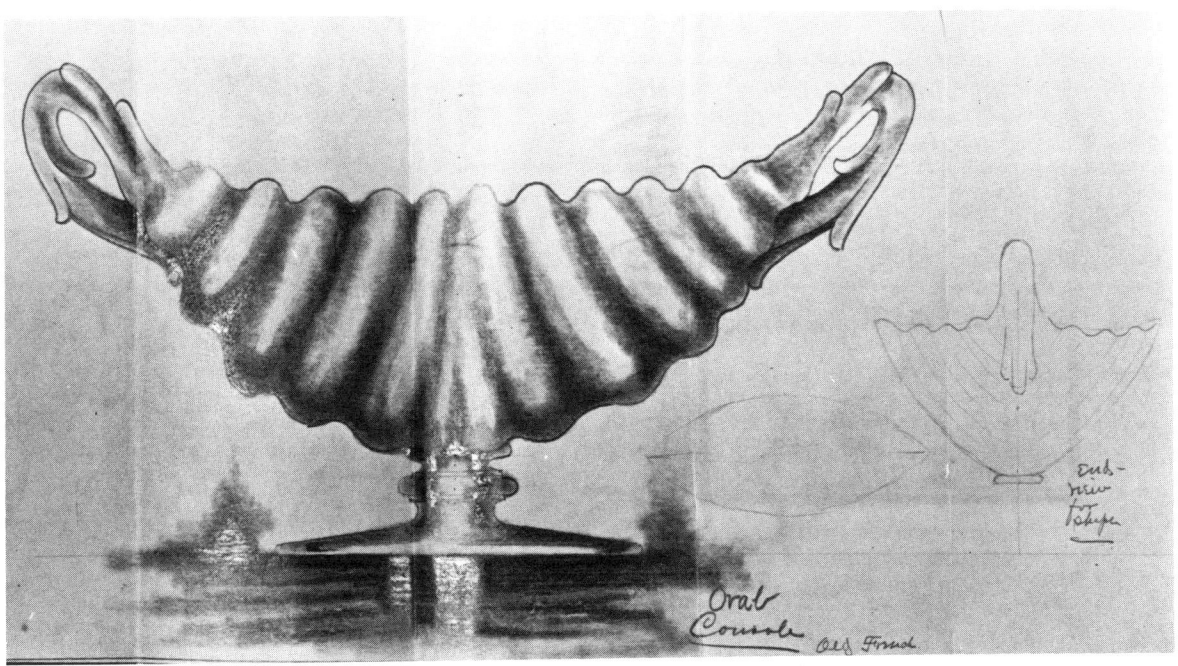

Sketch for unusual Crab console bowl, which never made the Fenton line.

brought in some old molds in 1936 and asked the company to make reproductions of an antique hobnail barber bottle. Only enough were manufactured for Wright's use, but Frank L. Fenton did have one sitting on his desk when Martin Simpson happened by. Simpson took the bottle back to Chicago with him and a Wrisley buyer saw it in his office. Wrisley was looking for something original in perfume bottles, because what apparently sold perfume was not the perfume, but the bottle the perfume was in. The Wrisley man asked Simpson if FAGCO could mass produce the barber bottle at a low price, and the representative replied, "Let's ask them."

When the Fenton company first talked with Wrisley about the barber bottle sometime in the winter of 1937-1938, Frank L. stated flatly that a bottle of this type was an expensive item and could not possibly be sold at the price Wrisley was suggesting. However, he added, modifications could be made in it which would bring down the cost appreciably without detracting too much from the appearance. This was acceptable to the perfume people, so FAGCO went ahead and designed an item similar to the barber bottle, but with a shorter neck, a wider opening, and a wooden stopper. Thus the #289 bottle was born.

A quantity of the bottles were shipped to Wrisley, who filled them with colored cologne, tied a matching ribbon around the top, and test marketed them in the spring and summer of 1938. When the results of the tests came back, both Wrisley and Fenton were dumbfounded. The tests indicated that the perfume bottles would sell far better than it was thought any such product could possibly sell. "The projections seemingly could not be that big." In spite of these misgivings, the glass company was instructed to make additional molds and start production. If the tests were correct new orders would be forthcoming; if the tests were in error, the whole matter would be forgotten.

The tests were correct. Wrisley perfume, in the new bottles, sold exceptionally well. FAGCO could not keep up with the flood of orders that poured in. Each week saw additional shops assigned solely to perfume bottles. The Wrisley company, which was not even listed in 1938 *Financial Records,* suddenly burst forth on the customer list of 1939 with a record-shattering account of $125,975, almost 30 percent of all 1939 sales. Although the account dropped off to $80,000 in 1940, it was still three times as great as any other. "Butch" Malone, long time Fenton employee mentioned in the first book, was laid off in the Depression year of 1933, and came back to work permanently for Fentons in 1939 on the wave of the Wrisley account.

Within a year or so, however, Fenton's costs rose so high that Wrisley went to a machine manufacturer for their bottle supply. One of the changes made by the new company was the substitution of a milk glass stopper for the wooden stopper. In addition to the perfume bottle, FAGCO also made a #289 puff box for Wrisley. This item had a wooden cover with a wooden knob, which matched the wooden stopper of the #289 bottle. Fentons also made a small salt jar for Wrisley which was used for bath salts. While the puff box and salt jar sold well, they did not compare to the perfume bottle.

Fenton's future in hobnail was secure. The company began making other hobnail items—vases, bowls, creamers, etc.—all of which sold very well. The outbreak of World War II hurt sales to some extent, but hobnail continued to move well. In 1943 when Anchor Hocking began to machine produce hobnail and sell it in dime stores, the Fenton people thought that this would knock the bottom out of the business, as it had done to so many other products. But it did not work that way this time. The machine product was not successful and was pulled out of the stores, while the handmade business continued to prosper.

Payroll records reveal in dramatic fashion the impact of the #289 bottle. Throughout much of the Depression one finds big gaps in the payroll books, where shops did not work at all or picked up only a smattering of turns. Then in the spring of 1939 one begins to notice a mass of shop activity. The empty pages give way to a solid array of #289 bottle shops, and one senses that prosperity is returning. The peak period was reached in October and November, when from six to eight shops worked on nothing but perfume bottles. On November 27, 28, and 29, eight shops were in continual operation. Although the move was 360 for the #289 bottle, it was a rare shop that made less than 550 items per turn. This was how the Allen B. Wrisley Company, perfume manufacturers, caused an unforgettable surge of production in 1939 and 1940.

Naturally, one should not assume from what has been said about Dormeyer and Wrisley, that FAGCO would not have survived the Depression without their business. There was a chance of failure, but the two Chicago accounts removed that possibility. Among other customers of the thirties, the Woolworth chain provided the biggest market for FAGCO products. The value of their purchases was only $14,000 in 1931 and 1933, but from 1934 through 1937, the annual average fluctuated between $70,000 and $100,000. "We cut prices and went after their business," Frank M. Fenton recalled. "It didn't do much for profit, but it helped keep the place alive." The most important items sold to Woolworth were the #848 console sets and ashtrays and the "Fenton Basket," After 1939, with the acquisition of new customers who could no longer import glass products from Europe because of the war, sales to Woolworth fell off significantly.

Among other large accounts during the decade, two in particular, S. S. Kresge of Detroit and S. H. Kress of New York, both of whom Fenton also deliberately solicited, stood out from the rest. Major buyers until 1938, they too played an important role in helping Fenton through the difficult years. Value of goods bought by Kress in 1931 was $59,000, in 1932 $10,300, in 1933 $9,100, in 1934 $20,300, in 1935 $16,200, and in 1937 $7,000. 1938 saw Kress purchases drop to $658 and the entire account was lost in the war-time boom. Kresge purchased $19,000 in FAGCO products in 1931, $10,300 in 1932, $22,000 in 1934, $19,800 in 1935, $7,000 in 1937, and $4,000 in 1938. The #848 console sets and ashtrays were among their largest purchases. Like Kress, the Kresge account also disappeared during World War II. Marshall Field was another good customer in the middle thirties, averaging $13,000 for 1933, 1934, and 1935.

* * * *

In addition to the Wrisley 289 bottle, 1938 saw the further development of the Daisy and Button line, and a new line of various sized hats and vase shapes made in cranberry red, French opalescent spiral, and in blue opalescent (Steigel blue). A new grouping of tableware items was tried that year, the #1720 line, but it did not prove very successful and was not expanded. Daisy and Button remained strong, although the satin finish pieces were beginning to taper off.

While 1939 was the big year for the Wrisley bottle, it marked the end of the Georgian, Lincoln Inn, Plymouth, and Daisy and Button patterns. They would be replaced in 1940 by hobnail of all shapes and descriptions. But there was already hobnail in 1939, plus Blue Ridge, Cranberry Red in spiral, Steigel Blue, Peach Blow, and Green Opalescent. By 1940 hobnail expanded to Cranberry, Blue Opalescent, French Opalescent, and Topaz Opalescent. Bowls, vases, and baskets in Peach Crest, Aqua Crest, and Ivory Crest appeared and sold well through the war years.

With the outbreak of war in September, 1939, the Fenton company began to receive a number of new accounts from New York importers of European glass products. Finding their sources of supply suddenly cut off, they turned in desperation to domestic manufacturers. For example, one A. A. Arditti, representing Edward P. Paul Company of New York, appeared at the Fenton offices late in 1939 to see what he could get. He eventually purchased $19,119 worth of products for 1940. Other New York firms in the same category were Jay Willfred Company and Weil Ceramics, who became large purchasers through 1946.

Frequently during those years Frank L. and Robert C. Fenton asked the import companies what would happen when the war was over. Would they continue to buy from Fenton and other domestic producers or return to their traditional European suppliers? The Fentons were assured in terms of undying fealty that they would always deal with those American companies which had saved them in their moment of need. "The truth was," reflected Frank M. Fenton, "that in 1946 they dropped us like a hot potato, and within months their business with us was dead."

During the 1940 presidential election campaign when Wendell Willkie, who had lately joined the Republican Party, was seeking to foil Franklin D. Roosevelt's third term effort, certain rumors got around the FAGCO factory that Frank L. Fenton wanted the employees to support Willkie. This prompted him to post a notice on November 4, shortly before election day, dispelling such stories. In his 35 years as an employer, he said, he had never asked for an employee's vote and did not propose to begin then. Everyone should vote as his own conscience and self-interest dictated. He pointed out that the company's current good fortune was due to (1) the cessation of foreign imports, (2) the quality of "our new designs, colors, and workmanship," and (3) an efficient sales organization. At the bottom of this interesting document, Mr. Fenton made the following observation:

> Due to the fact that the present administration, under Mr. Hull's reciprocal treaties, has reduced the tariff on glass from Czechoslovakia from 60 per cent to 35 per cent, which if it were not for the war in Europe would have put practically every hand plant in the United States out of business, and that Wendell Willkie has promised to protect small industries from the competition of cheap labor from Europe, as for me and my house, we are going to vote for Wendell Willkie for President of the United States for the next four years.

* * * *

Statistics certainly illustrate the difficulties confronting the company during the Depression, but they fail utterly to convey the personal hardships which the glassworkers themselves experienced. When sales dropped, as they did with authority in 1933, fewer products were made, fewer turns were worked, and fewer people were employed. Fortunately, the agreement negotiated between the American Flint Glass Workers Union and the glass companies stipulated a "spread the work" policy in hard times, which enabled everyone to get some turns, although no one would get too many turns. A man would work one day and another would take his place the following day. Lawrence Badgely recalls that a crowd of workers used to congregate in Jimmy George's hamburger emporium on Greene Street in Marietta and twice a day someone would call Fentons from Uncle Bill's Drug Store ("the only place which had a free phone") to see who would be needed on the next turn. Those who were to work would hop the street car and cross over to Williamstown, while the others would resume their game of cards or "cinch and pin."

1932 was the worst year in Henry Snyder's experience. He earned only $552 on which to support his wife and five children. "I couldn't live on it," he recalled with feeling. The fact that the Snyders also lost a son that year added grief to the mounting financial pain. Snyder left the company and worked on a PWA project, but went back to FAGCO after five weeks. Doc Bennett also left Fentons in 1933 and worked at a glass house in New Martinsville until business picked up back in Williamstown. Pete Raymond summed it up pretty well when he said "you had a job, but you didn't work. When you worked you made enough money, but you didn't work." Like everyone else, Raymond lost a lot of turns, a fact which did not completely displease his friendly rival, Charlie Hummel. When asked by a friend how he was getting on, Hummel replied, "Oh, I'm doing pretty good; I got as much time last week as Pete Raymond."

Strangely, in the company's worst year—1933— the year that men like Bennett, Snyder, and Malone left the factory because of insufficient work, young Austin "Pete" Dallison got a job at FAGCO. It was not much—carrying in/over—and he was lucky to pull five turns a week, but it was a job, and he was mighty thankful for it. Whereas married men with families had difficulty getting along on this skimpy work schedule and sometimes sought other employment, the income was sufficient for the unattached Dallison. Although he could not explain why he was hired when others were being laid off, the fact that he was a miscellaneous worker replacing another miscellaneous worker who left for insufficient work, might supply a clue.

A survey of annual incomes for the decade demonstrates what the workers were up against. It must be kept in mind, of course, that these figures do not mean that wage rates were lowered, but simply that the men worked fewer hours. The general pattern was for earnings to drop substantially in 1932 and 1933, rise to an almost acceptable plateau in the middle years, and begin a steady rise in 1938. The highest paid worker in 1931 earned $1,920, but his income dropped nearly 50 per cent by 1933, and he never returned to the 1931 figure until World War II. Another worker earned $1,812 in 1931, was down to $1,072 in 1933, but was up over $2,000 in 1939. Still a third man earned $1,582, $730, and $1,995 for the years 1931, 1933, and 1939 respectively. Only three workers made over $1,000 in 1933.

In the wake of the efforts of the Roosevelt Administration to guarantee a working man certain minimum rights and to uplift organized labor generally, the Fenton Company, in 1937, adopted a new pay system for its factory personnel. Prior to that time a worker had no guaranteed minimum wage and was only paid for the good pieces he made. He could conceivably earn as little as one dollar or two dollars a turn if a number of bad pieces came out of his batch. In 1937, however, an "unlimited turn work" method of payment was instituted, under which the piece-work incentive was retained, but now underwritten by a guaranteed wage per turn. For example, a worker might receive five dollars a turn irrespective of how many bad pieces he made, but he could earn perhaps $7.50 or $10 if he produced an extra quantity of good ones.

* * * *

It was during this period of ferment in the labor movement that one of the three major strikes in Fenton history occurred. The skilled workers had organized Local Number 22 of the AFGWU at the time the Williamstown plant opened, but the miscellaneous workers—warming-in boys, carrying-in boys, etc.—had never been organized, and it was the attempt to unionize them that sparked the trouble. The origins of Local 20156, the miscellaneous—or industrial—union, are obscure. Perhaps the January, 1933 wage cut, which did not affect Local 22, was a stimulant. Or it may be that the passage of the National Industrial Recovery Act in May, 1933, a law which for the first time gave federal governmental approval to the principle of labor unionization, provided the impetus.

According to one story, Local 20156 was founded in 1933 and remained affiliated with the AFGWU until May, 1935. At that time it broke off and pursued an independent course and finally, "seemed to drop out of the picture." Then in April, 1936, it was revived, linking itself with the American Federation of Labor. However, Henry Snyder, president of Local 22 in May, 1936, when the strike erupted, doubts that the miscellaneous workers had a union prior to April of that year.

Be that as it may, the strike grew out of the re-organization—or organization—of Local 20156 in the spring of 1936. At the recently-held convention of the AFGWU, that body of skilled workers had overridden internal opposition in deciding to promote the formation of local unions of unskilled workers. Spurred on by the pro-union philosophy of the New Deal, the AFGWU had come to the conclusion that even skilled workers would benefit if the unskilled men were organized. Not only were they all brothers marching together in one great cause, but also a dispute affecting the miscellaneous people just as certainly affected the fortunes of the skilled people as well. As a consequence of this decision by the AFGWU, all locals were instructed to initiate the organization of industrial unions—referring to the miscellaneous workers—in their own plants. In April, 1936, Olin Twyman, vice-president of Local 22 at Fentons, began working with the unskilled employees there, familiarizing them with the AFGWU ritual, advising them on the responsibilities of union membership, and finally administering the "obligation" to them. The obligation was an oath of allegiance and loyalty to the union.

Soon after the reorganization, a number of disputes arose between Local 20156 and the company. "Labor trouble had been brewing . . . for some time," reported the *Marietta Times* after the strike had begun. The three specific issues were preferential treatment of union members, the re-hiring of a dismissed worker in the cutting department, and a 20 per cent wage increase. On Monday, May 4, the popular union president, Hubert Patterson, issued an ultimatum to the company, that unless the terms were met by noon Tuesday, a strike would be called. The company rejected the conditions and in order to avoid violence, announced that the plant would be closed down following the morning turn on Tuesday.

Around eleven-thirty Tuesday morning 20 pickets began parading up and down Caroline Avenue opposite the entrances to the office and the factory. Tents were set up on Caroline outside the factory for shelter for the pickets. Certain office and supervisory personnel were allowed through the lines, but no other attempts were made to get into the plant. Railroad cars were generally admitted to the siding to deliver goods, but no loaded cars were permitted out. Pickets were stationed at the switch to prevent any from escaping.

Although Local 22 was in no way involved in the dispute, many of its members were in sympathy with the strikers. They had counselled the miscellaneous people to negotiate peacefully for their objectives, but when these could not be obtained in this fashion, they agreed that a strike was the only recourse. While the walk-out was in progress, Henry Snyder, who lived on Caroline Avenue directly across from the plant, had frequent contact with the strikers. He ran an electric wire across the street enabling the pickets to plug in a small radio in their tent. Pickets lounged around the Snyder porch and under the shade trees in the yard. Passers-by asked Snyder if he was not fearful of recriminations from the company for giving aid and comfort "to the enemy." He doubted whether the company would say anything about it and he was right; no reference was ever made to the matter.

Meanwhile, efforts to settle the dispute commenced on Wednesday, May 6, with the arrival of Robert E. Mythen, a federal conciliator, dispatched to Williamstown by the National Labor Relations Board. High-ranking officials in the AFGWU, Harry Cook and Coleman Claherty, had also come down from their Toledo headquarters to counsel the strikers. As proceedings got underway Cook, AFGWU vice-president, presented the workers' case, whereupon Frank L. Fenton observed, "that's a nice story, Mr. Cook." Frank L. then set forth the company's position, after which Cook commented, "that's a nice story, Mr. Fenton." Following this exchange of amenities the negotiations moved ahead, and by Thursday, May 7, the conferees had hammered out a compromise settlement.

By the terms of the agreement, FAGCO granted the request for preferential treatment and agreed to rehire the dismissed employee, while the union dropped its 20 per cent wage increase demand. The wage demand had never been a serious matter anyhow, the union having thrown it in largely for bargaining effect. It was also established that when future disputes arose they would be submitted to arbitration between the union and the company, and that work should continue while the negotiations were taking place. And finally, an effort would "be made to affiliate the ... union ... with the American Flint Glass Workers Union Local No. 22." What eventually happened was that the industrial union was re-numbered Local 508 of the AFGWU and the two unions lived together happily ever after.

Fenton's big strike of three days passed into history, but a better understanding of the problems of the other side was gained by both the company and the workers. And by no means the least significant aspect of the affair was the mature and responsible attitude with which both management and labor conducted themselves during the crisis. That there was no violence, no destruction of property, and not even much ill-will, reflected favorably on the common sense and good judgment of everyone involved in the dispute.

Chapter Six
THE DAY THE STACK FELL

George Pickens, a veteran Fenton finisher, was strolling leisurely along 4½ Street one warm Saturday afternoon in the summer of 1940, when he suddenly observed the factory's huge chimney twist around in its place—"almost a quarter of a turn"—and then drop straight down. As it collapsed in a tremendous pile of rubble in the center of the hot metal works, it tore out the ceiling beams which were tied in to it and killed a young man who had only started to work that morning.

The day the stack fell, June 29, 1940, naturally was the most unforgettable moment in the company's history, and all those who were present during the disaster have vivid recollections of the day's events. Yet reconstruction was completed within several weeks, full production resumed by September 1, and the profit and loss statement of 1940 gives no indication that anything out of the ordinary had occurred. But something out of the ordinary had occurred. One person was dead, several others badly hurt, and every man and woman in the Fenton organization had been through an experience that would leave its mark. What was the story behind the story?

The stack was part of the original plant erected in 1906. It was 80 feet high, contained an estimated 75,000 bricks, and weighed about 280 tons. As the photographs show, all the roof beams of the plant were joined directly to the stack. Inside the chimney there was a "crown," or slanted roof which rose to a height of about 12 feet at the center and sloped gently downward toward the outside walls. An intense flame—normally at 2400 degrees fahrenheit—burns inside the crown, the fumes from which escape through exhaust flues near the walls and are carried up the chimney. Positioned at regular intervals under the crown are 12 "pots," or earthen ovens, which are enclosed on all sides except that facing the outside of the furnace. The glassworker handles his materials and tools in an opening in the pot at that point. The flame inside the crown does not play directly on the glass in the pots, although the pot itself is as hot as if the glass was in the flame. Pots are changed after about eight or ten months' use, but the flame under the crown is never extinguished. Even during the annual summer shutdown, a fire is kept burning.

While Fenton's original stack was still in use in 1940, it had been repaired several times. Seven or eight years is the normal period between repairs. When repairs are undertaken, the plant is closed down, the crown fire is put out, the furnace is permitted to cool, and mortarmen methodically examine the entire chimney. Bricks are replaced, joints and seams are pointed, and other danger spots are attended to. The Fenton stack had probably—there is no absolute documentation—been checked over at least three times, 1915, 1923, and 1930 being the most likely dates. Another overhaul was due in the late thirties, but because of the Depression the job had been delayed. As we now know it was delayed too long.

Frank L. Fenton and his brothers were well aware that something needed to be done and plans were made for stack repairs during the summer shutdown in 1940. The plant is always closed during the first two weeks of July and the entire work force goes on vacation at that time. Consequently, by Saturday, June 29, 1940, the factory had ceased operations, the crown fire was out, and all materials needed for the repairs, which were to commence on Monday, July 1, were on hand. The chief reason the rebuilding job

Scene of the disaster, facing North from the lehrs.

proceeded so smoothly later was because preparations for the repairs had been completed.

Henry Snyder apparently was more aware of the dangerous condition of the stack than anyone else. He had told several people that the chimney looked bad and that he did not want to be around when they started the repairs. He and Mrs. Snyder went to the factory on Friday evening, June 28, and watched as the fire was extinguished. Snyder observed a crack in the furnace wall—"you could have laid a match stem in it"—and commented to his wife that he was afraid of what he saw. On Saturday morning he again visited the factory and noticed that the crack "had opened until you could lay your hand in it." Snyder asked George Thompson, who was standing nearby, if he intended to remain around the chimney the rest of the day. "If so,". he continued, "you had better stay back from the chimney. I'm afraid that thing is going to fall over. If I was going to stay here today, I'd want to be clear out on the streetcar track." "Doc" Bennett also attests to Snyder's gift of prophecy. Henry told him that "when they tear those pillows out from under the crown I don't want to be in here. I'm afraid it's going to fall down."

The fire in the furnace had been put out Friday night, and by Saturday morning a crew of workers began to remove the pots and loose bricks laying inside the stack. By mid-afternoon the crown had been knocked in and was about to be hauled away. A number of men and boys—Wilmer "Bill" Fenton, Fred Fenton, Dale Cox, Bob Smith, Eddy Fenton, Homer Cummings, and Harley Noland, among them—were actually inside the furnace when the stack made its strange "quarter of a turn" and plummeted down. Those who were not inside the crown at that moment could not imagine what it was like, and even those who were have had some difficulty in reconstructing what happened. But let's follow Bill Fenton's account:

"I was inside the furnace when the thing started to fall; it sounded like a rifle crack and someone yelled 'run.' I don't know why I ran in the direction I did, but I just instinctively ran on out one of the pot openings in the furnace, across the floor and toward the windows in the west wall. It seemed as though the pressure from the collapsing stack just shoved me along; it felt like somebody had his hands on my shoulders pushing me. I dove through a window—I couldn't have stopped; I just had to go through that window—and at that moment the wall in which the window was set, caved outward and I rode down on the crumbling bricks to the railroad tracks about ten feet below. I had so much weight on my legs that I could feel nothing from the waist down and thought my legs had been cut off. The window frame had ridden right down with me and protected my head so there was no weight there, and luckily no broken bones at all. Dale Cox who had jumped out of a window at the first rumble was unhurt and he came over and helped pull me out. On his way over to help me he stepped on a nail which ran clear through his foot. I couldn't see very well, because of all the furnace soot in my

Further damage at the scene, facing almost East from the railroad tracks.

eyes and had to wear dark glasses for several weeks."

Homer Cummings, who would later marry one of the Fenton sisters, instead of moving toward the outer walls when the "rifle crack" sounded, ran toward the office area, but luckily tripped over some bricks and fell between the lehrs. Just as he hit the floor, a hugh ceiling beam came crashing down on the lehrs, and while it partly caved the lehrs in, it did not reach Cummings, who was able to crawl to safety. He probably would have been killed by the beam had he not fallen between the lehrs. Fred Fenton was pinned down by a few bricks and beams and received electrical shocks from fallen wires. He understandably shouted for someone to "turn off the electricity." He spent several weeks in bed with electrical burns. A number of others suffered cuts and scratches, but nothing of a serious nature.

The one casualty was Robert Eugene Smith, who was on this very Saturday celebrating his eighteenth birthday as well as his first day of work at the company. So many ironies are connected to the Smith story that his death strikes one as almost predestined. Bob had been trying to get a job for some time, but there was no spot for him. He kept up the pressure, however, and finally James Fenton, who was in charge of maintenance, told him to come on in. He did, on Saturday, June 29. And then only 15 minutes before tragedy struck, the crew was taking a break prior to removing the dismantled crown. Young Smith gazed at the towering column and commented, "I'd like to see one of these things fall in. I don't mean this one," he hastened to add, "but you know you see newsreels of large buildings being demolished? Well, I'd like to see something like this one go down that way." But Bob Smith never saw the Fenton tower collapse. After it was over, he was dug out of the rubble right at the spot where he had been standing inside the furnace a few minutes before. He either did not hear the warning shout to "run," or was struck by some flying object before he could escape.

While turmoil prevailed inside the factory, what was going on outside? George Pickens, who described the twist of the stack, immediately raced to the gas house on Caroline Avenue, broke the lock and shut off the gas. His quick thinking averted a fire and possibly much more serious damage. Frank L. Fenton was golfing at the Parkersburg Country Club that Saturday afternoon, but Frank M. Fenton was sitting in his office going over payroll accounts, when he heard what sounded like a wheelbarrow rolling across the rough wooden floor on the outside corridor. The office lights flicked off for two or three seconds and went back on, followed by the sound of running water, Frank M. decided it was time to investigate, so he casually arose and wandered out into the factory. Suddenly he saw nothing but blue sky overhead which was strange because there was supposed to be a roof overhead. His first thoughts were of fire, but he quickly saw that the stack and the roof had fallen in. He cannot recall what his actions were for the next half hour or so, but he does remember taking a head count of the work crew and accounting for all of its members except Bob Smith.

Henry Snyder, as one might suspect, was far away from the factory when the collapse occurred. His absence, however, was not a result of his running away, in spite of what he said about removing himself from the vicinity of the repair operations. The fact was that Snyder had been elected by Local 22 to represent it at the annual convention of the AFGWU in Alton, Illinois, and had left Williamstown with his wife by automobile around noon on Saturday, June 29. He had reached Cincinnati by late afternoon when the stack fell in, but he did not learn about it until Sunday afternoon when he arrived in Alton. Harry Cook, International President, showed Snyder a copy of the Sunday *Parkersburg News,* which carried the full story. Though shocked, he was not surprised, having expected and predicted it.

No estimates of the damage were published in the press, but the losses must have been considerable. The stack itself was a substantial item, the roof was destroyed, and all the glory hole furnaces had been knocked off their platforms as if some giant broom had swept them away. And just one look at the piles of broken bricks and concrete, the battered beams, the twisted steel supports, and the tons of miscellaneous debris, must have caused the stoutest heart to wonder if anything could be salvaged from the ruins. Lem Lewis, viewing the situation with Frank L. Fenton, who had been hastily summoned from his golf match, commented sadly, "Frank, I don't see how you're gonna do it."

"Well, Lem, somebody's got to do some tall thinking," was the firm reply. To a reporter he remarked that he hoped to have the greater part of his work force back in harness in three weeks, but he certainly must have had his doubts about that.

The first order of business, of course, was to clear away the wreckage. "Oney" Gabbert, a local construction man, was called in to organize the work, and clean-up crews composed of factory employees were mobilized within several hours. Eight-hour shifts were set up and the work, begun by Saturday evening, continued around the clock—Saturday night, all day Sunday and throughout Sunday night. By Monday morning, the originally-scheduled time for the stack repairs to commence, the rubble had been cleared out of the factory area and all was in readiness for the reconstruction. Cleaning up was a monumental job, but through "some tall thinking," and the loyal, hard-working efforts of the company personnel, it was accomplished in about 36 hours.

Although reconstruction could have begun on Monday, July 1, the work was delayed to permit a more careful study of the design of the new stack. Foundation construction demanded attention, and the question was also raised about using steel instead of wood, which had been employed almost exclusively in the original plant. Steel had been used in the supports around the pot openings in the furnace, but not in the factory itself. At a special directors' meeting on Tuesday, July 2, it was decided to rebuild with steel, and the Dowling Construction Company was given the contract. Dowling was unable to obtain the steel at once, however, which caused another delay, but eventually the materials arrived and reconstruction moved rapidly ahead.

Meanwhile, however, someone conceived the idea of manufacturing glass solely in the daytanks, which had survived the stack collapse. Daytanks are large, square enclosed ovens in which the fire plays directly on the glass, in contrast to the pots where the oven protects the glass from the direct flame. Certain types of glassware cannot be produced in the daytanks, but partial production could be resumed by utilizing them. In the Fenton factory the daytanks, five in number, were located in the tankroom, a shed-like structure along the north wall, outside the central area. Consequently the tanks were covered not by the main roof, but by a sloping piece of metal which was joined to the main roof. When the main roof fell in with the stack, it carried down with it the inner portions of the sheet metal, but left it in place where it was connected to the outer wall. It was not too difficult a task, therefore, to disconnect the sheet metal from the ruins of the old roof and jack it up into its original position over the daytanks. Within three weeks glass was being manufactured in the daytanks.

Snyder and Pete Raymond were among those who went to work when operations were begun in the daytanks in the latter part of July. Everyone seemed to think it was going to be great fun working out in the open air, with the cool breezes providing welcome relief from the torrid temperatures which normally

Another view of the collapse looking toward the lehrs from railroad track.

After the cleanup—picture of where the stack originally stood, as taken from the water tower

prevail in a glass factory. But it was not to be. Not only was the heat from the daytanks as bad as ever, but the heat from the sun was even worse. Working without shirts a considerable number of employees suffered severe sunburns. Snyder recalled, "that was the hottest place I was ever in. A lot of us couldn't take it except in the forenoon. We couldn't work in the afternoon."

During the reconstruction days of July and August several glory holes were also rebuilt and put into operation. Carrying-over boys took the glass from the daytanks across the 60 feet or so of open space directly to the lehrs, or perhaps to the glory holes when additional work was needed on the pieces there. Occasionally it rained and all work was suspended. By August, however, temporary covered runways were constructed from the daytanks across to the lehrs and shelters were erected over the glory holes, so production could proceed without interruption.

Scattered news reports traced the progress of reconstruction. On July 6 it was stated that rapid strides were being taken and that a new roof would be built. A week later the daytank roof was back in place and plans were being made to resume production there. The new factory building design had been approved and was slated to be "superior in every way." It would be of steel and brick and completely fireproofed. By July 23 the new stack was up and work on the walls and roof was next on the agenda. At the directors' monthly meeting in early August, all the members expressed extreme satisfaction over the progress being made in rebuilding the factory. And a month later President Frank L. Fenton reported that the plant had been put into operation on a 100 per cent basis as of September 2. The directors responded by congratulating the president on the speed and efficiency of the job. As we know, 1940 was one of Fenton's most prosperous years, so the stack collapse hardly caused a ripple in the company's financial operations.

But what had happened? What had caused the chimney to twist and then fall to pieces? This was highly unusual behavior for a chimney, because as "Doc" Bennett noted, "generally when they have to destroy them, they dynamite them." One theory advanced in the newspapers suggested that "the bricks lining the inside of the big furnace had become devitalized by reason of the intense heat to which

The Fenton brothers after the cleanup of the disaster rubble—(left to right) James E., Robert C. and Frank L. Fenton.

they had been subjected and that this may have been responsible for undermining the big stack." Frank M. Fenton thinks that perhaps after the pots had been pulled out, some water might have been applied to the bricks on the inside of the stack to cool them faster, and that the water may have softened up certain key points of the inner wall. At any rate, he is the first to admit that the big mistake was in postponing the time for repairs.

"It wasn't anybody's fault; it was simply that we'd been through the Depression years where we just couldn't spend any money on repairs. We just didn't have it to spend. By 1939 we could see that the furnace was in bad shape, and by then we were able to do something about it. So we ordered all the materials and planned a complete overhaul during the summer shutdown in 1940. But we were too late."

So the stack fell, Bob Smith tragically died, a new and better factory rose up from the ruins, and the most unforgettable chapter in the Fenton Company's history had ended.

Chapter Seven
END OF AN ERA

The 1940's marked a watershed in Fenton history. World War II surprisingly brought the company an unprecedented prosperity, and the good times continued well into the post-war years. But then in the late forties the seller's market broke, and soon all hand glass operated companies were fighting for survival; many lost the battle. At this moment, unhappily for Fentons, the two men who had guided the company's destinies through the painful days of adolescence into the sunny years of success both passed from the scene. Frank L. Fenton died in May, 1948, to be followed within six months by his older brother and close colleague, Robert C., and control settled into the relatively inexperienced hands of Frank's two sons, Frank M., who was 32, and Wilmer C., who was only 24. The difficulties these two young executives encountered in mastering their trade under unfavorable business conditions will be narrated in the next chapter. Here will be set forth the history of the company during the last, best years of Frank L. Fenton's presidency.

* * * *

In 1941, the second full year of war in Europe, Fenton sales continued to increase, and while 1942 was a period of leveling off, 1943 witnessed the greatest jump in sales in the company's history. Gross sales of a million dollars or more were attained several times in the decade, but profits did not keep pace with sales. The wartime excess profits tax, geared to a pre-war base period when sales were not high, meant that all income above that base average was taxed at a 95 per cent rate. Thus, most of the money which poured in, poured right out again into the United States Treasury. Annual expenses during the 1940's increased at a more gradual pace than did sales, but in the post-war years they remained well above the figures reached during the war itself. Factory labor was the most inflationary item here, with more people now employed and higher hourly rates being paid.

Perhaps it seems odd that a great war stimulated a boom in something as unwarlike as the hand made art glass industry. After all, materials and labor were scarce, wages and prices frozen, glass-making was not essential to the national economy, and art glass did not seem to be the type of investment a war weary nation would want to make in its search for diversion and relaxation. Yet none of these adverse factors had any appreciable bearing on the business. Although wages were frozen, overtime pay stuffed the pockets of workers; and even though rationing limited what a consumer could buy, art glass was not rationed.

Consequently money was plentiful and people wanted art glass items. "We could sell anything we could make," recalled Frank M. Fenton. Unprofitable items were dropped and the company "concentrated only on profitable lines." Fred Muhleman, Mrs. Frank L. Fenton's brother and a manufacturer's representative in those years, reminisced that "during the war I sold more lamps than I ever sold before." Retailers and jobbers kept pressing for articles of every description. It made little difference what the article was; orders were months in arrears. In the mad rush to supply jobbers and fill shelves, even a small amount of glass which normally would have been rejected was shipped.

The character of the line in the forties had changed considerably from the thirties. More emphasis was placed on Victorian styling and coloring. At the beginning of the war Fenton colors in use were Ruby Overlay, Aqua Crest, Peach Crest, Crystal Crest, and Mulberry. Crystal Crest—forerunner of the present Silver Crest—was opal glass with a crystal ring spun around the edge and a second ring of opal around that

Fenton "finisher" Jimmy Coen preparing a No. 1522 COIN DOT basket for the "handler", circa 1950.

edge. It was in the line for only a year when the company switched to Silver Crest, eliminating the outer edge of opal. The latter proved popular and was easier to produce.

Mulberry was a cased glass with gold ruby on the inside covered with light blue glass, the same light blue which was used for Aqua Crest. This glass was blown in a diamond optic mould first and then blown in the various other moulds that were in use at that time, most of which were melon-shaped vases, pitchers, and bowls. Hobnail was produced in the various Opalescents—French, Blue, Topaz, and Cranberry. In 1943 Fentons moved to Blue Overlay, Rose Overlay, and Ruby Overlay, which again was a diamond optic pattern. In addition, Silver Crest, Gold Crest, and Peach Crest were produced in the melon-shaped patterns of the #192 line. Hobnail was still made in the opalescents. There were some real bargains that year. A group of opalescent miniature vases about two inches tall retailed at 25 cents each. Small miniature baskets were sold for 50 cents. It would cost ten times that amount to produce those miniatures today.

* * * *

One of the problems which Fenton and other art glass manufacturers were faced with in meeting the wartime demand was the shortage of essential ingredients. The basic materials—sand, soda ash, and lime—were plentiful, but chemicals needed to develop the different colors were not. Arsenic, for example, was necessary in the manufacture of some glass, but periodically it would be unobtainable. When arsenic could not be had, antimony oxide was employed as a substitute. Or, when tin oxide ran out an ersatz variety was fabricated by "powdering" molten solder in a sack. By this time arsenic might be again available, but something else, for example selenium, or perhaps cobalt, might be unavailable. Cryolite, a whitening agent ("opacifier"), was frequently short, as was manganese. Producers would just shift around, using what materials were available and dropping those lines they could not manufacture at the moment. In the case of certain ingredients like arsenic, the material would be stockpiled over a period of time and when a sufficient quantity had been accumulated, arsenic items would be produced. Suppliers would often alert the companies as to forthcoming shortages, so that production schedules could make allowances for those shortages.

Although sand was plentiful during the war, on several occasions boxcars in which the sand was shipped were unavailable. Fenton's chief sand supplier, the Pennsylvania Glass Sand Company of Berkeley Springs, West Virginia, with ample sand on hand, at one time was unable to send any of it to Williamstown. FAGCO thereupon turned to the Central Silica Company in Zanesville, Ohio, which although it produced a less pure quality of sand than at Berkeley Springs, could at least get boxcars. As far as the quality of the sand was concerned, Frank M. Fenton remembered that the company "would take anything it could get." Fenton stayed with Central Silica until the Zanesville firm also ran into a boxcar problem, by which time Pennsylvania Glass Sand could, fortunately, again obtain boxcars. FAGCO consequently resumed its old relationship with the people in Berkeley Springs.

Cast iron for new moulds was also difficult to secure. As the moulds then being worked wore out, the company concentrated on their replacement rather than the manufacture of new moulds. Thus little that was different could be added to the line in 1944, 1945, or 1946. Mulberry went out of the line in 1944, and Rose Crest made its debut in 1945. Overall, however, the shapes and styles were much the same.

* * * *

If the reader of this history has not as yet concluded that Frank L. Fenton was an enlightened and fair-minded employer, the following stories should make the point clear. In the first week of July, 1944, the AFGWU held its 68th annual convention in Marietta, at which time most of the debates centered on the wisdom of calling a national strike. The delegates were not in a happy mood, and some fighting speeches were delivered on the convention floor. In spite of this sullen spirit, however, two events occurred which reflected Mr. Fenton's respect for the union and the union's respect for him. As president of the Marietta Rotary Club, Frank L. invited the president of the International Union, Harry H. Cook, and the other officers, to be his guests at the Rotary luncheon on July 6. Traditionally union officials were about as appropriate at a Rotary meeting as communists at a session of the United States Chamber of Commerce.

Mr. Fenton broke through this custom and even had Cook deliver the main speech. In his remarks the union executive reported favorably on the machinery employed to settle labor disputes in the glass industry, paying special tribute to the National Association of Manufacturers of Pressed and Blown Glassware—the organization of the companies—for its fine attitude in making the machinery work well. He also commended Mr. Fenton "as an enlightened employer of labor" and reminded his listeners that Mr. Fenton always had approached "any labor problem sympathetically and with a full understanding of the workers' aims and aspirations."

That evening the two Williamstown local unions—22 and 508—sponsored a banquet in honor of Frank L. Fenton at the Betsy Mills Club in Marietta, and invited all the convention delegates to attend. It was a happy occasion for the 250 people who were present, and an especially happy one for Mr. Fenton. After the dinner and the distribution of favors—"baskets made by the workers at the Fenton plant"—there was an old-fashioned "sing," followed by a series of speeches eulogizing the company's president. "In the memory of the oldest delegate present," wrote the correspondent for *China and Glass,* monthly journal of the industry,

"no man associated with the glass industry was ever praised by the workers of the industry in such a manner as Frank Fenton was lauded by the various speakers at this dinner. It will be an event to be remembered by those who honored one of their fellow men and a cherished hour for Mr. Fenton, who received such a tribute from those who labor in our industry."

* * * *

Since 1944 through 1948 were the biggest sales years of the decade, customer accounts reflected the trend. By far the best individual customer of the war and post-war years was Abels, Wasserberg and Company of New York City. Abels was a decorating company, which bought glass products and decorated them much like Fenton had done in its infant days at Martins Ferry. They also made lamps which contained glass parts. First appearing on the Fenton books in 1940 and 1941 with small accounts of less than $1,000, Abels began to blossom in 1942 and from 1943 through 1949 never bought less than $22,000 worth of FAGCO products. For three years running —1944, 1945, and 1946—they were over the $30,000 figure, reaching a peak of $39,277 in 1946. Their total for the decade was $220,000, almost $50,000 above the next best customer.

It was noted in Chapter Five that one of the big stimulants to the American art glass industry after the outbreak of the war in Europe in 1939 was the shutting off of European suppliers to American importers—companies like Jay-Willfred, Edward P. Paul, Weil Ceramics, and Koscheraks. There was a difference between the kinds of purchases that Abels Wasserberg made in the war years and those of the companies just mentioned. While Abels bought items that were regularly in the Fenton line, the importers preferred something that was not currently being offered by Fenton. This might involve employing moulds that had not been used in recent years and making the pieces in the present Fenton colors, or taking the moulds then in use and making the pieces in colors not in the current line. No attempt has been made in this book to deal with products made for the importers. That is another field of research.

Whatever the items sold to the importers may have been, the income from those sales was good. Jay-Willfred first appeared in 1939 with a modest account of $7,000, which doubled within two years. In 1944 Jay-Willfred was second to Abels as FAGCO's best customer. Their total for the nine years, 1940 to 1948, was $105,000, seventh highest for the decade. Edward P. Paul & Co., on the other hand, experienced a much more meteoric relationship with Fenton, bursting forth with three big years early in the war, and then subsiding rapidly in the last two years of the war. Paul first appeared on the records in 1940 with $19,000, but it skyrocketed to $58,000 in 1942, by far the biggest single account for any of the war years. Unaccountably, however, their purchases dropped off in the next two years and disappeared from the list of major accounts.

Fenton's second best customer in the forties was A. C. McClurg, Chicago jobbers. McClurg was a very steady account with their annual purchases averaging about $19,000. The nine year total was slightly above A. L. Randall, another Chicago jobbing concern, which was third on the Fenton list. Randall's performance was not unusual in the war years, but the company moved into a class by itself in 1948. From that year through 1950 its purchases totaled nearly $120,000,

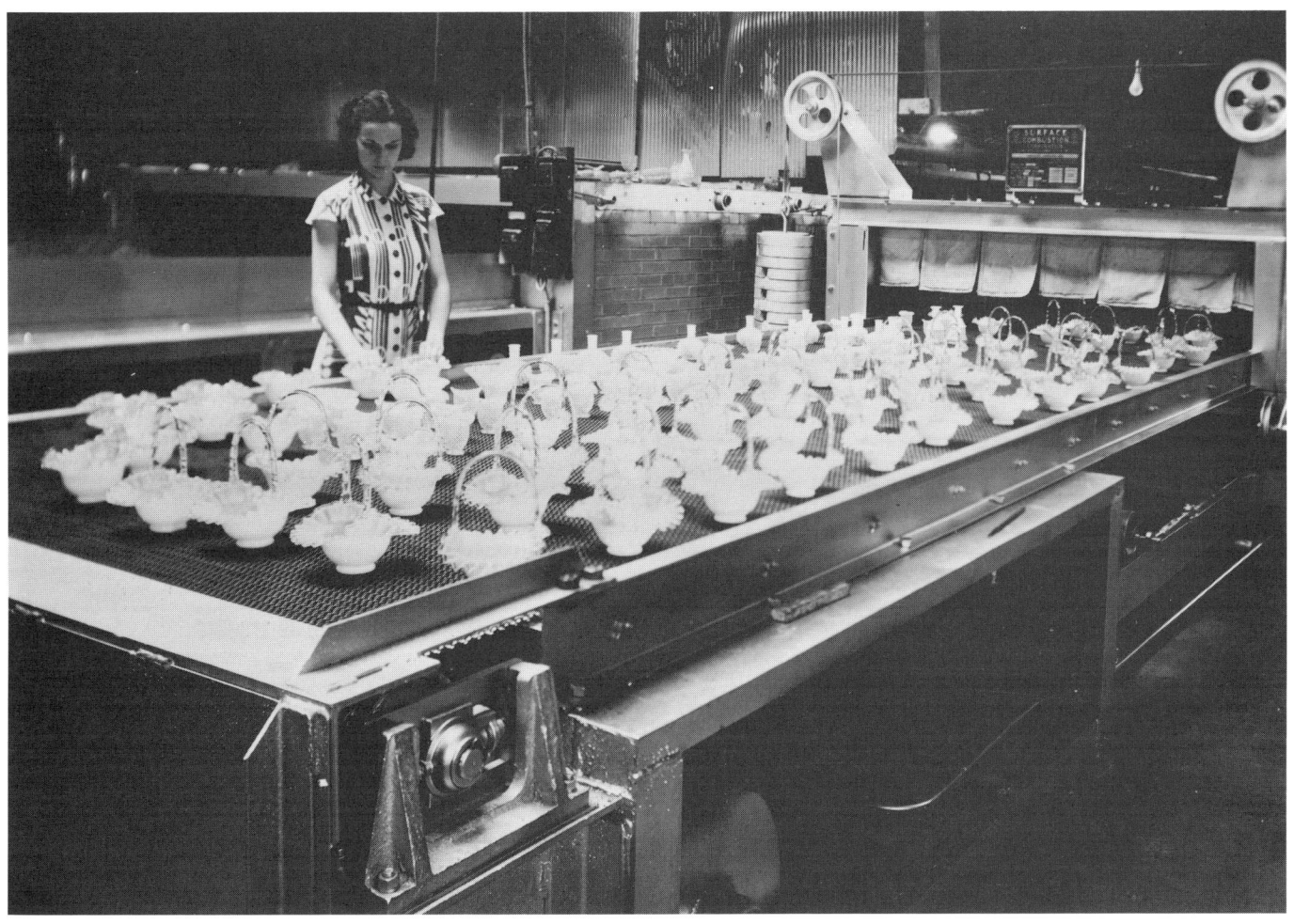

Employee Betty Jane Dulin is shown standing here at the new annealing lehr, circa 1941; photo is dated by the line of glassware shown here, the No. 192 10" baskets and No. 389 Hobnail cologne bottles.

with a $50,000 high in 1949. The latter figure ranks next to Edward Paul's great year of 1942. Other good accounts for the decade were Sears Roebuck of Chicago, and four jobbing concerns: Bechtel, Lutz, and Jost of Reading, Pennsylvania, Seller-Lowengart of San Francisco, Blackwell Wielandy of St. Louis, and T. M. James of Kansas City, Missouri.

The war ended in 1945, but the seller's market continued and the company entered 1947 with a year's backlog of orders. Then the buyer's market arrived, and by the end of 1947 the backlog had been eliminated. The only new addition to the line in 1947 was the Coin Dot pattern, which remained strong in 1948 in French Opalescent, Blue Opalescent, and Cranberry. A Honeysuckle Coin Dot was also introduced that year. It was a cased glass with amber on the inside and French Opalescent on the outside. In addition, 1948 witnessed the advent of the four piece *Diamond Lace* epergne set made in French Opalescent and Blue Opalescent. The former had an applied blue edge and the latter a crystal edge. This item was the hit of the year's glass show and proved a good seller.

* * * *

Plant improvements had to be postponed in the forties because of wartime shortages. One major project was undertaken by sheer necessity, but otherwise it was another period of minor "patching up and making do." The one big job was the replacement of the day-tank room. When the stack collapsed, it will be recalled, the roof of the tank room was also dragged down. The roof was temporarily propped up and production was resumed in the undamaged day tanks. Then when the new stack was built, the old tank roof remained somewhat precariously attached, although not closely joined to it. Within a year or so, however, it became obvious that a permanent tank roof would have to be installed. But the problem by this time was one of materials. FAGCO officials wanted to rebuild with steel as they had done with the stack, but the contractors they approached doubted whether any steel was available.

They next called on Blair Plate of the Plate Construction Company in Parkersburg. An application for steel was made to the War Production Board, again with the proofs that the material was essential for the company to maintain employment at a certain level, and with Plate's help the application was approved. In 1944 the tank room roof was replaced and enlarged, using steel and concrete construction. Other improvements in the war and post-war years included air conditioning and the installation of acoustical ceilings in the offices, and some exterior work on the Caroline Avenue side of the building. Silos and a new mixer were also put in during 1949 to reduce handling costs in the mixing operation. However, a major renovation and expansion program would have to await the 1950's and 1960's.

In 1934 Clarence Rosenthal, mould shop foreman since the company opened its doors and one of its oldest employees, died. Francis Lehew, who had been a lathe hand in the shop for almost 20 years, was slated for the vacancy and fully expected it, but he did not get it. Frank L. Fenton told him why: "Anyone could be a foreman, but good lathe hands were hard to obtain." Mollified by such faint praise and also by the fact that he was named assistant mould shop foreman and was to be paid eight dollars more per week than the new foreman, Lehew remained a lathe hand. The new foreman, a 63-year old man named Harry Bridges, was brought in from the outside and served from 1934 until 1949. In the latter year he retired and Lehew finally became mould shop foreman, a job he held until his own retirement in 1964.

Up to 1949 Lehew had been active in union affairs and was secretary of local 22 at the moment of his promotion to foreman. Foremen, of course, were ineligible for union membership. His appointment was made in the middle of the week, and a day or two later Lawrence Badegly brought in a mould which needed some immediate attention. Without thinking, Lehew put it in a vise, took a file and went to work on it. Almost immediately, Shirley Bee, the shop committeeman came rushing over, shouting, "Hey, you can't do that, you're the boss now; you can't work on moulds!"

"Is that so?" replied the surprised Lehew.

"Yes, sir!"

"O.K., here's the file," said the new foreman, "now you go ahead and file it. And don't take too much off or you've lost yourself a job." For the next year whenever a "hot job" came into the shop, Lehew made Bee do it.

Chapter Eight
THE OLD ORDER CHANGETH

Frank Leslie Fenton, co-founder of the Fenton company and its guiding genius since 1910, died Tuesday morning, May 18, 1948, from complications which followed a heart attack. He had been stricken on April 23 and rushed to Parkersburg's Camden-Clark Hospital, but his condition deteriorated steadily. He was 68. This was a serious loss for the company under any circumstances, but it was particularly acute at this time as the boom in the hand glass business was rapidly leveling off. The good war years were over and competition was again keen, not only from other hand glass plants but also from machine glass factories. Firm, experienced hands were needed at the controls, but Robert C., the surviving brother, was over 80, and the sons of Frank L., Frank M. and Wilmer C. ("Bill"), while familiar with specialized aspects of the business, had only limited knowledge of overall operations.

But Mr. Fenton's passing was felt well beyond the confines of Caroline and 4½ Street in Williamstown. His contributions to the industry at large and to the communities of Marietta and Williamstown were not unrecognized. The *Marietta Times* noted that he "was a leader in his home town industry and finance, in the promotion of its development along good lines . . . a leader in developing the community spirit between Williamstown and Marietta that has been of marked benefit to both . . . His influence was great and he exercised it well for the public's benefit, as a good man and a good citizen should." The *Parkersburg*

(continued on page 115)

Bill and Frank M. Fenton busy with their responsibilities managing the company, circa 1951.

News added that Mr. Fenton "gave Williamstown the first and largest manufacturing industry it ever has had and which gave employment to several hundred persons... The industry which he started seemed to bring new life to that community and today Williamstown is one of the most prosperous and attractive little cities in West Virginia." Since his arrival in Williamstown, the *News* concluded, he "certainly has done as much for the benefit of that historic little city as any man who has lived there."

Among assorted testimonials in the company archives is one from the Associated Glass and Pottery Manufacturers, and another from the Farmers and Mechanics National Bank of Williamstown. The former observed that "Mr. Fenton served with us as a Director ... for many years, giving us sound and wise counsel, enthusiastic inspiration and cooperation, sincere support ... all to the end that his name has been written indelibly in the minds and hearts of each of us." The bank directors praised Mr. Fenton for his energies in organizing and leading the institution for almost 30 years, stating that

> "it has been largely through his civic-mindedness and our reliance upon his excellent judgment and unselfish devotion to the cause of the Bank and the sound banking principles which he maintained that this institution has been carried to a larger, stronger and more secure place in our community life."

The Fenton Board of Directors held an emergency meeting on May 24, 1948, and named Frank M. Fenton as acting treasurer, one of his father's two positions, until the regular monthly session. At the regular meeting on June 1, presided over by Robert C. Sr., the principal item was the election of a new president. Robert himself was nominated first, but recognizing this as a gesture of respect to him for his years of service to the company, he declined. He "thanked the directors for their confidence in him, but thought it best that a younger man assume this responsibility." He then put the name of Frank M. Fenton in nomination for both president and treasurer, and the eldest son of Frank L. was unanimously elected to those two offices. Robert C. stayed on as vice-president and sales manager.

Robert, however, was not in good health and his last illness set in within several months of his brother's death. He lingered for some while, but finally succumbed on November 26, 1948, in his home at 211 Fourth Street in Williamstown. James E. Fenton, the fifth brother connected with the company, who had handled maintenance matters for many years, had died almost one year to the day before Robert, so now the first generation of Fenton officials was gone. John, it will be recalled, departed after a policy dispute in 1910, and Charles died in 1936. The one remaining brother, Will, never left Indiana, Pennsylvania, outliving all of the others. At the first directors' meeting following the 1949 stockholders session, Wilmer C. Fenton, Frank L's. youngest son, was elected to succeed his uncle as vice-president and secretary. At that time Frank M. was also given the job of general manager in addition to his other duties. Hence by 1949 a second generation of Fentons had taken over management of the glass plant from the old order.

Frank M. Fenton, fifth child and first son of Frank L., was born at the original family home on Williams Avenue on December 1, 1915. He attended grade school in Williamstown, but crossed over to Marietta for his high school work. He entered Marietta College in September, 1932, in the depths of the Depression, and graduated with a bachelor of arts degree in 1936. At Marietta he majored in chemistry, captained the crew, and played center on the Pioneers' 1935-1936 Ohio Conference Championship basketball team. At 6'7" Frank was probably one of the game's first long men. He pledged Delta Upsilon social fraternity and was elected to the Gold Key honorary.

Frank M. experienced his first real contact with the company while attending Marietta College. For several years he had urged his father to hire him in the summer months, but Frank L. always turned him down on the theory that "other people need the work a lot more than you do. You can pull weeds at home." At length he sought out his Uncle Jim who told him to come to work the next day. Frank M. observed that night to his parents that he had been "asking the wrong guy" for a job and announced that he was forever done with weed pulling. He reported to his uncle the next morning and was put to work down by the railroad siding. What did he do? He pulled weeds. A short time later he was sent up on the roof with a bucket of tar to patch holes. Once, long after he became president, he was asked "did you start at the bottom and work up?" Frank replied with a chuckle, "no, I started at the top—patching the roof—and worked down."

The real apprenticeship for Frank M. began in June, 1936, when he graduated from college. During that summer he did maintenance work in the hot metal department, but in the fall he went into the office to master the company's books. He worked with Grace Sayre, learning the union's rules and regulations for pay incentives and soon was preparing the payroll. For the next seven or eight years drawing up the payroll remained one of his chief responsibilities. A silent understanding gradually developed between father and son during these years that the latter would move into the former's shoes at some unspecified, future time.

In mastering the company's affairs Frank studied

the financial records, investigated union relations, and examined many other facets of the business. As the years passed he developed a reasonably good grasp of how things were done. "I began to learn," he recalled, "what was going on out there mainly by observation, not by actually doing it. I began to know all the people and their backgrounds; I dealt with the men and now when they had complaints they began to come to me. It was a gradual growth process." In January, 1942, Frank M. was elected "Assistant General Manager," which he remained until he became president. He learned a great deal about the operations of a glass plant during his "apprenticeship," but there was still much that his father and uncle shielded from him until it was too late. This would cause problems in 1948 and after.

Wilmer C. "Bill" Fenton, Frank's youngest son, was born on November 13, 1923. He graduated from Williamstown High School in 1940, where he captained the basketball team, and attended Marietta College from 1940 to 1943. With the local draft board closing in on him during the winter of 1942-1943, he began to work part time at the glass plant during the spring term and await his "Greetings." He was called by his draft board in June, 1943. Prior to this time he worked summers with the company's maintenance crew and in the hot metals department. In fact, he had been working less than a month during his first summer when the stack collapsed literally over his head.

Following three years of military service, Bill was demobilized in the early spring of 1946 and went back to work at the company on May 8. While he was still in the army, a comrade from Portsmouth, Ohio, had invited him to become a business partner after their respective discharges. He was greatly tempted. Bill wrote to his father, remarking that there appeared little opportunity for him at the company and asking what Mr. Fenton thought of his going to Portsmouth. Frank L. replied promptly that they had plans for him at the factory, and that he should advise his Portsmouth friend to recruit someone else. So Bill started on the job in May, expecting to assist his cousin, Robert C. Jr., in sales. However Bob Jr. died of a heart attack, and Bill never had the opportunity to work with him.

It is not easy to speculate how the new table of organization would have looked had Bob Jr. lived. Born in Marion, Ohio, in 1902, he came to Williamstown when his father decided to join forces with Frank L. in 1909. He graduated from Williamstown High School in 1920 and then attended the Marietta

The newly remodeled home of F. L. Fenton, circa 1925. This is where Bill and Frank (M.) Fenton were raised.

Business College and Marietta College for several years. In the mid-twenties he joined the company full time in the sales division, working very closely with his father. As the years passed Bob Jr. took over more and more of the sales work and in 1940 was named sales manager. He loved selling and had soon mastered the techniques of salesmanship. He made a point of knowing his buyers, knowing what merchandise they could handle, and he never "oversold" his product. His unexpected death from a heart attack in the summer of 1946 was a severe loss to the company and made the burden which would fall on Frank L.'s sons two years later, a little heavier.

Although the position of sales manager was not continued at this time, the sales duties were thrust into Bill's untrained hands. But working with his Uncle Bob, who had handled the job for several decades before Bob Jr. was elevated to the post in 1940, he gradually learned the art of selling. His first trip was one he would never forget. Loading 150 to 200 pieces of Fentonware into the back of his car he set out alone for Pittsburgh one summer's day in 1946. Unable to get a room at the classy William Penn Hotel, he had to settle for the rather dingy Fort Pitt, downtown. With the aid of a porter, he dug out some dusty old tables from the basement, cleaned them off and set them up in his display room, covered them with bedsheets, and put up his exhibits.

But now doubt gripped him — it was his first selling experience and he was ashamed to bring any buyers into his Fort Pitt headquarters, and he decided on a quick phone call to Williamstown. Frank L. was told by his 23-year old son that he did not think he could go through with it. Several well-chosen fatherly words restored the young man's confidence, and the next day he went out and looked up Joseph Horn Jr., buyer for Joseph Horn and Company of Pittsburgh. Bill apologized for being at the Fort Pitt Hotel, but that apparently mattered little to Horn, who came over and in a friendly, reassuring manner, placed a very large order. The worst was over for the new salesman.

* * * *

In view of the outstanding success the Fenton company has enjoyed in the years after 1950, it might surprise one that doubts about its future were widely-held at the time control changed hands. Yet this was the case. Frank M. would be stopped on the streets of Marietta and told that he had assumed an awesome responsibility and did he think he could handle it? Rumors of an imminent sale of the plant circulated freely. Stockholders began to press Frank M. about finances. One cousin, who was not associated with the company but who owned some stock, came in shortly after the changeover. Fearful that his stock, which he had used to secure a bank loan, would depreciate and thereby jeopardize his loan, he inquired if Frank would want to buy his shares. He certainly did. Although there was the problem of raising funds on short notice, he was able to do this and buy the stock. Another close relative who owned important stock demanded to see the books and was not reassured until she had studied the records for the previous five years and found that all was in order. Paul Rosenthal not only wanted to sell his stock, but decided that since the old order was gone he might just as well quit too. He did in 1949.

Why the panic? The two points cited at the outset of the chapter well sum it up: first, a serious decline in the hand glass industry set in during the late forties and continued on for a few years; second, just at this time new and fairly inexperienced men became the chief executive officers of the company. Frank M. was 32 years old and Bill was only 24 at the time of the changeover, and it was perfectly natural that some shareholders, long used to the familiar, comfortable old personnel and business methods, were skeptical about the future. They simply did not believe the new leaders had enough experience and know-how to make the company prosper, and they wanted to get out before trouble developed. Some of them did, but they might have had second thoughts as the company bounced back from its temporary decline and moved onward and upward.

An early problem developed under the new management in the wake of Paul Rosenthal's retirement. The trouble centered on the old formulas which Jake Rosenthal had developed, passed on to Paul, and which had been improved upon by Paul in his 20 years as factory manager, from 1929 to 1949. Some time before his retirement Paul had been asked to turn over the formulas to the company, but he was reluctant to do so, arguing that they were his own private property. The matter was dropped. Then at the time he left the company he was offered a generous sum of money for the formulas, which he accepted. The company thus acquired full title to 40 or 50 distinctive glass formulas.

Fenton's "glassmaker" at the time was Harold Riggle, Rosenthal's son-in-law, who had been with the company for seven or eight years. Several months after Paul's departure, instructions came from the front office which required Riggle to keep a record of the chemical ingredients which went into each batch. In the next few weeks it became apparent that one particular batch was not turning out right. Frank M. went out into the hot metal works and asked to see the records, but to his dismay he found that none had been kept. Moreover, Riggle advised him, none would be kept. The need for such records was explained, but Riggle remained adamant. He would quit before he would write down any list of chemicals. Told one last time that he must keep the records, he gave Frank M. his notice. No problem of secrecy was involved since the company already had the formulas; it was a matter of simple bookkeeping.

But there was no official glassmaker. Consequently, Frank M. hastened to the mixing room himself, and with Lawrence Badgely at his side, went to work. Frank had with him the Rosenthal formula for the batch which had been causing Riggle so much trouble, and he was going to solve the mystery if he possibly could. The batch turned out beautifully. Then more problems developed, and they could not get another good batch for the next few weeks. For some time the results continued to be unsatisfactory, although eventually the source of the difficulty was eliminated. As Frank M. continued to keep a close eye on the chemical-mixing operation, Badgely remained temporary glassmaker. Meanwhile a search was launched for a "glass technologist."

In the spring of 1950 when the Fenton company began its earnest quest for a glass technologist, Isaac Willard was a young married man, a senior at the University of Pittsburgh, majoring in chemical engineering. After graduation in June, he planned to locate in the Pittsburgh area with one of the industrial organizations to whom he had submitted job applications. In late March or early April, however, George Tabler, a sales representative for Solvay Sales Company and a close friend of Willard's in-laws, informed Willard that there was an opening for a young chemist at the Fenton glass factory in Williamstown. Tabler visited FAGCO frequently in his travels and had been asked by Frank M. to recommend someone for the job. He recommended Willard. Although he knew nothing about glass-making and had never imagined that he would work in a glass plant, "Ike" sent his credentials to the company.

In about three weeks he received an invitation from Frank M. to come to Williamstown for an interview, an invitation he quickly accepted. He was quite enthusiastic about the company and its facilities during his visit, and he decided to accept the job if it was offered to him. When Frank M. was in Pittsburgh some weeks later on business, he met Willard and told him the job was his if he wanted it, which he did. He began work at Fentons in the second week of July, 1950.

When asked what caused himself and his brother the greatest concern at the time of the takeover, Frank M. cited the following four problems: (1) ignorance of the company's sales structure; (2) labor relations; (3) design of the "line;" and (4) expansion. Perhaps the chief shortcoming in the new leaders was their unfamiliarity with the sales organization. This had been the private preserve of the Bobs, Senior and Junior, and although Bill by now had several years of sales experience under his belt, neither he nor Frank had a very clear idea of how the sales end was administered. "We didn't even know what our west coast representative looked like," Frank recalled. "We knew so little that we got a Dun and Bradstreet report to learn more about them." So they muddled along as best they could, picking up a few ideas here and there. In time, trips to various parts of the country gradually cemented the ties between the new Fentons and the old sales outlets.

But after their basic training in sales organization had been completed, Bill and Frank found several things they did not like. Chief among these was the "jobbing" system. We have already described how jobbers operated. A jobber was a middleman, who would buy assortments of items from a manufacturer at a discount, mark up the prices, and resell the merchandise to his own customers. It was an easy, convenient way for small concerns, which could not afford elaborate sales forces, to market their product. A jobber had numerous contacts, was familiar with the sales potential of different items, and paid his bill as soon as he received the goods. All of this simplified the manufacturer's task.

But the jobber was often in direct competition with a Fenton salesman. The salesman perhaps had arranged with a gift shop to carry the Fenton line as long as no other local outlet had it. Then along came the jobber who, interested only in another account, would bypass the gift store and put a Fenton assortment in the store directly across the street. The gift shop proprietor would conclude that the salesman had broken the agreement and withdraw the Fentonware from his shelves. It was exceedingly difficult to coordinate the activities of salesmen and jobbers, even though both might represent the same company. Since their operations were independent of one another, they became competitors, and the end result was frequently harmful to the company.

For this reason, therefore, it was decided in the early 1950's to abandon the jobbers and sell solely through manufacturer's representatives. The step was not taken without some soul-searching, however, because it meant the rupture of a number of close personal relationships dating well back into the elder Fentons' days. "It was not easy," Bill recollected, "to tell a man like Crawford James that we were not going to sell to him anymore." Crawford James represented the T. M. James Company, Kansas City jobbers, who had handled Fentonware in the midwest for many years. It seemed that every spring at the Pittsburgh Glass Show the first order received by Fentons would be placed by Crawford James. He worked closely with Robert C. Fenton Sr. for a long while and continued his collaboration with Bill when he became sales chief. Thus dropping the jobbers was unpleasant business, but it was a move dictated by the needs of the time.

Taking over for the jobber was the manufacturer's representative (MR). The company employed MR's from the early years, but they always shared the field with the jobber, and both of them were assisted occasionally by someone like Bob Sr. or Jr., making special trips of their own into the field. Now everything would be in the hands of the MR. An MR generally specialized in one area, say art glass or glass lamps, and represented a number of companies producing that type of product. The MR would send an order to the company, which would ship the goods directly to the customer. He received a commission on the transaction when the order left the factory.

Unexpected difficulties emerged, however, as the Fenton company began to rebuild its sales program with MR's. Many of them, in the company's pay for decades, had lost their vitality and it was necessary to replace them. Not only were better salesmen recruited, but a new incentive system was adopted, which further stimulated the men in the field. Quotas were assigned to all MR's, and anything sold above that figure would bring a higher commission. The yearly quota deadline was set for July, which served to promote greater activity in the spring months, normally the hardest time to sell art glass. Furthermore, if an MR made no contact with a customer for two years after the original order was placed, and the orders kept coming in, he could no longer claim a commission on that order. He must keep up his visitations. In addition to all this, regular conferences of FAGCO MR's were inaugurated in Williamstown, which helped provide a much more closely-knit organization than ever before.

A short run experiment with national consumer advertising was made in 1950-1952. The elder Fentons had opposed such advertising as money down the drain, but their successors felt that it was worth trying. Not much money was actually budgeted for

(continued on page 145)

Fenton Glass in color

1 — No. 1720 (1757) DIAMOND OPTIC 7½" vase in opalescent cranberry, missing satin finish, circa 1951-54
2 — No. 1763 DIAMOND OPTIC cruet in cranberry opalescent satin, original stopper, circa 1952-53; this color was originally called "satin rose"
3 — No. 203 (1437) 7" cranberry opalescent handled basket in COIN DOT pattern, circa 1947-64
4 — No. 2005 SWIRLED FEATHER perfume bottle to vanity set, circa 1953-54, in cranberry opal satin
5 — No. 2090 (electrified) or No. 2092 (with candleholder) SWIRLED FEATHER fairy lamp, circa 1953-54, in cranberry opalescent satin finish
6 — No. 3903 cranberry opalescent HOBNAIL jam set with original white opalescent lid, circa 1950-56

Mandarin Red & "Flame"

Illustrated above are a number of items in the popular Mandarin Red, also known as "red slag". Also pictured are Figures 7, 15 and 16 in what collectors call Fenton's "Flame" color. These three items appeared in inventory records from 1924 to 1926 in a color listed as "orange". This "Flame" color slightly resembles Northwood's Chinese Coral color from the mid-1920's. Figures 11 and 17 appear to be poor batches of what was meant to be Mandarin Red. This Northwood "red slag" has a redder color and less variegation.

7 — No. 636 one-pound candy jar, 10½" high, almost identical to Northwood's. See Book 1, Figure 382 for the difference between the two, circa 1924.

8 — No. 791 flared Peacock vase, 7½" tall, circa 1934.

9 — No. 891 vase, 12" tall, circa 1933

10 — No. 1681 BIG COOKIES wicker handled basket, 10½" x 5", circa 1933

11 — No. 1681 macaroon jar, 7" tall, circa 1933

12 — No. 846 cupped bowl on black 5-legged pedestal, 6½" diameter, circa 1933

13 — No. 1093 FENTON BASKET 5½" vase, circa 1933

14 — No. 1684 macaroon jar, 6½" tall, circa 1933

15 — No. 549 candlestick in Flame color, 8" tall, circa 1924-26

16 — No. 2007 shallow cupped bowl, 9" diameter, circa 1924-26

17 — No. 847 flared bowl, 7½" diameter, circa 1933

Mongolian Green
Periwinkle Blue

18 — No. 1684 macaroon jar, 6½" tall, circa 1935
19 — No. 901 DANCING LADIES 8½" flared vase, circa 1935
20 — No. 847 fan-shaped vase, 5½" tall, circa 1934
21 — No. 791 flared Peacock vase, 7½" tall, circa 1935
22 — Same as Figure 21, except color is different
23 — No. 621 flared vase, 6" tall, circa 1935
24 — Possibly No. 621 flared vase, 8½" tall, circa 1935
25 — No. 901 DANCING LADIES 9" vase with plain rim possibly designed for a lamp base, circa 1935
26 — No. 847 crimped bowl, 8½" diameter, circa 1935
27 — Unusual figural whiskey bottle, elephant shape, circa 1935
28 — No. 847 crimped vase, 6½" tall, circa 1935
29 — No. 1684 macaroon jar, 6½" tall, circa 1935

30 — No. 8 half-pound decorated candy jar, 9" tall, circa 1925
31 — No. 449 decorated candlesticks, 8½" tall, circa 1925
32 — No. 607 cupped bowl, 8" diameter, circa 1925
33 — No. 919 MIKADO pattern compote, 7" tall, 10" diameter, quite rare in Ebony, circa 1935. The exterior pattern is known as FENTON CHERRIES. See Book 1, Fig. 182, for detail of the interior pattern.
34 — No. 1608 oval footed bowl, dolphin-handled, silver decorated, circa 1934. This same number was used earlier to designate the STAG & HOLLY pattern bowl.
35 — No. 1681 macaroon jar in BIG COOKIES pattern, 7" tall, circa 1933
36 — No. 1601 dolphin-handled footed bowl, 11" diameter, circa 1934
37 — No. 1532 dolphin-handled candy jar, circa 1928
38 — No. 1618 ELEPHANT flower bowl, 8½" diameter, rare in Ebony, circa 1928
39 — No. 1092 FENTON BASKET 6" cupped bowl, circa 1936
40 — No. 844 covered candy bowl, 6¼" tall, circa 1928

Jade Green

Chinese Yellow

41 — No. 184 vase, 12" tall, circa 1931; also made in other sizes

42 — No. 2318 candelabra, 6" tall, circa 1933

43 — No. 1618 ELEPHANT flower bowl, 7" tall, circa 1928

44 — No. 1639 sherbert with ebony stem and base, 3" tall, circa 1931

45 — No. 1639 creamer with ebony stem and base, 4" tall, circa 1931

46 — No. 1700 LINCOLN INN wine or cocktail, 4" tall, circa 1931

47 — No. 1639 footed tumbler in ebony with jade green stem and base, 5½" tall, circa 1931

48 — No. 1616 ice bucket, 6½" tall, circa 1931

49 — No. 1563 large oval two-handled bowl, 17" long, circa 1931; the mold on this item was probably acquired from the Northwood factory, originally made there in the mid-1920's.

50 — No. 1611 GEORGIAN tumbler, 5" tall, circa 1931-38

51 — No. 107 tulip vase, 6½" tall, circa 1932

52 — No. 846 cupped bowl and ebony base, 6" tall, circa 1932

53 — No. 1504-A dolphin-handled cupped bowl with ebony base, 5" tall, circa 1931

54 — No. 900 DANCING LADIES oval flared bowl, 11" wide, circa 1934

55 — No. 315 candlestick, 3½" tall, circa 1925

29

Fenton Ruby

56 — No. 1800 SHEFFIELD 10″ plate, circa 1936

57 — No. 1800 SHEFFIELD 3-toed flared bowl, 7″ diameter, circa 1936

58 — No. 1800 vase, SHEFFIELD pattern, 6¼″ tall, circa 1936

59 — No. 1502 DIAMOND OPTIC fan vase, 8½″ tall, circa 1928

60 — No. 1502 DIAMOND OPTIC goblet, 7″ tall, circa 1928

61 — No. 1933 3-toed flared bowl, 7″ diameter, circa 1932

62 — No. 1933 tumbler, 4¼″ tall, circa 1933

63 — No. 1639 open sugar with crystal base, 3½″ tall, circa 1930

64 — No. 1639 creamer, 4″ tall, circa 1930

65 — No. 1620 PLYMOUTH pattern goblet, 5¾″ tall, circa 1933-39

66 — No. 1620 PLYMOUTH pattern sherbert, 4¼″ tall, circa 1933-39

67 — No. 1620 PLYMOUTH pattern tall tumbler, 6″ tall, circa 1933-39

68 — No. 1700 LINCOLN INN cup and saucer, circa 1928-38

69 — No. 1700 LINCOLN INN footed tumbler, 5¼″ tall, circa 1928-38

70 — No. 1700 LINCOLN INN iced tea, 6″ tall, circa 1928-38

71 — No. 1611 GEORGIAN pattern 21 oz. decanter, circa 1931-38

72 — No. 1611 GEORGIAN pattern salt shaker, original top, 4½″ tall, circa 1931-38

73 — No. 1611 GEORGIAN pattern cup, 3¼″ diameter, circa 1931-38

74 — No. 1611 GEORGIAN pattern 9 oz. footed tumbler, 5½″ tall, circa 1931-38

75 — No. 184 engraved vase, 12" tall, circa 1931
76 — No. 2000A FENTON PINEAPPLE crimped bowl, 3-toed, 11" diameter, circa 1937
77 — No. 249 candlesticks, circa 1933
78 — No. 901 DANCING LADIES vase, 9" tall, circa 1933
79 — No. 1681 BIG COOKIES 10½" wicker-handled basket, circa 1933
80 — No. 1608 dolphin-handled compote, 10" diameter, circa 1933
81 — No. 857 flared bowl, 10" diameter, circa 1933
82 — No. 1639 two-handled plate, 12" diameter, circa 1932
83 — No. 848 ash tray, three-footed, circa 1934
84 — No. 705 ivy ball, 5" diameter, circa 1933
85 — Tiny 3½" shell, with embossed letters LOBSTER POUND on surface, circa 1936
86 — No. 175 leaf-shaped tray, 8½" long, circa 1936

Royal Blue

87 — No. 1621E dolphin-handled etched 5½" square bonbon, circa 1936

88 — No. 1621E dolphin-handled etched 9½" square bowl, circa 1936

89 — No. 1502 DIAMOND OPTIC 11½" rolled rim bowl, circa 1928

90 — No. 184 engraved vase, 12" tall, circa 1933

91 — No. 901 DANCING LADIES 8½" tall vase, circa 1933

92 — No. 848 3-footed ash tray, 4" diameter, circa 1934

93 — No. 107 tulip vase, 6½" tall, circa 1932; same design as #1933 tumbler

94 — No. 1611 GEORGIAN pattern cupped sherbert, 3" tall, circa 1931-38

95 — No. 1611 GEORGIAN cocktail glass, 4" tall, circa 1931-38

96 — No. 1611 GEORGIAN tumbler, 9 oz. size, circa 1931-38

97 — No. 1611 GEORGIAN 54 oz. water pitcher, 7" tall, circa 1931-38

98 — No. 848 flower form bowl, 9" diameter, circa 1932

99 — No. 848 candleholder, 4" diameter, circa 1932

100-101 — No. 950 cornucopia shaped console set, 11" oval centerpiece, 5" tall candlesticks, circa 1934

Ming & San Toy

102 — No. 1653 pitcher in Ming rose color with rare black handle, 10" tall, circa 1934

103 — No. 249 three-footed bowl, Ming rose color, 9" diameter, circa 1934

104 — No. 750 Ming green octagonal-shape bowl, 9¼" diameter, circa 1935

105 — No. 1653 Ming green 10" pitcher, circa 1934

106 — SAN TOY design on 4½" jar to bathroom set, circa 1936

107 — No. 950 centerpiece bowl to console set, SAN TOY design on green, circa 1936

108 — No. 1684 macaroon jar in MING rose color, 6½" tall, handle missing, circa 1935

109 — No. 621 cupped vase in Ming rose, 6½" tall, circa 1935

110 — No. 1621 dolphin-handled 6½" Ming Rose bon-bon, circa 1935

111 — No. 950 Ming rose cornucopia candlestick, 5½" tall, circa 1935

112 — No. 1663 centerpiece bowl in Ming Rose, 12" oval, circa 1935

Fenton Rose

113 — No. 1412 ORANGE TREE goblet, 5" tall, circa 1930
114 — No. 1700 LINCOLN INN 8" plate, circa 1928-32
115 — No. 1700S LINCOLN INN oval compote, circa 1928-32
116 — No. 1621-1703 dolphin-handled 9" cut bowl, circa 1928
117 — No. 100 Octagon bowl, 8½" diameter, circa 1930
118 — No. 5 swan bon-bon, 6" diameter, circa 1938
119 — No. 6 swan candlestick, 6½" tall, circa 1938
120-121 — No. 1611 GEORGIAN 6 oz. high footed sherbet and 5 oz. juice glass, circa 1931
122-123 — No. 1502 DIAMOND OPTIC creamer and open sugar, 3½" tall, circa 1927
124 — No. 1502 DIAMOND OPTIC vanity set, circa 1927
125 — No. 1621-1703 dolphin-handled cut bowl, 8" diameter, circa 1928
126-128 — No. 1900 Daisy & Button vanity set on No. 957 fan-shaped tray, circa 1937

Fenton Amber

129—No. 6 swan bowl, 11½" oval, circa 1938

130-131—No. 950 console bowl, 11" oval, and single candlestick, 5" tall, circa 1935

132—No. 1620 PLYMOUTH 8 oz. highball, circa 1933-38

133—No. 1800 SHEFFIELD tumbler, 4¼" tall, circa 1936

134-136—No. 1611 GEORGIAN pattern cocktail, cup and whiskey, circa 1931-38

137—No. 5595 planter bookend, two pieces, 7" tall, circa 1953

138-140—No. 1900 DAISY & BUTTON vanity set (missing one perfume) on #957 fan-shaped tray, circa 1937

142—No. 1002 SILVERTONE pattern 9" flared bowl, circa 1937

141-143—No. 1010 three-toed SILVERTONE candleholders, one flared, one tri-cornered, circa 1937

Mulberry & Amethyst

144 — No. 192 DIAMOND OPTIC pitcher in rare Mulberry color, 5" tall, circa 1942

145 — No. 192 DIAMOND OPTIC basket, 10½" diameter, Mulberry color, circa 1942

146 — No. 192 DIAMOND OPTIC 9" vase in Mulberry color, circa 1942

147 — No. 1800 SHEFFIELD amethyst tumbler, 4" tall, circa 1936

148 — No. 1021 footed ivy ball, 8½" tall, amethyst & milk circa 1953

149 — No. 957 DAISY & BUTTON fan-shaped dresser tray, 10¾" diameter, circa 1937

150 — No. 6 Swan bowl, 11½" diameter, circa 1938

151 — No. 100 amethyst opalescent crimped bowl, 7" diameter, circa 1932

152 — No. 1004 cupped bowl, 7" diameter, circa 1934, SILVERTONE pattern

153 — No. 1009 flat plate in SILVERTONE pattern, 7½" diameter, circa 1934

154 — No. 1005 SILVERTONE flared bowl, 6½" diameter, circa 1934

155 — No. 1007 cupped bowl in SILVERTONE pattern, 5" diameter, circa 1934

Satin Poinsettia & Silvertone

156 — No. 1352 Iced Tea Pitcher with SILVERTONE etching, circa 1937; do not confuse for the pressed SILVERTONE pattern on opposite page

157 — No. 1352 Iced tea tumbler with Silvertone etching, 5¼" tall, circa 1937

158 — No. 1800 SHEFFIELD 8" three-footed plate with SILVERTONE etching, circa 1937

159 — No. 1800 SHEFFIELD 14" underplate to salad bowl, SILVERTONE etching, circa 1937

160 — No. 1616 basket, 6½"x9½", with #43 POINSETTIA etching, circa 1939

161 — No. 349 bowl with #43 POINSETTIA etching, 10½" diameter, circa 1939

162 — No. 183 vase, 6½" tall, with POINSETTIA etching, circa 1939

163 — No. 1800 three-toed SHEFFIELD bowl, unknown etched design, triangular shapes, 7" diameter, circa 1937

164 — No. 950 cornucopia centerpiece with SILVERTONE etching, 11" long, circa 1936

165 — No. 950 cornucopia candleholder with SILVERTONE design, circa 1936

166 — No. 107 footed plate with unlisted etched design, 8" diameter, circa 1936

Satin Wistaria & Ming

167 — No. 184 vase with WISTARIA etching, 11½" tall, circa 1938

168 — No. 1354 iced tea pitcher with WISTARIA design, 10½" tall, circa 1937

169-170 — No. 200 night set or tumble-up (tumbler fits inside 7" tall pitcher), WISTARIA design, circa 1937

171-172 — #1934 decanter with Ming decoration, 9¼" tall with 2½" jigger glass, circa 1935

173 — #349 fan vase with WISTARIA decoration, 8" tall, circa 1937

174-176 — Possibly No. 604 punch bowl and cups with WISTARIA etched design, bowl is 12½" diameter, circa 1937

177 — No. 1616 ice pail with WISTARIA etching, 5¾" tall, circa 1938

178-179 — No. 349 creamer and open sugar with WISTARIA etching, both 3¼" tall, circa 1937

180 — No. 1684 basket with WISTARIA design, circa 1936

181 — No. 2000 candelabra to console set, 5" tall, circa 1936, MING decoration

Satin San Toy & Velvatone

182 — No. 898 vase with SAN TOY etching, 11½" tall, circa 1936
183 — No. 1590 coaster, with SAN TOY design, 4" diameter, circa 1936
184 — No. 1616 ice pail with SAN TOY etching, 6" tall, circa 1936
185 — No. 349 bowl, 8½" diameter, with SAN TOY design, circa 1937
186-187 — No. 35 whiskey and No. 33 cocktail shaker, circa 1936
188 — No. 249 candlestick with SAN TOY etching, 6" tall, circa 1936
189 — No. 950 cornucopia centerpiece with SAN TOY design, 11" oval, circa 1936
190 — No. 844 covered bon-bon, 6" tall with SAN TOY etching, circa 1936
191 — No. 107 three-footed plate, 8" diameter, circa 1938, SAN TOY etching
192 — No. 1934 triangle vase, 5" tall, circa 1938, VELVATONE design
193 — No. 846 covered bon-bon, 5" tall with VELVATONE etching, circa 1938
194 — No. 200 vase, 7" tall with VELVATONE design, circa 1938
195 — No. 1800 footed bon-bon, three-footed with HALO etching, 7" diameter, circa 1937

39

Miscellaneous Satin

- **196** — No. 901 DANCING LADIES vase, 9" tall, circa 1934
- **197** — No. 2000A center bowl to console set, 12½" diameter, FENTON PINEAPPLE pattern, circa 1938
- **198** — No. 1517 LINCOLN INN 11" plate with satin three-fruits center, circa 1935
- **199** — No. 1110 LATTICE & GRAPE 11½" tall vase, circa 1934
- **200** — No. 2000 PINEAPPLE compote, 5¼" diameter, circa 1938
- **201** — No. 2000 salver in Fenton's PINEAPPLE pattern, 7" diameter, circa 1938
- **202** — No. 2000 candlestick to console set, 5½" tall, circa 1938
- **203** — No. 2000 triangle bowl in PINEAPPLE pattern, 7" diameter, circa 1938
- **204** — No. 2000 compote, 5½" tall, unusual tall stem, circa 1938
- **205** — No. 1623 dolphin candlestick, 4" tall, circa 1937
- **206-207** — No. 900 DANCING LADIES console set, 11½" (900) centerpiece, 4¼" (901) footed vases, circa 1935
- **208** — No. 4 SWAN novelty, 4" tall, circa 1938

Pekin Blue

Blue Overlay

209 — No. 549 candlesticks, 8" tall, circa 1924
210 — No. 1663 oval bowl, 12½" diameter, circa 1933
211 — No. 643 salver, 6¼" diameter, circa 1924
212 — No. 621 vase, 6" tall, circa 1933
213 — No. 318 candlestick, 3" tall, circa 1933
214-215 — No. 53 dresser set, Pekin Blue with Moonstone lid and stoppers, circa 1926

216 — No. 192 handled jug, 6" tall, circa 1943
217 — No. 192 squat jug, 5¼" tall, circa 1943
218 — No. 203 handled basket, 7¼" diameter, circa 1943
219 — No. 1924 handled basket, 5" diameter, circa 1943
220-221 — No. 192A three-piece vanity set, circa 1943
222 — No. 192A handled jug, 8½" tall, circa 1943

41

Fenton Green

223 — No. 194 vase in ivy, 11" tall, circa 1949-52

224 — No. 1925 vase in ivy, 6¼" tall, circa 1949-52

225 — No. 1924 vase, 3½" tall, circa 1950-51, ivy color

226 — No. 711 rose bowl, 5" tall, in ivy, circa 1949-51

227 — No. 711 Peacock bookend in light green satin, 5¾" tall, circa 1935

228 — No. 1729 pipe ashtray in green marble, 4½" diameter, circa 1950-53

229 — No. 752 candle holder to console set, emerald green, circa 1951-52

230 — No. 711 handled creamer in light green overlay, 4" tall, circa 1949

231 — No. 1522 emerald green SNOWCREST bowl, 10" diameter, circa 1950

232 — No. 5185 covered chick, 5½" long, emerald green top on milk base, circa 1953

233-237 — No. 1700 LINCOLN INN service in emerald green, sometime between 1928-1938

Green & Lime Opalescent Hobnail

The HOBNAIL pattern is without a doubt the single line most often associated with the Fenton name. The story of how Fenton entered the Hobnail business is well documented in the Murdock history of the company. Any attempt to accurately date a single piece of Fenton Hobnail is no simple task. Many items remained in the line for twenty years or more. Others were introduced to the line in 1940, pulled out a few years later, and then re-introduced in other colors at later dates. For example, green opalescent Hobnail was made in 1940 and 41. The items returned to the line in 1952 as Lime opalescent, a similar color made by casing dark green inside French opalescent. A careful study of the catalogues reprinted in this book will reveal the same items in the 1940, 1948, 1950, 1953 and 1955 offerings. However, the colors offered might vary and the stoppers in the cruets and perfumes can differ. It is almost impossible to determine by color depth, weight or age wear whether any Hobnail item with a long production life is from the early forties or the late fifties. All Hobnail made before 1953 was assigned the Number 389.

238 — No. 389 double-crimp 6″ vase circa 1940-41 in green opalescent, shown here in lime opalescent, circa 1952-54; No. 3856 after 1952

239 — No. 389 (No. 3855 after 1952) 4″ miniature vase, tri-cornered, circa 1940-41 in green opalescent, circa 1952-54 in Lime opalescent shown here

240 — No. 389 (No. 3854 after 1952) double crimp 4½″ vase, circa 1940-41 in g.o., circa 1952-54 in Lime opalescent shown here; this shape still made in milk glass

241 — No. 389 (No. 3863 after 1952) 6″ cruet in Lime opalescent, circa 1952-54

242 — No. 389 (No. 3865 later) perfume with 1940 stopper, 4½″ tall, shown here in green opalescent — two other possible stoppers in later years; not made in Lime opalescent

243 — No. 389 (No. 3964 after 1952) 5½″ handled jug with crimp top, circa 1940-41 in g.o., circa 1952-54 in Lime opalescent

Cranberry Opalescent Hobnail

244 — 8½" tall vase, circa 1940-1961; No. 3859 after 1952
245 — 5" tall double crimped vase, circa 1940-1977; No. 3850 after 1952
246 — Reproduction hobnail barber bottle which started Fenton into the Hobnail business; made for L. G. Wright in late thirties from a mold found at Indiana, Pennsylvania. Northwood made the original around 1900, probably from an old Hobbs mold.
247 — 11" crimped bowl, circa 1940-1977; No. 3924 after 1952
248 — 4½" handled basket, circa 1940-1956; No. 3834 after 1952
249 — 5½" handled basket, circa 1950-1955; No. 3835 after 1952
250 — 7" handled basket, circa 1941-1977; No. 3837 after 1952
251 — 5½" diameter bowl, No. 3927, circa 1941-1977
252 — 6" diameter bon-bon, circa 1940-1945
253 — 5½" jug, circa 1941-1954; No. 3964 after 1952
254 — 6" tall cruet, circa 1942-1977; No. 3863 after 1952
255 — 7" diameter oil lamp fount, circa 1950
256 — 5½" tall crimped vase, circa 1940-1956; No. 3856 after 1952
257 — 4" triangle miniature vase, circa 1940-1956; No. 3855 after 1952
258 — 3½" tall salt and pepper, No. 3806, circa 1955-1967

Blue Opalescent Hobnail

259 — 3½" tall 5 oz. tumbler, circa 1940-1954; No. 3945 after 1952
260 — 5½" tall squat jug, circa 1940-1954; No. 3965 after 1952
261 — 8" tall 80 oz. pitcher, circa 1940-1954; No. 3967 after 1952
262 — No. 3809 condiment set on No. 3879 chrome handled tray, circa 1950-1953
263 — No. 3986 (after 1952) vanity boxtle, 7½" tall, circa 1953 only
264 — No. 3837 basket, 7½" diameter, circa 1940-1954
265 — 4½" tall cup flared vase, circa 1940-1945
266 — No. 397 (after 1952) Miniature cornucopia, circa 1940-1954
267 — 4" ash tray, circa 1940-54; No. 3873 after 1952
268 — 4½" diameter handled basket, circa 1948-1954; No. 3834 after 1952
269 — 7" crimped bowl, circa 1940-54; No. 3827 after 1952
270 — 4" miniature vase, circa 1940-45
271 — 3½" salt and pepper, circa 1950-1954; No. 3806 after 1952
272 — 2½" hat-shaped cigarette holder, circa 1940-1953; No. 3992 after 1952
273 — 5½" fan ash tray, circa 1941-1954; No. 3872 after 1952
274 — 10½" fan tray, circa 1941-1954

Topaz & French Opalescent

275 — No. 1948 DIAMOND LACE epergne in French opalescent with applied aqua rim, circa 1948-54

276 — No. 389 HOBNAIL 15" tall basket in Topaz opalescent, 11" diameter, circa 1940-43

277 — No. 1948A DIAMOND LACE apartment size epergne in Topaz opalescent, made in flint and blue opalescent beginning in 1948, made in Topaz opalescent for AA Sales in 1970

278-279 — No. 1948 three-piece DIAMOND LACE console set in flint opalescent, circa 1949-1953; No. 4804 after 1952

280 — No. 389 HOBNAIL 5" crimp vase in flint opalescent, circa 1941-1949

281 — No. 389 HOBNAIL 8¼" fan vase in French opalescent, circa 1941-1945

282 — No. 389 slipper in Topaz opalescent, 6" long, circa 1941-1943

283 — No. 389 HOBNAIL candlestick in Topaz opalescent, 4½" diameter, circa 1941-1943

284 — No. 389 hand vase in Topaz opalescent, 6" tall, circa 1942-1943

285 — No. 389 HOBNAIL 5½" pitcher in Topaz opalescent, circa 1941-1943

286 — No. 3870 HOBNAIL candlestick in French opalescent, 1953 only

287 — No. 289 HOBNAIL cologne bottle in French opalescent made exclusively for Wrisley, with original wooden stopper, circa 1939-1940

Aqua Crest & Emerald Crest

288 — No. 1923 AQUA CREST 10″ tall basket, circa 1941-1942

289 — No. 37 AQUA CREST 4″ miniature fan basket, circa 1942

290 — No. 1523 AQUA CREST large 13″ tall basket, circa 1941-1942

291 — No. 36 AQUA CREST 4½″ tall oval vase, circa 1941

292 — No. 1353 AQUA CREST triangular vase, 10½″ tall, circa 1942

293 — No. 401 EMERALD CREST pot and attached saucer, 4½″ tall, circa 1951-1955 (#7299 after 1952)

294 — No. 7296 EMERALD CREST 2-tier tidbit tray, circa 1954-1955; the No. 680 2-tier tray made earlier was larger in size

295 — No. 680 EMERALD CREST 3″ tall open sugar (#7231 after 1952), circa 1951-1955

296 — No. 680 EMERALD CREST 3¼″ tall creamer (#7261 after 1952), circa 1951-1955

297 — No. 680 EMERALD CREST 5½″ soup bowl (#7320 after 1952) circa 1951-1954

298 — No. 36 EMERALD CREST 6″ crimped vase (#7356 after 1952), circa 1951-1955

299 — No. 680 AQUA CREST cup and saucer (#7208 after 1952), circa 1948-1953

300 — No. 37 AQUA CREST miniature vase, circa 1942

301 — No. 680 AQUA CREST 8½″ plate (#7217 after 1952) circa 1948-1953

302 — No. 1924 AQUA CREST 3¼″ top hat, circa 1942

303 — No. 1523 AQUA CREST 5″ candlestick, circa 1941-42 and again in 1951

304 — No. 36 AQUA CREST 4″ triangle vase, circa 1941-42

Peach Blow, Peach Crest & Black Rose

- **305** — Unusual patterned PEACH BLOW vase or bottle, possibly made for a lamp base, from the 1950's
- **306** — No. 192 PEACH CREST 10" basket with milk handle made in 1948 only; the earlier baskets in this pattern, circa 1942-1947, had crystal handles
- **307** — No. 193 PEACH CREST 10¼" hand vase, circa 1942-1943; No. 5155 from 1953-54 had a different crimp on the upper rim
- **308** — No. 7398 BLACK ROSE globe to hurricane lamp, circa 1953
- **309** — No. 7250 BLACK ROSE 8½" tulip vase, circa 1953-1954
- **310** — No. 5155 BLACK ROSE 10½" hand vase, circa 1953-1954
- **311** — No. 9020 PEACH CREST 10¼" shell bowl, circa 1955-1964; made in peach satin and green satin in 1953 and 1954
- **312** — No. 203 decorated PEACH CREST 7" basket with milk handle, circa 1948; the following three years, 1949-1951, the No. 711 beaded melon mold was used on this basket
- **313** — No. 6056 PEACH CREST 6" vase, circa 1955-1962
- **314** — No. 203 PEACH CREST basket (#7237 after 1952) with crystal handle, circa 1940-1947 and again from 1952-1969
- **315** — No. 186 PEACH CREST 8" crimped triangle vase, circa 1941-1945; in 1953-1954 this same mold was made only in a double crimp (#7258) and crimp tulip vase (#7250)
- **316** — No. 203 PEACH CREST 7½" square bowl, circa 1940-1944
- **317** — No. 1522 PEACH CREST 10" eight-point crimped bowl, 1940 only
- **318** — No. 1523 PEACH CREST candlestick, 5" tall, circa 1940-1953 (#7270 after 1952)
- **319** — No. 186 PEACH BLOW 8½" tulip vase, circa 1939
- **320** — No. 187 PEACH CREST 5" triangle vase, circa 1940-1943

Fenton Crest Lines

321—No. 192 ROSE CREST 8½" double crimp vase, circa 1945-1947

322—No. 192 ROSE CREST 10" tall basket, circa 1945-1947

323—No. 192 ROSE CREST 6½" vase, circa 1945-1947

324—No. 573 GOLD CREST 8" crimped vase, circa 1943; rare vase of limited production

325—No. 192A SILVER CREST 9" handled jug, circa 1943-1948

326—No. 186 IVORY CREST 8" vase, circa 1940-1941

327-328—No. 1522-951 IVORY CREST 6-piece epergne set (one candlestick not shown), circa 1940-41

329—No. 1523 IVORY CREST cornucopia vase, circa 1940-1941

330—No. 203 GOLD CREST 6½" crimp triangle bowl, circa 1943-1944

331—No. 1924 GOLD CREST crimped top hat, circa 1943-1944

332—No. 192 CRYSTAL CREST 6½" double crimp vase, circa 1942

333—No. 682 IVORY CREST 10" bowl and 11½" plate, circa 1940-1941

Milk Glass & Moonstone

- **334** — No. 1929 DAISY AND BUTTON 11" oval bowl, circa 1953-1959 in milk only
- **335** — No. 1561 APPLE TREE 10" vase, circa 1933-1936
- **336** — No. 791 Peacock 4" vase, circa 1933-1934; also made in 6" and 8" sizes
- **337-338** — No. 5647 (6" tumbler) and No. 5667 (70 oz. jug) in BLOCK AND STAR, circa 1955, rare
- **339** — No. 6180 WAFFLE pattern sugar bowl, circa 1960; repro of early Beatty pattern
- **340** — No. 6601 RIB covered sugar bowl, circa 1958; repro of early Beatty pattern
- **341** — No. 1790 LEAF TIERS milk glass bowl, 10" diameter, circa 1934-1936
- **342** — No. 5156 fish vase, 6½" tall, 1953 only; also made in black with milk eyes and tail
- **343** — No. 6985 TEARDROP 6" candy box, circa 1955-56
- **344-345** — No. 752 console centerpiece and candlestick, circa 1951-1952
- **346** — No. 549 8" candlestick in Moonstone with ebony base, circa 1924
- **347** — No. 1611 GEORGIAN tumbler in Moonstone, circa 1933
- **348** — 3½" SHELL in Moonstone or Opaline color, made for Du-Arte, circa 1955

Rose Pastel & Rose Overlay

349 — No. 1957 DAISY & BUTTON 8″ cupped vase, circa 1954-1956

350 — No. 3924 HOBNAIL 9″ double crimp bowl, circa 1954-1956

351 — No. 9019 Rose Pastel "Backward C" plate with open edge, 9″ diameter, circa 1954-1956

352 — No. 3998 HOBNAIL hurricane chimney on plain base, Rose Pastel color, 1954 only

353 — No. 711 BEADED MELON 8″ vase in Rose Overlay, circa 1949; rare item in this color

354 — No. 4517 double crimp vase, 6½″ tall, made for Weil Ceramics in 1945

355 — No. 4516 handled jug, 8½″ tall, in Rose Overlay, also made for Weil Ceramics (1945)

356 — No. 192 Rose Overlay 8″ handled jug, circa 1943-1948

357 — No. 1924 Rose Overlay 5″ diameter basket, circa 1943-1948

358 — No. 192 Rose Overlay 5½″ jug, circa 1943-1948

359 — No. 5606 Rose Pastel BLOCK AND STAR salt shaker, circa 1955 — a rare sample

360 — No. 9026 Rose Pastel 8″ open edge bowl, circa 1954-1956

361-362 — No. 3906 Rose Pastel HOBNAIL creamer and open sugar, circa 1954-1956

Ruby Overlay

363 — No. 1353 DIAMOND OPTIC 70 oz. water pitcher (jug), circa 1942-1948
364 — No. 1353 tumbler, 4" tall (10 oz.) circa 1942-1948
365 — No. 170 DIAMOND OPTIC hurricane globe and milk base, 11" tall, circa 1951
366 — No. 7202 two-piece epergne, circa 1955-1959
367 — This is a private mold lamp shade made for the B & P Lamp Company
368 — No. 1721 pinch vase, 8¼" tall, circa 1952
369 — No. 192 DIAMOND OPTIC 5½" squat jug, circa 1942-1948
370 — No. 192 DIAMOND OPTIC 7½" double crimp vase, circa 1942-1948
371 — No. 192 DIAMOND OPTIC 8" handled jug, circa 1942-1948
372 — No. 1021 footed ivy ball, circa 1953-1966
373 — Another private mold item — a tumbler for L.G. Wright in DOT OPTIC
374 — No. 705 5" ivy ball, circa 1952
375 — No. 1924 top hat, 3" tall, circa 1942-1948
376 — No. 192 DIAMOND OPTIC 4¼" vase, circa 1943-1948
377 — No. 192 DIAMOND OPTIC 6" handled jug, circa 1942-1948

French Opalescent

378—No. 201 Ring pattern 7" water pitcher, circa late 30's
379—No. 1925 COIN DOT 6" vase, circa 1947-56; No. 1456 after 1952
380—No. 1522 COIN DOT 11" diameter basket, circa 1947-51
381—No. 1800 SHEFFIELD 12" crimped bowl, circa 1936-37
382—No. 1922B SPIRAL 6" tall flared vase in BLUE RIDGE, circa 1939
383—No. 894 SPIRAL 10½" triangle vase, in BLUE RIDGE, circa 1939
384-385—No. 1522 SPIRAL console 10½" bowl and No. 1523 candleholder, in BLUE RIDGE, circa 1939
386—No. 186 SPIRAL 8" vase in BLUE RIDGE, circa 1939
387—No. 1922 RIB OPTIC 6" tall top hat, 9" diameter, circa 1939
388—No. 38 miniature hand vase, 3½" tall, circa 1942-43
389-390—No. 1620 PLYMOUTH pattern 8" plate and 4" highball, circa 1935
391—Private mould atomizer bottle made for Devilbiss
392—No. 1923 RIB OPTIC 3½" tall top hat, 6" diameter, circa 1939

Cranberry Opalescent Rib Optic and Spiral

393-394 — No. 170 SPIRAL hurricane globe, 11" tall, with milk or cobalt base, circa 1939

395 — No. 898 SPIRAL 11½" vase, circa 1939

396 — No. 1667 RIB OPTIC 13½" wine bottle, circa 1953-62

397 — No. 3255 SPIRAL ribbed vase, 5" tall, circa 1955-58

398 — No. 3253 SPIRAL vase, 6½" tall, circa 1955-59

399 — Private mould lamp chimney made for either Quoizel or Billig

400 — No. 201 SPIRAL 5" diameter crimped rose bowl, circa 1939

401 — No. 3160 SPIRAL 6½" vase, circa 1953-59

402 — No. 510 (later #1658) RIB OPTIC satin vase, circa 1952-53

403 — No. 705 RIB OPTIC 4" ivy ball, without base, circa 1952-54; No. 1622 after 1952

404 — No. 1604 RIB OPTIC 4" creamer, circa 1953-54

405-406 — No. 1605 RIB OPTIC 5" salt and 4" pepper shaker, circa 1953-58

407 — No. 1669 RIB OPTIC 7" tall cruet, circa 1953-54

Cranberry Opalescent

408-409 — No. 1353 9" water pitcher and 4" tumbler in Dot Optic pattern, circa 1945

410 — No. 1353 (#1467 after 1953) 70 oz. COIN DOT water pitcher with ice lip, 9½" tall, circa 1949-1957

411 — No. 2221 POLKA DOT footed ivy ball, almost 9" tall, circa 1955-1956

412 — No. 2267 POLKA DOT 70 oz. jug, 9" tall, circa 1955-1956

413 — No. 3005 (later #1451) double crimp COIN DOT vase, 11" tall, circa 1952-1961

414 — No. 894 COIN DOT 12" decanter, circa 1947-1950

415 — No. 194 (No. 1459 after 1952) circa 1948-1958, COIN DOT 8½" vase

416 — No. 194 COIN DOT 11" vase two-handled vase, circa 1947-1950; also made with one handle and without handles

417 — No. 1925 COIN DOT 10½" tall basket, circa 1947-1951

418 — No. 1473 COIN DOT 7" cruet, circa 1953-1961; different from COIN DOT cruet shown in 1947 and 1950 catalogue

419 — No. 203 COIN DOT 7" tall basket (#1437 later), circa 1947-1964

420 — No. 1924 (later #1455) COIN DOT top hat, 3¼" tall, circa 1947-1954

421 — No. 1924 COIN DOT 4" cream pitcher (later #1461) circa 1947-1956

422 — No. 1924 Dot Optic cream pitcher, 4" tall, circa 1944

423 — No. 2293 POLKA DOT sugar shaker, 4½" tall, circa 1955-56

Green & Lime Opalescent

424—No. 184 RIB OPTIC 11" vase, circa 1939

425-426—No. 1647 RIB OPTIC 4" wine glass and 7" cruet, circa 1953

427-428—No. 1352 DOT OPTIC pattern 70 oz. 9" pitcher with ice lip and 4½" handled tumbler, with rare black handles, circa 1931

429—No. 3005 (later #1451) COIN DOT 11" vase, circa 1952-1954

430-431—No. 1604 RIB OPTIC open sugar and creamer, circa 1953-1954

432-433—No. 1605 RIB OPTIC 5" salt shaker and 4" pepper, circa 1953-1954

434-434A—SPIRAL OPTIC console set, No. 1523 4" candlesticks and No. 1522 9½" bowl, circa 1939

435-436—No. 2005 SWIRLED FEATHER vanity set, circa 1953; 6" cologne and 4" puff box

437—No. 2083 SWIRLED FEATHER 5½" diameter candy jar, circa 1953; this piece incorrectly placed here between the colognes

438—No. 2092 SWIRLED FEATHER fairy lamp, 6" tall, circa 1953

439—No. 2098 SWIRLED FEATHER chimney to hurricane lamp, 7½" tall, circa 1953

(Note: Figures 424, 427-428 and 434 set are green opalescent. All other items shown are lime opalescent)

Blue & Honeysuckle Opalescent

440 — No. 1353 COIN DOT 9" two-handled vase, double-crimp, circa 1947-1948

441 — No. 194 COIN DOT 6½" handled vase, circa 1948-1951

442 — No. 186 SPIRAL OPTIC 8½" tulip vase, circa 1939

443 — No. 1922 SPIRAL OPTIC 8" vase, circa 1939

444-445 — No. 1353 SPIRAL OPTIC 4" tumbler and 9" pitcher with ice lip, circa 1939

446 — No. 175 8" leaf-shaped plate, circa 1935

447 — No. 91 COIN DOT covered candy jar, circa 1947-1951

448-449 — No. 1924 COIN DOT creamer and open sugar, circa 1948-1954

450 — No. 1900 DAISY & BUTTON 3¾" top hat cigarette holder, circa 1939

451 — No. 6137 7" basket, circa 1960 — a reproduction of "Beatty Waffle" pattern

452 — No. 1924 SPIRAL OPTIC 3½" double crimped vase, circa 1939

453 — No. 203 COIN DOT 6" bowl in Honeysuckle, circa 1948-49

454 — No. 1925 COIN DOT 6" vase in Honeysuckle, circa 1948-49

455 — No. 1353 COIN DOT 12 oz. tumbler, 5¼" tall, in Honeysuckle, circa 1948-49

456 — No. 1924 COIN DOT 3¼" hat, circa 1948-1954, No. 1492 after 1952

Turquoise and Green Pastel

457—No. 7360 two-handled 10½" vase, circa 1955-1956
458—No. 5626 BLOCK & STAR 8½" bowl, circa 1955-1956
459—No. 4381 LAMB'S TONGUE 5½" tall candy jar, circa 1955-1956
460—No. 3869 HOBNAIL cruet, almost 5" tall, circa 1955-1956
461—No. 6909 TEARDROP condiment set, 7" to top of handle, circa 1955-1956
462—No. 1957 DAISY AND BUTTON 8½" vase in green pastel, circa 1955 only
463—No. 3883 HOBNAIL 5½" diameter candy jar in green pastel, circa 1955 only
464—No. 9019 open-edge "Backward C" 9" plate in green pastel, circa 1955 only
465—No. 9020 crimped 10" shell bowl in cased Lilac, circa 1955-1956
466—No. 9030 lacy edge shell, circa 1955-1956
467—No. 5606 BLOCK & STAR 3" salt and pepper, circa 1955-1956
468—No. 9015 SCROLL & EYE 8½" open-edge plate, circa 1955-1956
469—No. 3974 HOBNAIL candlestick, 4½" diameter, circa 1955-1958
470—No. 5603 BLOCK & STAR jam and jelly set, 9" x 6" circa 1955-1956

Miscellaneous Fenton

471 — No. 1921 top hat, 10" diameter, in cased green in white, circa 1940

472 — This blue and white 11½" cane was made to accompany #1921 top hat in blue cased in white; the cane to Figure 471 would be green and white

473 — No. 1561 APPLE TREE 10" vase in topaz opalescent, circa 1933

474 — Very rare engraved lamp in Venetian Red, circa 1926

475 — No. 612 decorated 6½" vase in Moonstone on five-legged Ebony base, circa 1933

476-477 — No. 11 BEADED MELON Gold Overlay 5½" bottle (no stopper) and 4" creamer, circa 1949

478 — No. 815 blue RIB SATIN cruet, 8½" tall to top of stopper, circa 1952

479 — No. 1720 blue DIAMOND SATIN pinch vase, 7½" tall, circa 1951

480 — No. 1562 decorated 13" diameter bowl in unusual yellow-orange color, a decided rarity

481 — No. 457 Refrigerator dish in Jade Green, circa 1934

482 — Fenton mixing bowl in Chinese Yellow, circa 1933

483 — No. 1700 LINCOLN INN 4¼" tall salt shaker, circa 1935

484 — No. 2 Mixing bowl Opaque Green, circa 1933

485 — Light blue opalescent atomizer bottle made for Devilbiss, circa 1941

Miscellaneous Fenton

486 — No. 1921 amber SNOWCREST 7" tall top hat, made in 1951 only

487 — No. 3001 yellow-cased 7" tall vase, circa 1950

488 — No. 1522 (No. 3124 after 1952) rose satin SNOWCREST 10" diameter bowl, circa 1951-1953

489 — No. 1721 (No. 3152 after 1952) emerald green SNOW-CREST 8½" pinch vase, circa 1951-1953

490 — No. 1890 PRISCILLA emerald green 9" cupped bowl, circa 1951-1952

491 — No. 1890 PRISCILLA light blue 4" high sherbet, circa 1951-1952

492 — No. 1565 amber TURTLE flower bowl circa 1929

493-495 — No. 1900 DAISY & BUTTON in Colonial blue; 7½" tall basket, 2½" toothpick, 6¼" Cornucopia vase, circa 1937-1939

496-497 — No. 1700 LINCOLN INN Aquamarine blue cup, saucer and #1700S oval sherbet, circa 1928-39

498-503 — No. 1900 DAISY & BUTTON in light blue, circa 1938-1939; cup and saucer, creamer and open sugar, 2½" toothpick, 7½" plate and 1½" salt shaker

Miscellaneous Fenton

504 — No. 6137 green opalescent 7" diameter basket, circa 1960

505 — No. 7237 BLACK ROSE 7" diameter basket with black handle, circa 1953-1954

506 — No. 711 BEADED MELON basket in blue overlay, circa 1949-1951

507 — No. 36 4½" ROSE CREST basket, circa 1946

508 — No. 1924 AQUA CREST 5" handled basket, circa 1942

509 — No. 4306 LAMB'S TONGUE salt and pepper in blue pastel, circa 1954

510 — No. 4381 LAMB'S TONGUE candy jar in green pastel, circa 1954-55

511 — No. 6068 cased LILAC 6½" handled jug, circa 1955-56

512 — No. 2083 SWIRLED FEATHER blue satin candy jar, circa 1953-54

513 — No. 711 BEADED MELON 5½" tulip vase in IVY green, circa 1950

514 — No. 711 BEADED MELON miniature vase in GOLD OVERLAY, circa 1949

515 — No. 5188 "Chickenserver" in milk glass with green, circa 1953-54; made in solid milk glass in 1955-56 (No. 5189)

516 — No. 5156 FISH vase in milk with ebony, 7" tall, circa 1953

517 — No. 711 BEADED MELON 6" handled jug in Emerald Crest, circa 1950-1952

518 — No. 7398 BLACK ROSE hurricane lamp, circa 1953-54

Fenton Rarities

519 — No. 893 decorated Mandarin red ginger jar on pedestal, very rare, circa 1934

520 — No. 604 large two-piece punch bowl with crimp in Florentine green, circa 1924

521 — No. 562 fan vase in Velva rose color, decorated with "Spirit of St. Louis", circa 1927

522 — No. 1124 or 1125 PANTHER bowl with BUTTERFLY AND BERRY exterior, extremely rare color for Fenton, very similar to Rosenthal's Nile Green made at Greentown, believed to have been made circa 1924

523 — No. 602 flared vase with outstanding gold decoration, unique green opaque color unlike anything else made at Fenton, circa 1930

524 — No. 562 decorated fan vase in Ebony color, very rare, circa 1926

525 — No. 350 FENTON DRAPERY small spittoon formed from a tumbler mold, green opalescent, circa 1910

Miscellaneous Fenton

526 — No. 184 cased 10" vase, rare ruby over milk, circa 1933

527 — No. 893 6½" vase or ginger jar, unusual color treatment similar to Periwinkle Blue, appears to be experimental and not a major Fenton line, circa 1935

528 — No. 898 11½" vase, very rare cased blue over white with cut-back floral design, not a major part of the Fenton line, but a superb example of the talent available at the time, circa 1935

529-530 — Possibly No. 1829 CANNONBALL decorated pitcher with FENTON DRAPERY interior in scarce ruby; the tumbler is No. 350, usually found in opalescent; circa 1914

531 — Ruby stretch covered bon-bon, circa 1921, probably made by Diamond Glass Co.; very similar to Fenton's #643

532 — No. 103 ruby stretch sherbert, missing underplate, circa 1921

533 — No. 9 ruby stretch ¾ pound covered candy jar, circa 1924

534 — No. 249 6½" tall candlestick, circa 1921, in ruby stretch

535 — No. 184 ruby engraved 6" vase, circa 1934

536 — No. 1934 7½" vase with unusual decorative treatment, circa 1935

537 — No. 1900 ruby slipper, DAISY AND BUTTON with KITTEN, year unknown, possibly 1970

538 — No. 1774 4½" ORANGE TREE (exterior) nappy with SAILBOATS interior in amberina, circa 1915

539 — No. 920 GRAPE AND CABLE orange bowl with PERSIAN MEDALLION interior, 10" diameter in unusual amberina, non-iridescent, circa 1915

540 — No. 935 ruby non-iridescent GRAPE AND CABLE bowl, circa 1915

Miscellaneous Fenton

541—No. 466 VINTAGE pattern blue opalescent ruffled bowl, incorrectly attributed by most to Northwood, circa 1910

542—No. 37 blue opalescent 2½" miniature basket, circa 1942-44

543—No. 352 amethyst opalescent DOT OPTIC water pitcher, rare color, circa 1910

544—No. 38 blue opalescent HAND vase, circa 1942-44

545—BOGGY BAYOU vase in blue opalescent, attributed to Fenton based on the amethyst opalescent pieces found in this pattern, and the photo on page 127 of the first Fenton book; this vase is formed from the REVERSE DRAPERY mold, also known in amethyst opalescent

546—No. 215 amethyst opalescent grape juice pitcher, circa 1921

547—No. 37 blue opalescent miniature triangle vase, circa 1942-44, often found today in collections of toothpick holders; shown here with original paper label

548—No. 401 green opalescent RIB OPTIC two-piece night set, circa 1927

549—No. 8 WATER LILY AND CATTAILS novelty vase formed from berry mold, green opalescent, circa 1908

550—Extremely rare chocolate glass vase, known as IDYLL in carnival glass, a variant of WATERLILY AND CATTAILS, made by Fenton, circa 1908

551—No. 847 fan vase in rare Lilac color, circa 1932

552—No. 848 Lilac bowl on five-legged ebony pedestal, circa 1932

553—No. 1952 clusteretes flower candleholder set, unusual purple slag treatment, circa 1952

554—No. 598 PERSIAN MEDALLION rose bowl in Persian blue color, circa 1915

555—No. 595 ORANGE TREE mug in Persian blue decorated, circa 1915

556—No. 592 BLACKBERRY SPRAY tulip vase in Persian blue, circa 1915

557—No. 597 WATER LILY oval bon-bon in Persian blue, circa 1915

559—No. 1729 green marble ash tray, circa 1951

Ad & Catalogue Reprints in Color 1930-1955

Royal Blue Assortment of Fenton's #1639
(also made in ruby with crystal feet, jade green
with ebony feet, and ebony with jade green feet
and jade green with moonstone feet)

Circa 1933-35

(Above & Below) Large assortment of Jade Green items

Circa 1931

Circa 1934

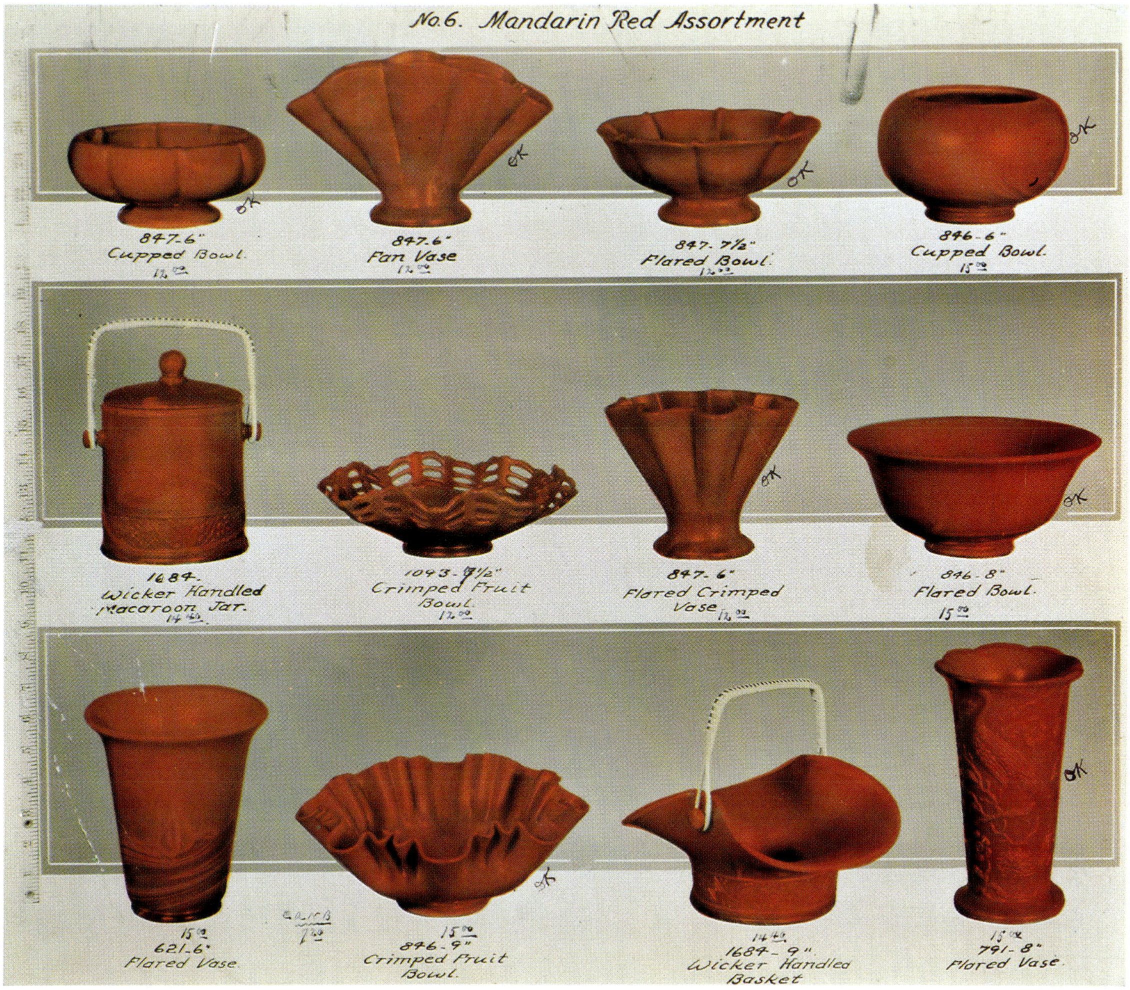

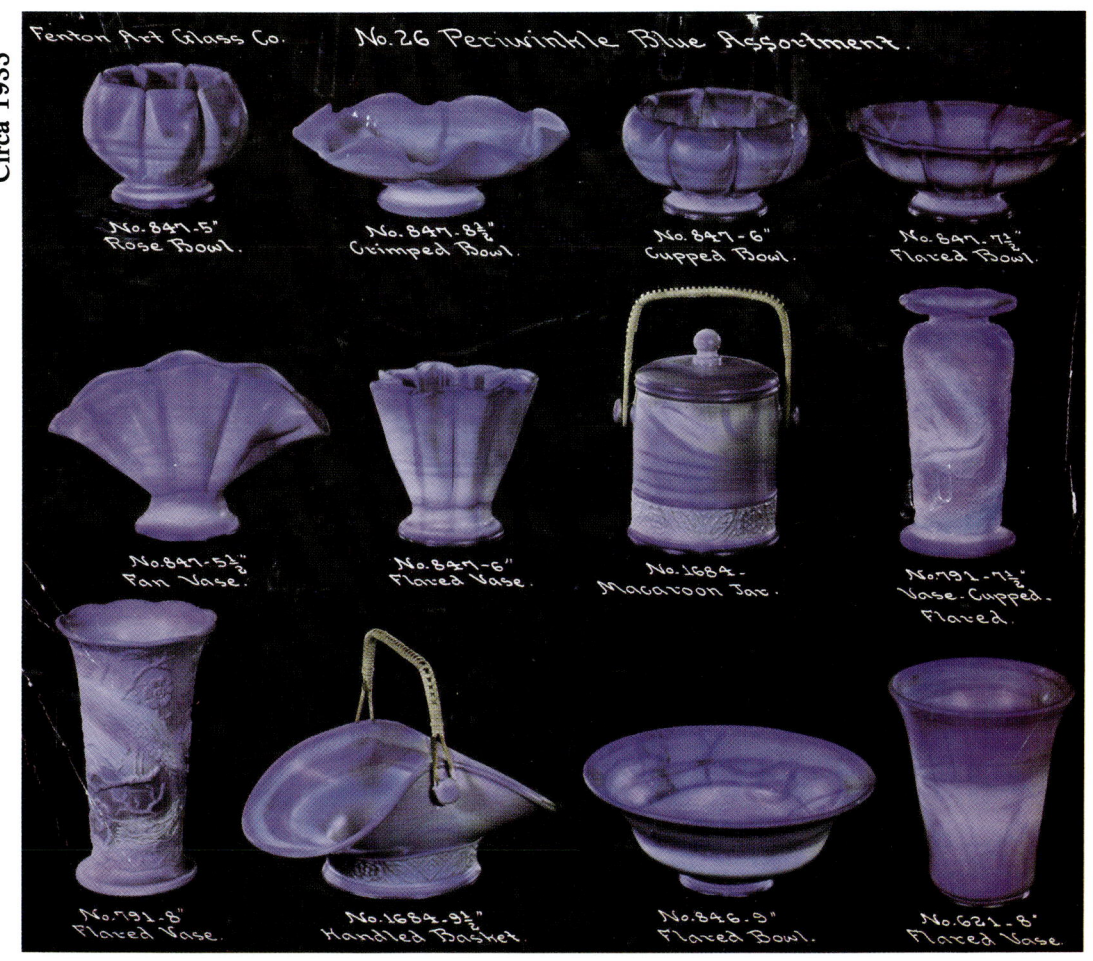

Original catalogue pages featuring an assortment of Mandarin Red (above) and Periwinkle Blue (below).

Circa 1935

Circa 1934-35

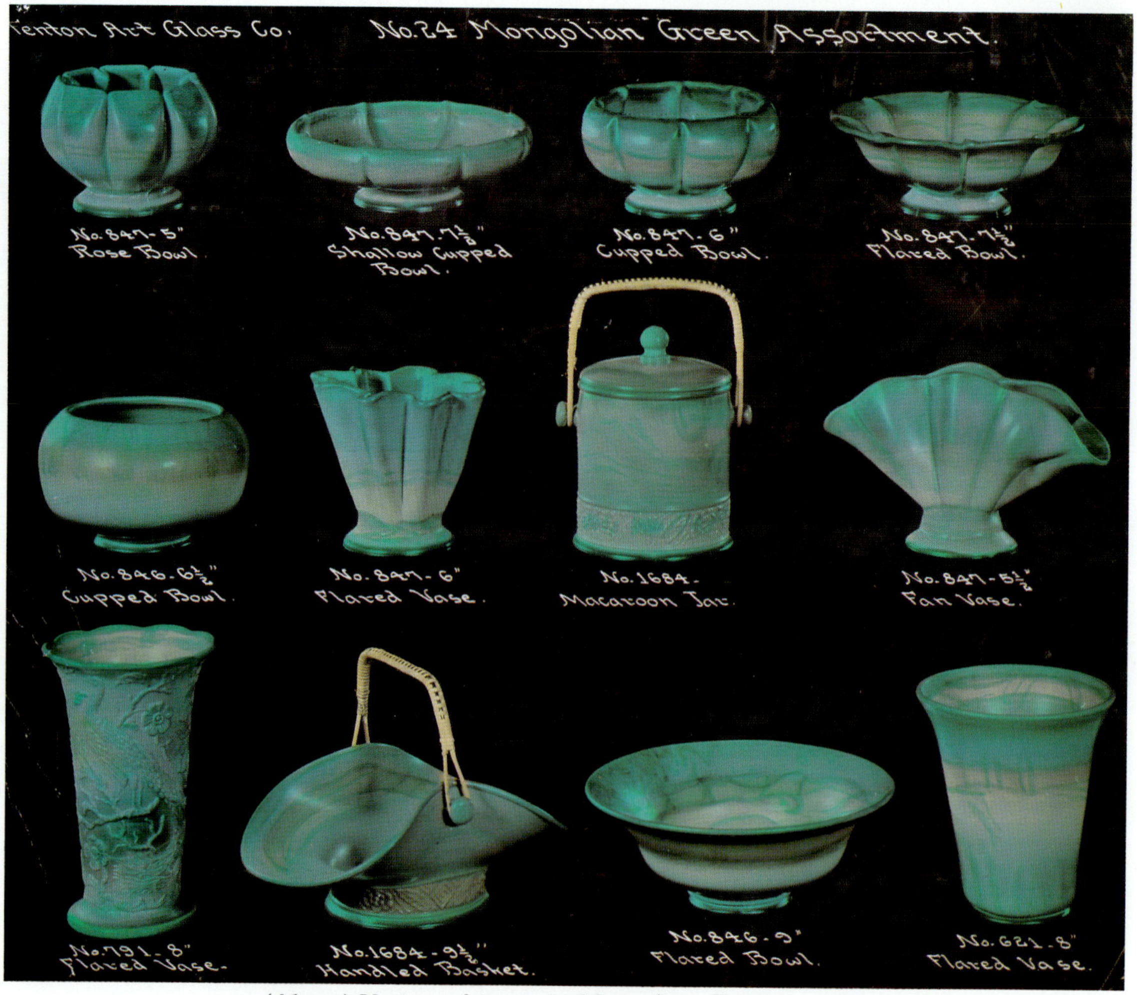

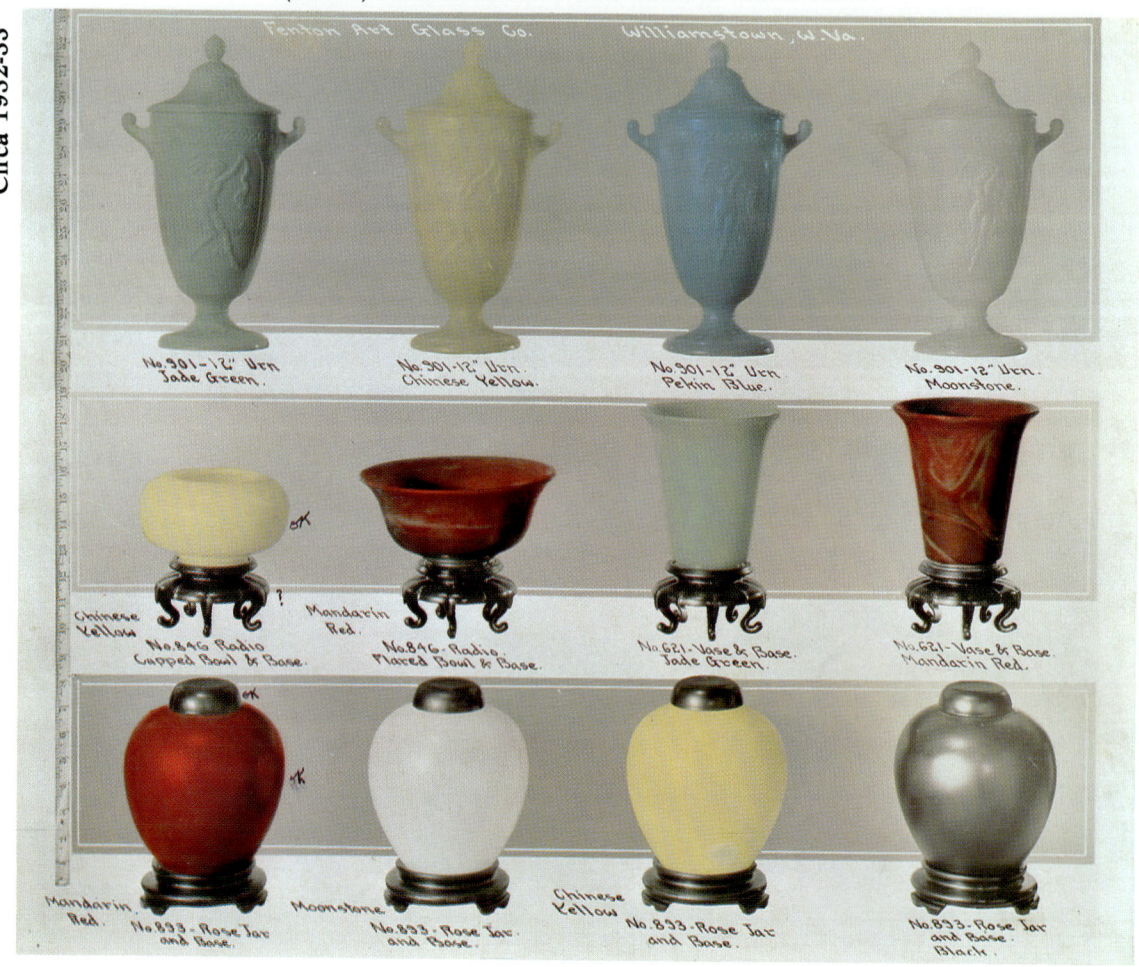

(Above) Variety of items in Mongolian Green.
(Below) Assortment of several colors in scarce items.

Circa 1932-33

Circa 1931-32

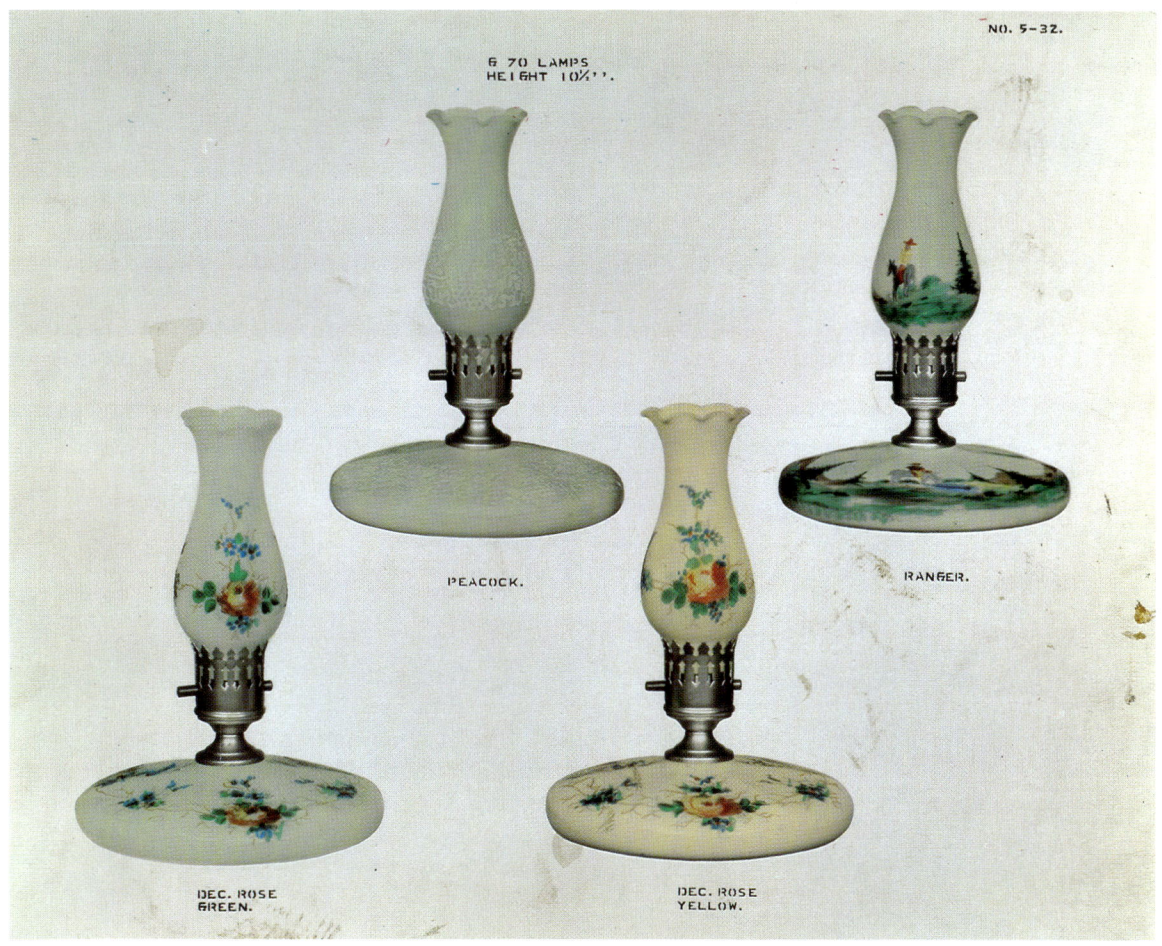

(Above) Assortment of Fenton lamps, some hand-decorated.
(Below) Variety of Fenton three-part lamps, all quite rare today.

Circa 1931-32

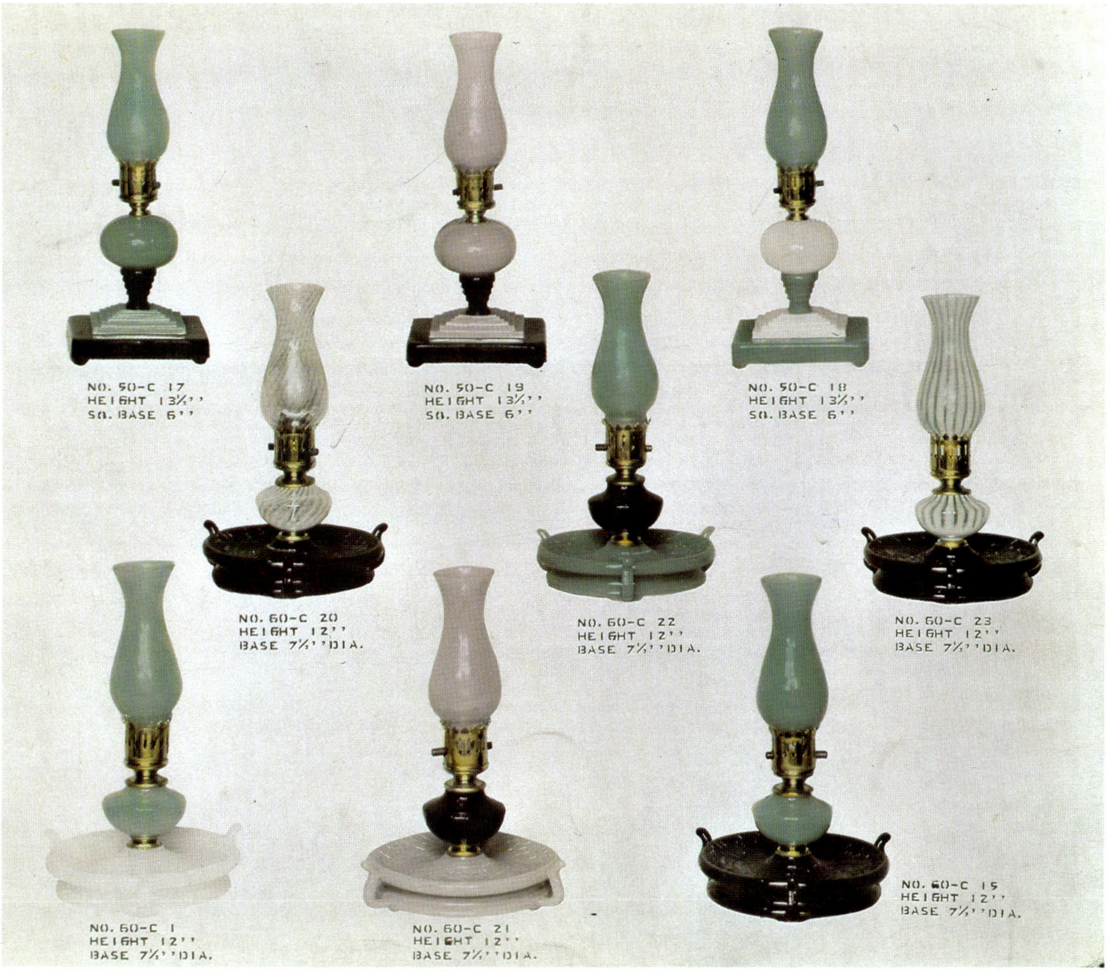

1939 Brochure

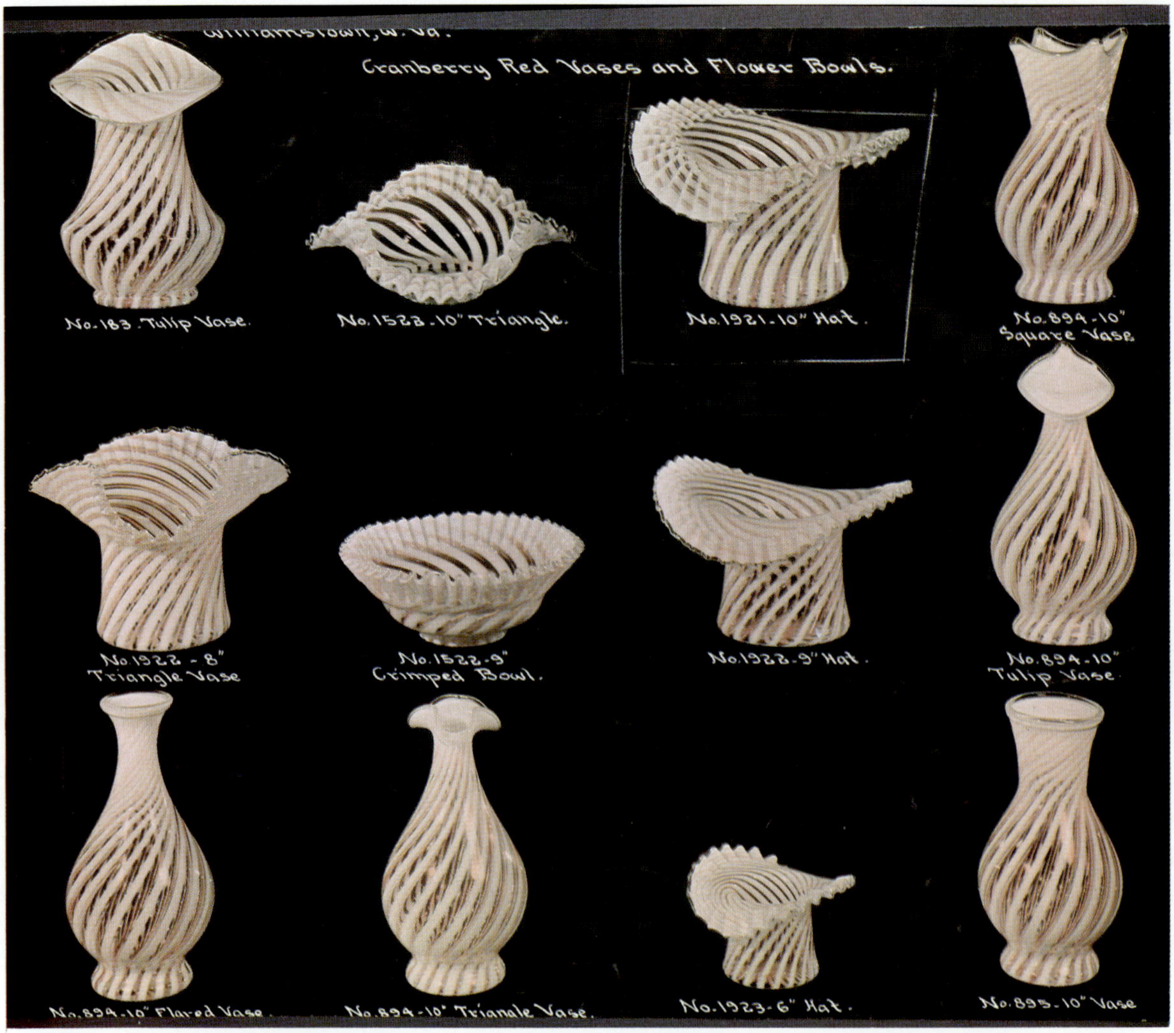

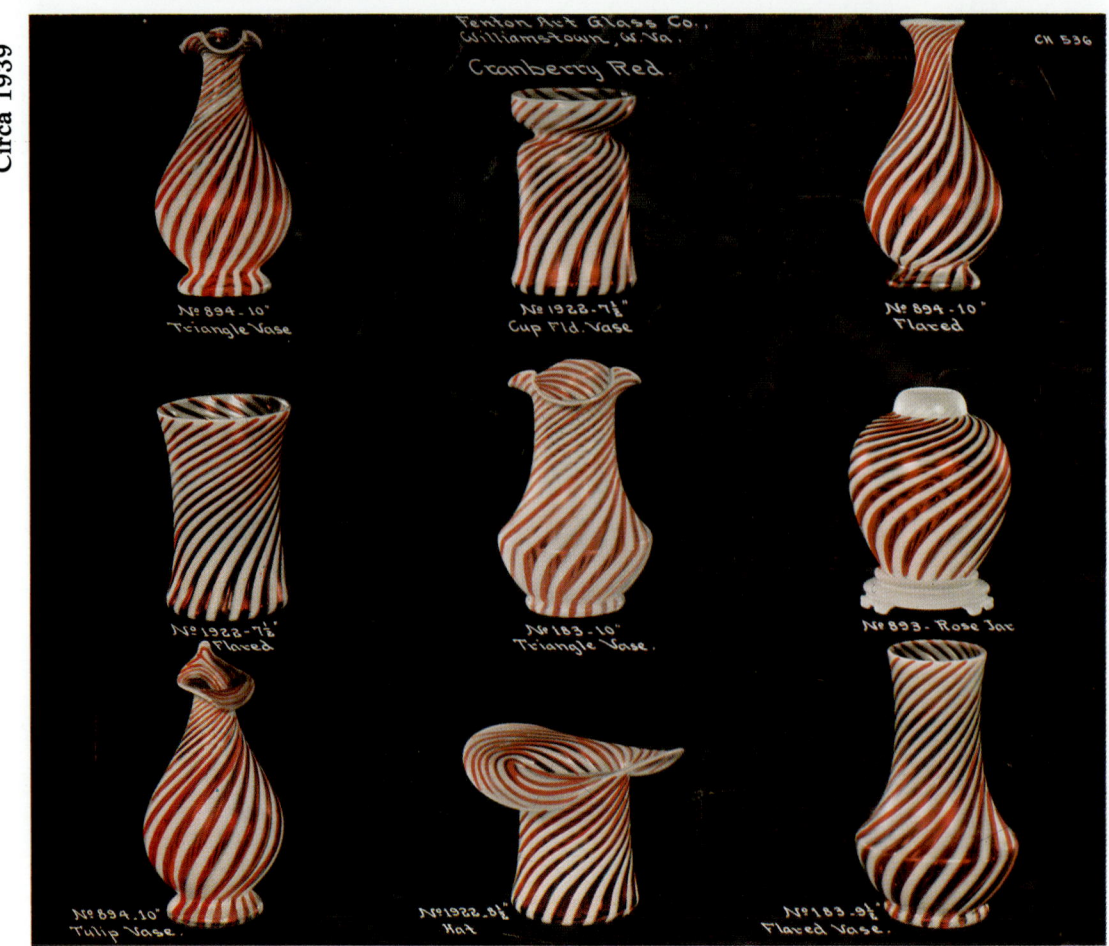

(Above and Below) Assortment of items in cranberry opalescent SPIRAL OPTIC.

Circa 1939

1939 Brochure

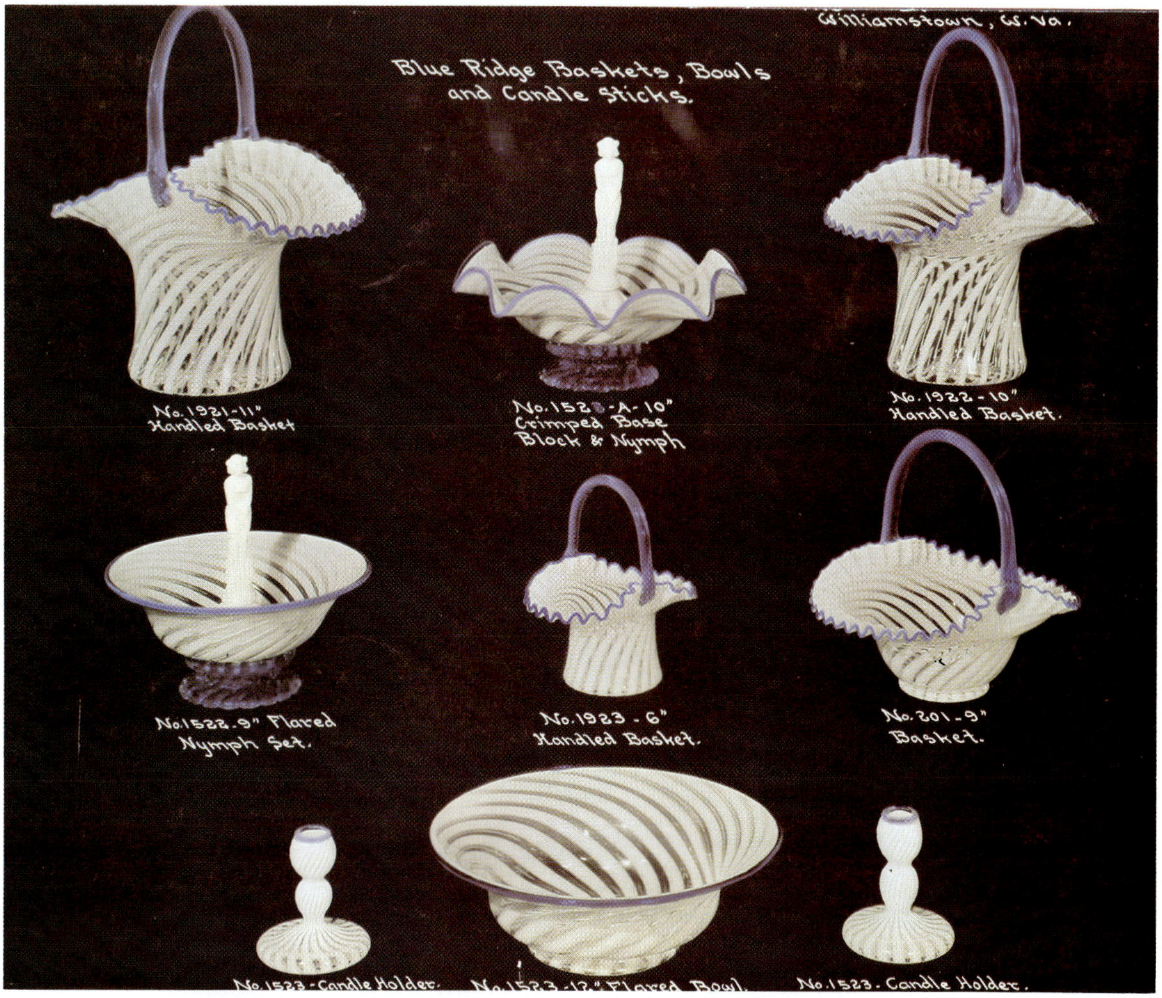

(Above) Assortment of BLUE RIDGE baskets, bowls and console sets.
(Below) Assortment of IVORY CREST vases.

Circa 1940

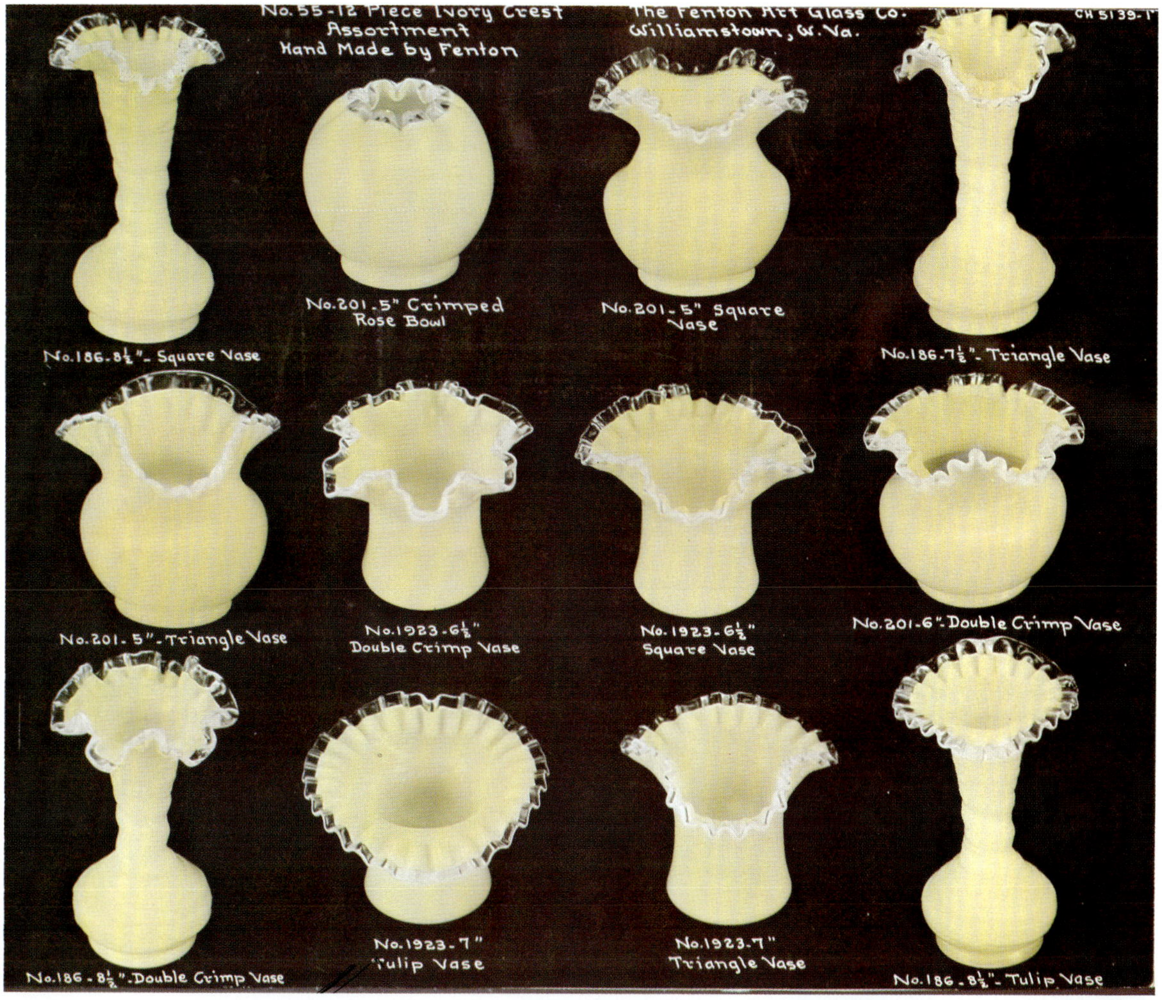

71

(Above) Assortment of Fenton's PEACH BLOW color.
(Below) Assortment of the popular PEACH CREST color.

Circa 1940

(Above and Below) Earliest assortments of Fenton's popular HOBNAIL—note the line was available in green opalescent in 1940 and in topaz opalescent in 1941.

Circa 1940-43

Circa 1940-43

NO. 389—HOBNAIL ITEMS—OPEN STOCK

	French Opal Blue Opal Topaz Opal	Cranberry Red	Rose Overlay
389—12" Footed Bowl—Double Crimp and Shallow	$26.40		
389—12" Footed Cake Plate	26.40		
389—6" Hand Vase (discontinued)			
389—Handled Decanter	39.60	$46.20	
389—Cruet	19.80	26.40	$26.40
389—5" Handled Bon Bon—Square and Oval	3.90		
389—6½" Handled Bon Bon—Square and Oval	4.50		
389—Miniature Cornucopia	3.30		
389—5-piece Condiment Set	30.00		
389—Oil Bottle	6.60		
389—Salt and Pepper	9.90		
389—Mustard and Spoon	6.60		
389—6¾" Crescent Tray (discontinued)			
389—Individual Sugar and Cream	6.00		
389—6½" Swung Vase	9.00		
389—Covered Candy Jar (new)	18.00		
389—7½" Flared Bowl (discontinued)			
389—6½" Fan Vase	9.00		

Plus Regular Package Charge—F. O. B. Williamstown, W. Va. Prices List per Dozen.

WHERE PRICE IS NOT SHOWN—ITEM NOT MADE IN THAT COLOR

2 *Hand Made in America by Fenton*

No. 389—HOBNAIL ITEMS—OPEN STOCK

	French Opal Blue Opal Topaz Opal	Cranberry Red	Rose Overlay
389—8½" Vase—Double Crimp	$26.40	$39.60	
389—8" Fan Vase	13.20		
389—9" Flared Vase	13.20		
389—10" Flared Vase (discontinued)			
389—10½" Fan Tray	9.90		
389—13½" Handled Basket	39.60	52.80	
389—80 oz. Jug	39.60	52.80	
389—12 oz. Tumbler	5.00	9.90	
389—5½" Jug	16.50	21.00	$21.00
389—4½" Jug	13.20	19.80	19.80
389—Footed Candy Jar (1941)	13.20		
389—Fan Ash Tray	3.30		
389—6-piece Cigarette Set, packed	15.90		
389—Round Ash Tray	2.20		
389—Slipper	5.00		
389—Oval Ash Tray	3.30		
389—No. 2 Hat	3.30		
389—No. 1 Hat	2.80		
389—6¼" Footed Vase—Flared, Triangle, Double Crimp and Fan	6.60		
389—5½"—Triangle, Flared, Square and Crimped	9.90	15.00	15.00

Plus Regular Package Charge—F. O. B. Williamstown, W. Va. Prices List per Dozen.

WHERE PRICE IS NOT SHOWN—ITEM NOT MADE IN THAT COLOR

Hand Made in America by Fenton 3

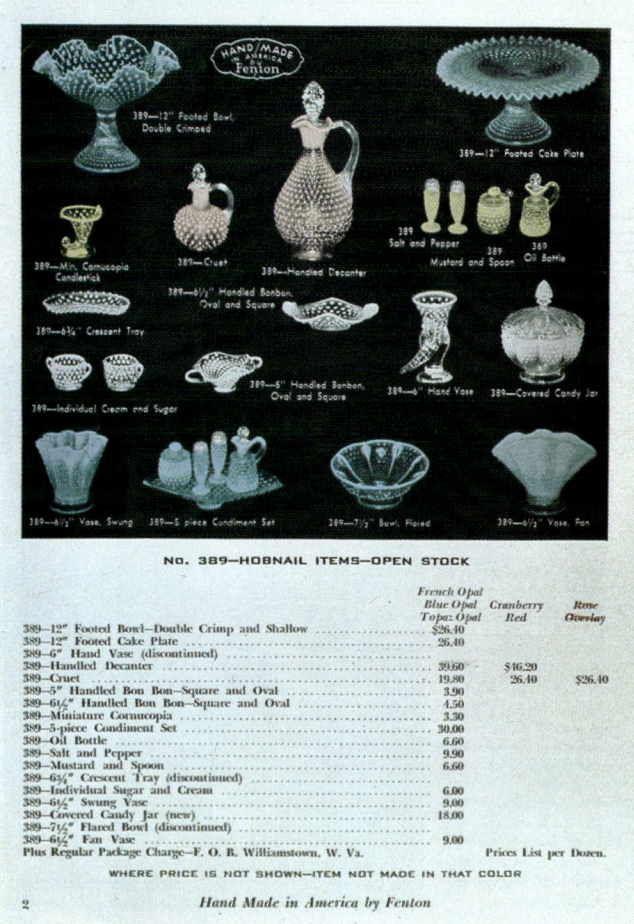

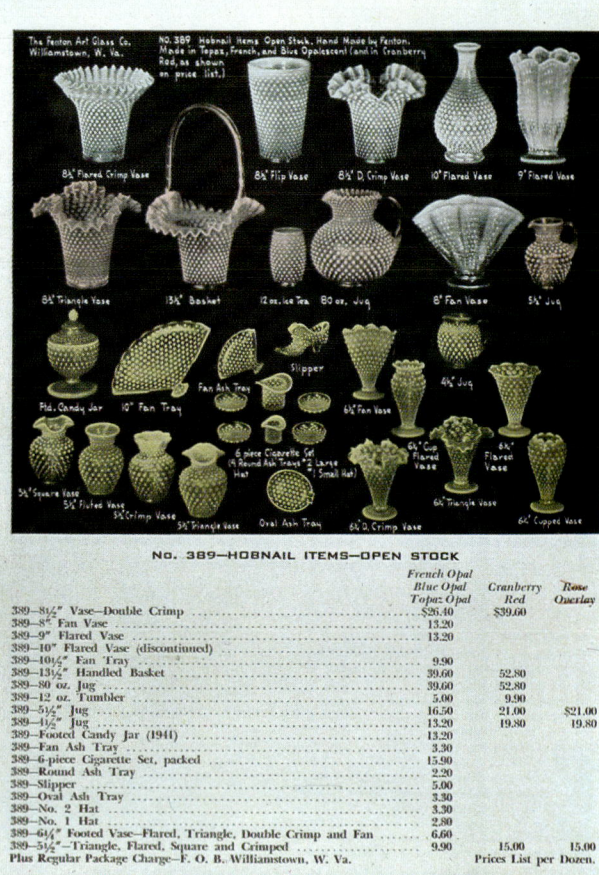

(Above) Additional assortment of Fenton with price list.
(Below) Variety of Fenton items from 1942 catalogue, including rare Mulberry.

Circa 1942

OPEN STOCK ITEMS

	Aqua Crest	Crystal Crest Ruby Overlay Mulberry	Peach Crest
192—Squat Jug	$18.00	$24.00	$30.00
192—10½" Handled Basket	33.00	36.00	39.60
192—8" Handled Jug	33.00	39.60	52.80
192—6" Handled Jug	19.80	26.40	33.00
203—7" Handled Basket	13.20	15.00	19.80
192—6" Regular Vase	13.20	19.80	26.40
192—10½" Double Crimp Bowl	19.80	24.00	36.00
203—7" Double Crimp Bowl		13.20	
1921—5" Handled Basket	9.90	13.20	15.00
1921—5" Top Hat	6.60	9.90	13.20
	Aqua Crest Crystal Crest	Ruby Overlay Mulberry	Peach Crest
1921—Handled Jug	$ 9.00	$13.20	$13.20
192-A—Vanity Bottle	14.00	16.00	21.00
192-A—3-piece Vanity Set	42.00	48.00	60.00
192-A—Puff Box	14.00	16.00	18.00
192—7" Bottle	18.00	21.00	30.00
192—5½" Bottle	15.00	18.00	24.00
192—Squat Cologne Bottle	15.00	18.00	21.00
192—Squat Candleholder	12.00	15.00	21.00
1353—70 oz. Jug		36.00	
1353—10 oz. Tumbler		8.00	
1353—7-piece Beverage Set		84.00	
1353—9" Vase—Double Crimp and Triangle		33.00	

Plus Regular Package Charge—F. O. B. Williamstown, W. Va. Prices List per Dozen.

Hand Made in America by Fenton

OPEN STOCK ITEMS

	Aqua Crest	Crystal Crest Ruby Overlay Mulberry	Peach Crest
192—6" Vase—Square, Double Crimp, Triangle, Tulip	$13.20	$19.80	$26.40
192—5" Vase—Square, Double Crimp, Triangle, Oval	13.20	19.80	26.40
192—8" Vase—Square, Double Crimp, Triangle, Tulip	19.80	26.40	39.60

ALL ITEMS MADE IN AQUA CREST, CRYSTAL CREST, RUBY OVERLAY, MULBERRY, PEACH CREST

Plus Regular Package Charge—F. O. B. Williamstown, W. Va. Prices List per Dozen.

WHERE PRICE IS NOT SHOWN—ITEM NOT MADE IN THAT COLOR

Hand Made in America by Fenton

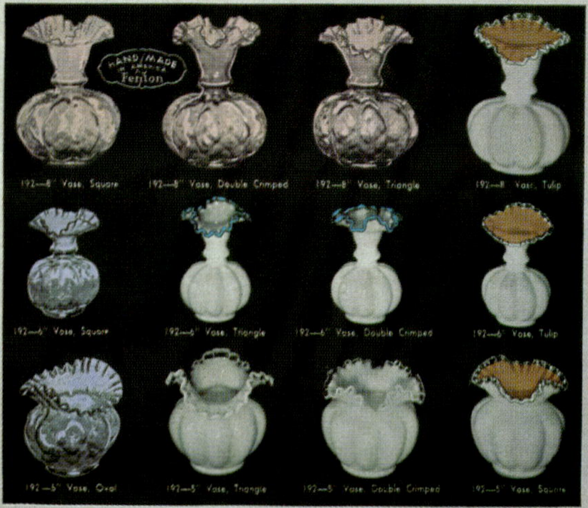

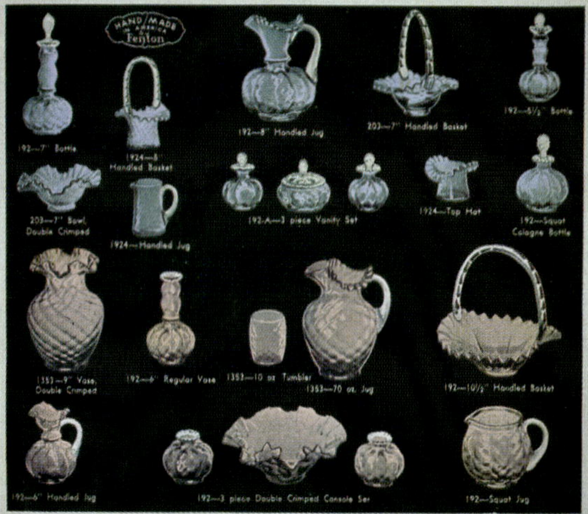

1949 Catalogue

INTRODUCING *Tiara* in *Crests* and *Overlays*

DESCRIPTION OF ITEM AND COLOR IN WHICH SHOWN.

Top Row:—Left to Right
711—5" Vase—Ivy
711—4" Rose Bowl—
　　Gold Overlay
711—5½" Hdl. Jug—
　　Blue Overlay
711—Covered Candy Jar—
　　Silver Crest
711—4" Handled Creamer—
　　Green Overlay

Middle Row:
711—6" Handled Jug—
　　Gold Overlay
711—Miniature Vase—
　　Peach Crest
711—8" Vase—Green Overlay
711—Miniature Vase—
　　Gold Overlay
711—7" Handled Basket—
　　Peach Crest

Bottom Row:
711—9" Vase—Peach Crest
711—Miniature Vase—
　　Blue Overlay
711—3 pc. Vanity Set—
　　Green Overlay
711—Miniature Vase—
　　Silver Crest
711—4" Handled Creamer—
　　Blue Overlay

COMPLETE LIST OF ITEMS MADE IN THE NEW TIARA LINE IS CONTAINED IN PRICE LIST.

(Above and Below) Wide assortment of Fenton's "Tiara" line and SNOWCREST in their Spiral Optic mold.

Circa 1949

75

1955 Golden Anniversary Color Catalogue

Illustrated on the next three pages are ten of the thirteen color pages from Fenton's golden anniversary full-color catalogue. Because of space limitations I did not include a one-page assortment, picturing a variety in every line, and a two-page display of Fenton's "Crest", the vast majority of which was previously illustrated in earlier catalogues.

1955 Catalogue

Page 6 — HOBNAIL — FINEST GLASS FOR FIFTY YEARS

- A. No. 3901-MI Sugar & Cream
- B. No. 3889-MI Mustard & Spoon
- C. No. 3873-FO Oval Ash Tray
- D. No. 3971-FO Min. Cornucopia
- E. No. 3926-RP 6" Bonbon
- F. No. 3834-RP 4½" Basket
- G. No. 3874-MI Candleholder
- H. No. 3870-CR Candleholder
- I. No. 3900-MI Sugar & Cream
- J. No. 3903-CR Jam Set
- K. No. 3863-CR Cruet
- L. No. 3917-MI Sugar & Cream
- M. No. 3977-MI ¼ lb. Cov. Butter
- N. No. 3835-PB 5½" Basket
- O. No. 3980-MI Ftd. Candy Jar
- P. No. 3886-MI Honey Jar
- Q. No. 3991-MI Hat
- R. No. 3859-CR 8" Vase
- S. No. 3856-PB 6" Vase
- T. No. 3817-MI 16" Torte Plate
- U. No. 3827-MI Punch Bowl
- V. No. 3807-MI 15 pc Punch Set
- W. No. 3847-MI Punch Cup
- X. No. 3913-FO Ftd. Cakeplate

Page 7 — DAISY and BUTTON — FINEST GLASS FOR FIFTY YEARS

- A. No. 1959-MI 9" Ftd. Fan Vase
- B. No. 1994-MI Bootee
- C. No. 1995-MI Slipper
- D. No. 1957-MI 8" Ftd. Vase
- E. No. 1903-MI Sugar & Cream
- F. No. 1958-MI 8" Ftd. Vase
- G. No. 1929-MI 9" Oval Bowl
- H. No. 1974-MI 2-Lt. Candleholder
- I. No. 1927-MI 7" Cupped Bowl
- J. No. 1953-MI 3" Vase
- K. No. 1954-MI 4" Vase
- L. No. 1920-MI 10½" Square Bowl
- M. No. 1993-MI #3 Hat
- N. No. 1992-MI #2 Hat
- O. No. 1935-MI 5" Basket
- P. No. 1922-MI Ftd. Bowl
- Q. No. 1937-MI 5½" Bonbon
- R. No. 1956-MI 6" Vase
- S. No. 1936-MI 6" Basket
- T. No. 1926-MI Ftd. Bowl
- U. No. 1924-MI Ftd. Bowl
- V. No. 1955-MI Ftd. Vase

1955 Catalogue

COIN DOT — FINEST GLASS FOR FIFTY YEARS

- A. No. 1469-CR 8" Bottle
- B. No. 1473-CR Cruet
- C. No. 1465-CR Vanity Bottle
- D. No. 1485-CR Puff Box
- E. No. 1405-CR 3 pc. Vanity Set
- F. No. 1461-CR Creamer
- G. No. 1459-CR 8" Vase
- H. No. 1457-CR 7½" Vase
- I. No. 1454-CR 4½" Vase
- J. No. 1435-CR 5" Basket
- K. No. 1427-CR 7" Bowl
- L. No. 1456-CR 6" Vase
- M. No. 1437-CR 7" Basket
- N. No. 1424-CR 10" Bowl
- O. No. 1450-CR 5" Vase
- P. No. 1451-CR 11" Vase
- Q. No. 1447-CR 12 oz. Tumbler
- R. No. 1467-CR 70 oz. Jug
- S. No. 1458-CR 8" Vase

BLOCK and STAR — FINEST GLASS FOR FIFTY YEARS

- A. No. 5671-MI Square Candleholder
- B. No. 5624-MI 9" Square Bowl
- C. No. 5601-MI Square Console Set
- D. No. 5603-MI Jam & Jelly
- E. No. 5635-MI Bonbon
- F. No. 5658-MI 8½" Vase
- G. No. 5609-MI Mayonnaise Set
- H. No. 5606-MI Salt & Pepper
- I. No. 5627-MI Sugar Bowl
- J. No. 5604-MI Sugar & Cream
- K. No. 5661-MI Creamer
- L. No. 5620-MI Square Dessert
- M. No. 5622-MI Cupped Dessert
- N. No. 5621-MI Flared Dessert
- O. No. 5659-MI 9" Vase
- P. No. 5602-MI Buffet Set
- Q. No. 5672-MI Flared Candleholder
- R. No. 5625-MI 11" Flared Bowl
- S. No. 5605-MI Flared Console Set
- T. No. 5673-MI Cupped Candleholder
- U. No. 5608-MI Cupped Console Set
- V. No. 5626-MI 10" Cupped Bowl
- W. No. 5600-MI 3 pc. Console Set
- X. No. 5670-MI Handled Candleholder
- Y. No. 5649-MI 9 oz. Tumbler
- Z. No. 5647-MI 12 oz. Tumbler
- AA. No. 5667-MI 70 oz. Jug

THIS 'n THAT — FINEST GLASS FOR FIFTY YEARS

- A. No. 1021-MR Ftd. Ivy Ball
- B. No. 7299-EC Pot & Saucer
- C. No. 3255-CR 5" Vase
- D. No. 7228-RP Ftd. Comport
- E. No. 3252-CR 8" Vase
- F. No. 3160-CR 5" Vase
- G. No. 6906-MI Salt & Pepper
- H. No. 6909-TU Condiment Set
- I. No. 7351-MI 3" Vase
- J. No. 3253-CR 6" Vase
- K. No. 7335-SC 7" Serving Bowl
- L. No. 7348-GP 6" Bud Vase
- M. No. 7202-RO Epergne Set
- N. No. 7349-RP 6½" Bud Vase
- O. No. 7333-SC Handled Relish
- P. No. 7328-MI Ftd. Bowl
- Q. No. 7331-MI 4" Basket
- R. No. 5116-MI 8" Leaf Plate
- S. No. 5118-MI 11" Leaf Plate

THIS 'n THAT — FINEST GLASS FOR FIFTY YEARS

- A. No. 7056-RP 6" Vase
- B. No. 7063-MI Cruet
- C. No. 5197-MI Bird
- D. No. 5508-MI Cigarette Set
- E. No. 7005-MI 3 pc. Vanity Set
- F. No. 4381-GP Candy Jar
- G. No. 7001-GP Salt & Pepper
- H. No. 4303-MI Mayonnaise Set
- I. No. 4306-MI Salt & Pepper
- J. No. 5185-MI Chick
- K. No. 5183-MI Hen on Basket
- L. No. 7302-GP Bathroom Set
- M. No. 7004-MI Mayonnaise Set
- N. No. 1605-CR Salt & Pepper
- O. No. 1667-CR Wine Bottle
- P. No. 5157-MI 6" Madonna Vase
- Q. No. 5808-MI Canasta Set
- R. No. 4801-MI Epergne Set
- S. No. 7073-GP Candleholder
- T. No. 7021-GP 11" Bowl
- U. No. 7003-GP 3 pc. Console Set
- V. No. 4802-FO Epergne Set
- W. No. 6549-MX 8 pc. Tumbler Set
- X. No. 6550-LG 10 oz. Tumbler
- Y. No. 5189-MI Chickenserver
- Z. No. 4808-EC Epergne Set

1955 Catalogue

POLKA DOT and OPEN EDGE

- A. No. 2257-CR 7½" Vase
- B. No. 2225-CR 5" Rose Bowl
- C. No. 2224-CR 4" Rose Bowl
- D. No. 9015-MI Scroll & Eye Plate
- E. No. 2293-CR Sugar Shaker
- F. No. 2204-CR Sugar & Cream
- G. No. 2261-CR Creamer
- H. No. 9018-TU 8" Plate
- I. No. 2206-CR Salt & Pepper
- J. No. 2273-CR Cruet
- K. No. 9021-MI Scroll & Eye Comport
- L. No. 2277-CR Butter & Cheese
- M. No. 9030-MI Lacy Edge Shell
- N. No. 2221-CR Ftd. Ivy Ball
- O. No. 9011-TU 11" Plate
- P. No. 2247-CR 12 oz. Tumbler
- Q. No. 2207-CR 7 pc. Ice Tea Set
- R. No. 2267-CR 70 oz. Jug

POLKA DOT and OPEN EDGE

- A. No. 2237-CR 7" Basket
- B. No. 2251-CR 8" DC Vase
- C. No. 2255-CR Vase
- D. No. 2250-CR 8" Vase Tulip
- E. No. 2227-CR 7" Bowl
- F. No. 9025-TU Scroll & Eye Bowl
- G. No. 9029-MI Ftd. Comport
- H. No. 9026-RP 8" C Bowl
- I. No. 2259-CR 8½" Vase
- J. No. 9012-RP 12" Plate
- K. No. 2258-CR 8" Vase
- L. No. 9024-MI Banana Bowl
- M. No. 2256-CR 6" Vase
- N. No. 9017-MI Ftd. Plate

HOBNAIL

- A. No. 3994-MI 4½" Jardiniere
- B. No. 3996-MI 6" Jardiniere
- C. No. 3880-MI Candy Jar
- D. No. 3990-GP Kettle
- E. No. 3853-CR 3" Vase
- F. No. 3935-MI 5" Bonbon
- G. No. 3855-MI Min. Vase
- H. No. 3956-MI 6¼" DC Vase (8"-3958)
- J. No. 3865-CR Vanity Bottle
- K. No. 3885-CR Puff Box
- L. No. 3805-CR 3 pc Vanity Set
- M. No. 3928-RP Berry Dish
- N. No. 3929-RP 9" Square Bowl
- O. No. 3957-MI 6¼" Fan Vase
- P. No. 3979-MI Mustard Kettle
- Q. No. 3837-GP 7" Basket
- R. No. 3810-FO Ash Tray Set
- S. No. 3916-MI Oil & Vinegar
- T. No. 3830-PB 10" Basket
- U. No. 3921-PB 5" Star Bonbon
- V. No. 3959-FO 8" Fan Vase
- W. No. 3840-MI Punch Cup
- X. No. 3820-MI Punch Bowl
- Y. No. 3913-MI 14-pc punch Set

HOBNAIL

- A. No. 3915-MI Jam & Jelly
- B. No. 3858-CR 8" Vase
- C. No. 3946-FO 16 oz. Tumbler
- D. No. 3942-FO 12 oz. Tumbler
- E. No. 3949-FO 9 oz. Tumbler
- F. No. 3945-MI 5 oz. Tumbler
- G. No. 3965-MI Squat Jug
- H. No. 3822-FO Relish
- I. No. 3843-FO Wine
- J. No. 3918-FO 8" Salad Plate
- K. No. 3869-FO Oil
- L. No. 3842-FO Ftd. Ice Tea
- M. No. 3845-MI Goblet
- N. No. 3825-MI Sherbet
- O. No. 3883-TU Candy Jar
- P. No. 3953-GP 4" Fan Vase
- Q. No. 3952-GP 4" DC Vase
- R. No. 3927-PB 7" Bowl
- S. No. 3912-MI 8½" Plate
- T. No. 3809-MI Condiment Set
- U. No. 3947-CR 12 oz. Tumbler
- V. No. 3967-CR 80 oz. Jug

1950 Advertisement

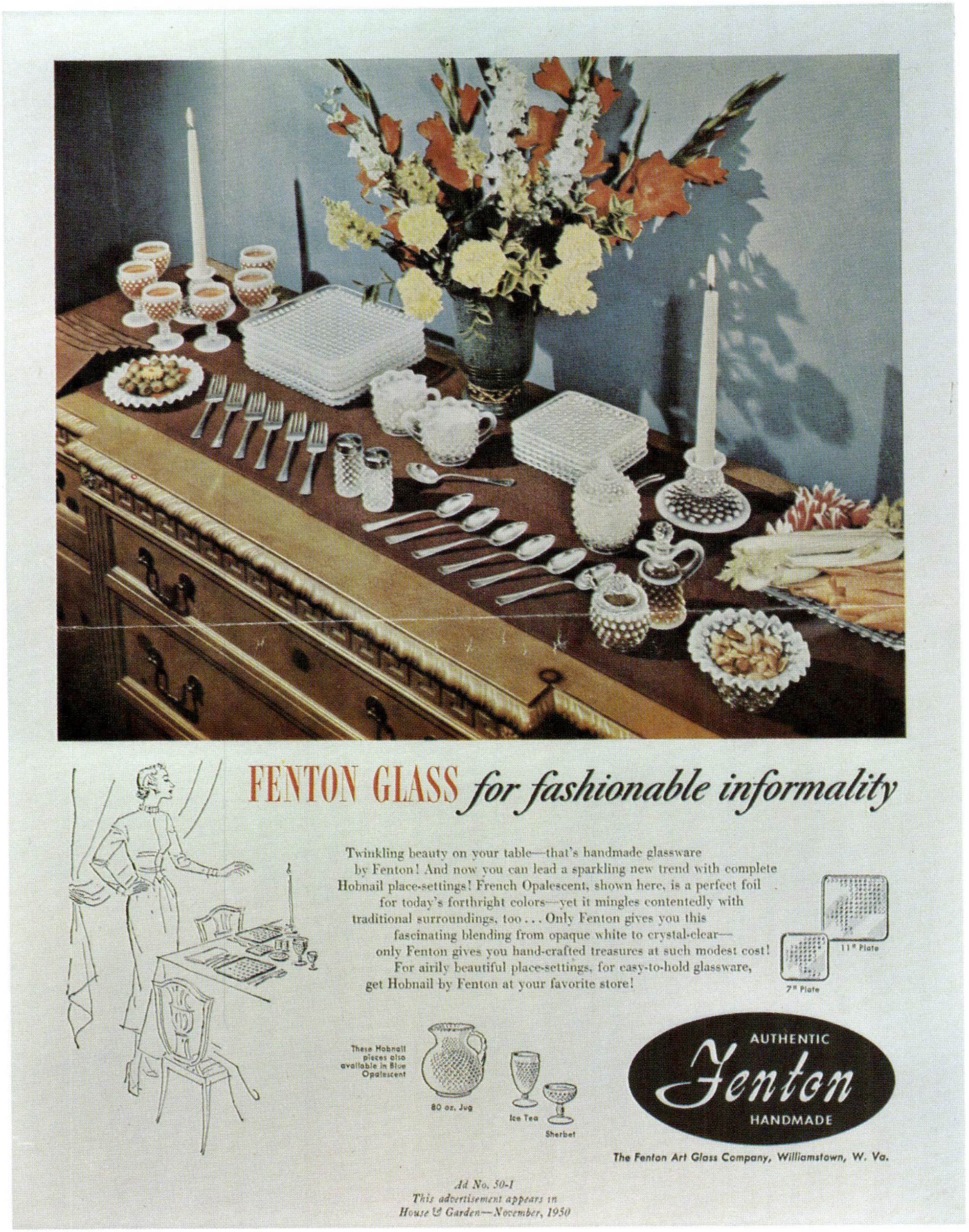
FENTON GLASS for fashionable informality
Twinkling beauty on your table—that's handmade glassware by Fenton! And now you can lead a sparkling new trend with complete Hobnail place-settings! French Opalescent, shown here, is a perfect foil for today's forthright colors—yet it mingles contentedly with traditional surroundings, too . . . Only Fenton gives you this fascinating blending from opaque white to crystal-clear—only Fenton gives you hand-crafted treasures at such modest cost! For airily beautiful place-settings, for easy-to-hold glassware, get Hobnail by Fenton at your favorite store!
11" Plate
7" Plate
These Hobnail pieces also available in Blue Opalescent
80 oz. Jug
Ice Tea
Sherbet
AUTHENTIC
Fenton
HANDMADE
The Fenton Art Glass Company, Williamstown, W. Va.
Ad No. 50-1
This advertisement appears in
House & Garden—November, 1950

1950 Advertisement

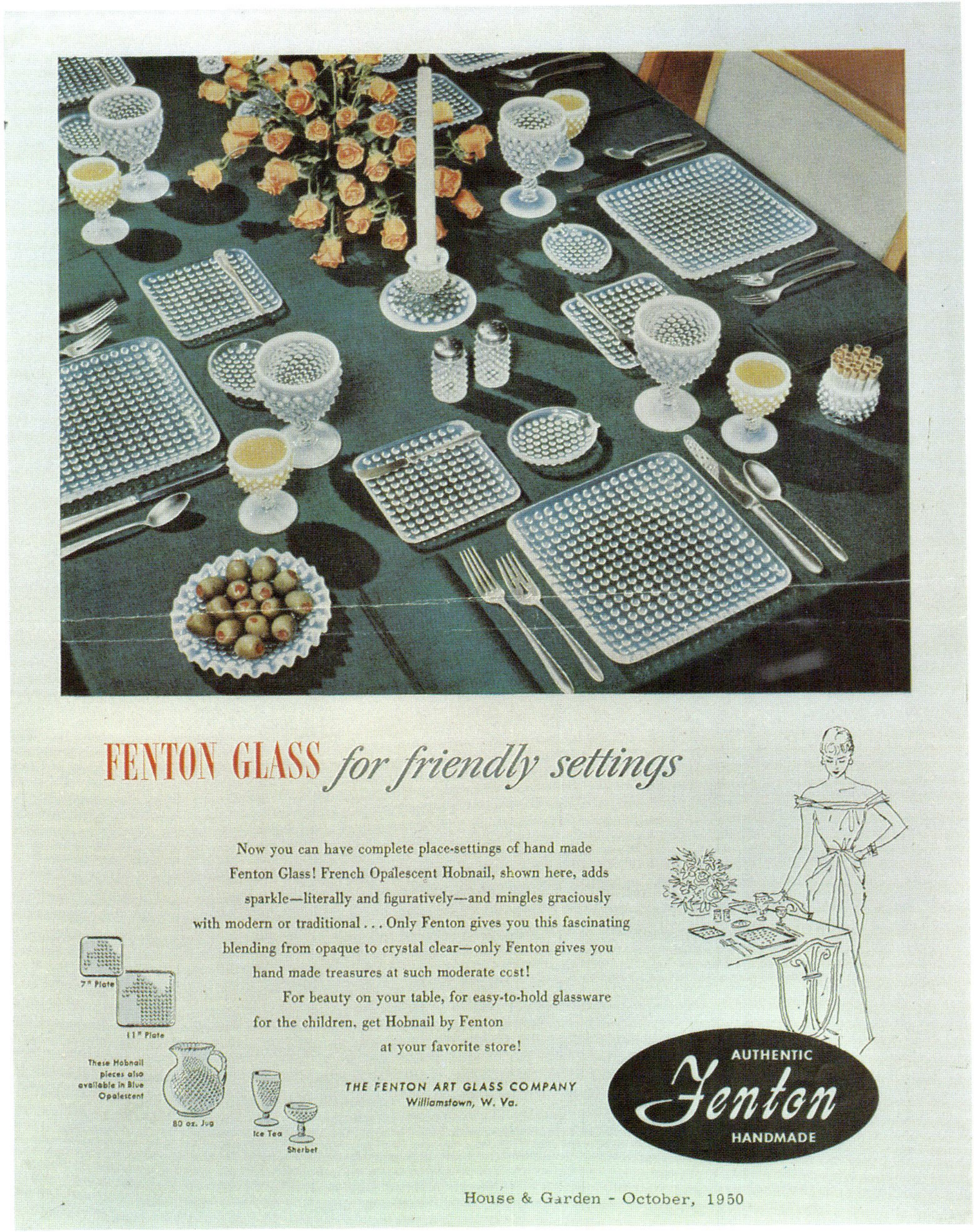
FENTON GLASS for friendly settings
Now you can have complete place-settings of hand made Fenton Glass! French Opalescent Hobnail, shown here, adds sparkle—literally and figuratively—and mingles graciously with modern or traditional . . . Only Fenton gives you this fascinating blending from opaque to crystal clear—only Fenton gives you hand made treasures at such moderate cost!
For beauty on your table, for easy-to-hold glassware for the children, get Hobnail by Fenton at your favorite store!
7" Plate
11" Plate
These Hobnail pieces also available in Blue Opalescent
80 oz. Jug
Ice Tea
Sherbet
THE FENTON ART GLASS COMPANY
Williamstown, W. Va.
AUTHENTIC
Fenton
HANDMADE
House & Garden - October, 1950

Glassware to make you proud, Handmade by *Fenton*

There's happiness, and charm, and cordiality in every authentic line of this sparkling handmade glassware by Fenton. Whether Cranberry is right for your color scheme, or whether you choose blue, emerald, yellow or clear, your selection is practically unlimited. Place settings, boudoir accessories, accent pieces—Hobnail, Coin Dot, Crest, Overlay, Diamond Lace—all delightful, all moderately priced. See them soon—for yourself and as gifts!

A—Top Hat—Cranberry Coin Dot
B—5" Basket—Cranberry Coin Dot
C—Cruet—Cranberry Hobnail
D—7½" Pinch Vase—Diamond Satin
E—7" Basket—Peach Crest
F—3 piece Jam Set—Cranberry Hobnail
G—7½" Vase—Ruby Snowcrest
H—6" Vase—Cranberry Coin Dot.

AUTHENTIC Fenton HANDMADE

THE FENTON ART GLASS COMPANY, WILLIAMSTOWN, W. VA.

Ad. No. 51-3
This advertisement appears in House Beautiful—November, 1951

Prepared by JOHN FALKNER ARNDT & COMPANY, INC. PHILADELPHIA

1951 Advertisement

Handmade *Fenton Glass*
luminous...lovely

Sparkling emerald accents... emerald with snow-white accents... white with clear accents... These, and a host of other delightful, authentic styles, patterns, and colors—all handmade by Fenton—lend charm and beauty to your surroundings, or the surroundings of those you love... See handmade Fenton glassware soon—the price is very moderate! Table settings, too!

A—Emerald Crest Tid-Bit Tray $8.00 • B—Ivy 6" Vase $2.75 • C—Emerald Crest 13" Footed Cake Plate $5.00 • D—Green Snowcrest 2 piece Hurricane Lamp $7.50 per pair • E—Green Snowcrest Pot & Saucer $2.25 • F—Emerald Crest Sherbet & 6½" Plate $2.10 per set • G—Green Snowcrest 8½" Pinch Vase $3.50. Prices slightly higher in the West.

AUTHENTIC Fenton HANDMADE

THE FENTON ART GLASS COMPANY, WILLIAMSTOWN, W. VA.

Advt. No. 51-4
House & Garden - October, 1951

Prepared by JOHN FALKNER ARNDT & COM. PHILADELPHIA

1951 Advertisement

Circa 1938

FEBRUARY SPECIAL
CRYSTAL, ROSE, VASELINE, AQUAMARINE

DAISY & BUTTON PATTERN

1900 SALAD SET

1—10" Bowl.   1—13" Plate.

*WRITE FOR SPECIAL PRICE
TO STIMULATE RETAIL SALES.*

FENTON ART GLASS CO.
WILLIAMSTOWN, W. VA.

More Reprints From Ads, Catalogues & Brochures 1930-1955

Illustrated in this section are a vast number of ad and catalogue reprints from the second twenty-five years. Those before 1939 are dated according to existing inventory records, and are to be considered an estimate of the earliest year of production. Always bear in mind that many items were continued in the line for several years. After 1938, the catalogues and brochures were usually dated, but you must still consider that just because an item is shown in a 1948 catalogue reprint it doesn't mean that same item could not have been made much earlier or later as well. Consult the listing of major Fenton lines on page 5 for further information. THIS REPRINT IS NOT COMPLETE. Many pages had to be passed over for reprint, especially in the case of duplicate offerings from previous catalogue. No catalogues were issued during the war years of 1944-1945 and the following 1946.

Circa 1934

81

1930 Brochure

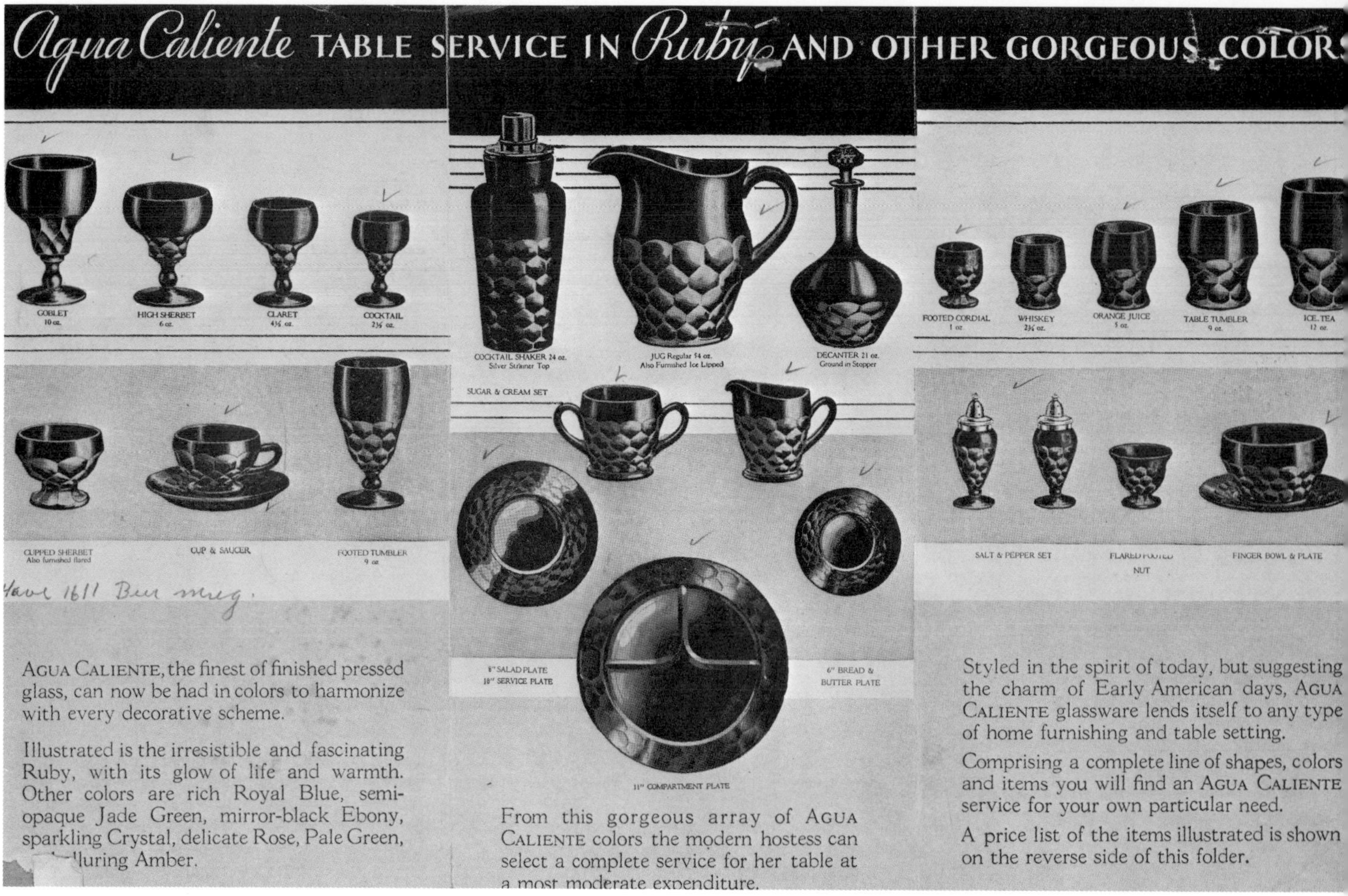
Agua Caliente TABLE SERVICE IN Ruby AND OTHER GORGEOUS COLORS
GOBLET 10 oz.
HIGH SHERBET 6 oz.
CLARET 4½ oz.
COCKTAIL 2½ oz.
COCKTAIL SHAKER 24 oz. Silver Strainer Top
JUG Regular 54 oz. Also Furnished Ice Lipped
DECANTER 21 oz. Ground in Stopper
FOOTED CORDIAL 1 oz.
WHISKEY 2½ oz.
ORANGE JUICE 5 oz.
TABLE TUMBLER 9 oz.
ICE TEA 12 oz.
CUPPED SHERBET Also furnished flared
CUP & SAUCER
FOOTED TUMBLER 9 oz.
SUGAR & CREAM SET
SALT & PEPPER SET
FINGER BOWL & PLATE
8" SALAD PLATE
10" SERVICE PLATE
6" BREAD & BUTTER PLATE
11" COMPARTMENT PLATE
AGUA CALIENTE, the finest of finished pressed glass, can now be had in colors to harmonize with every decorative scheme.
Illustrated is the irresistible and fascinating Ruby, with its glow of life and warmth. Other colors are rich Royal Blue, semi-opaque Jade Green, mirror-black Ebony, sparkling Crystal, delicate Rose, Pale Green, ...lluring Amber.
From this gorgeous array of AGUA CALIENTE colors the modern hostess can select a complete service for her table at a most moderate expenditure.
Styled in the spirit of today, but suggesting the charm of Early American days, AGUA CALIENTE glassware lends itself to any type of home furnishing and table setting.
Comprising a complete line of shapes, colors and items you will find an AGUA CALIENTE service for your own particular need.
A price list of the items illustrated is shown on the reverse side of this folder.

(Above & Below) Assortments of Georgian pattern, called Agua Caliente in early brochure—note the listing of colors made, some quite rare.

Circa 1930-35

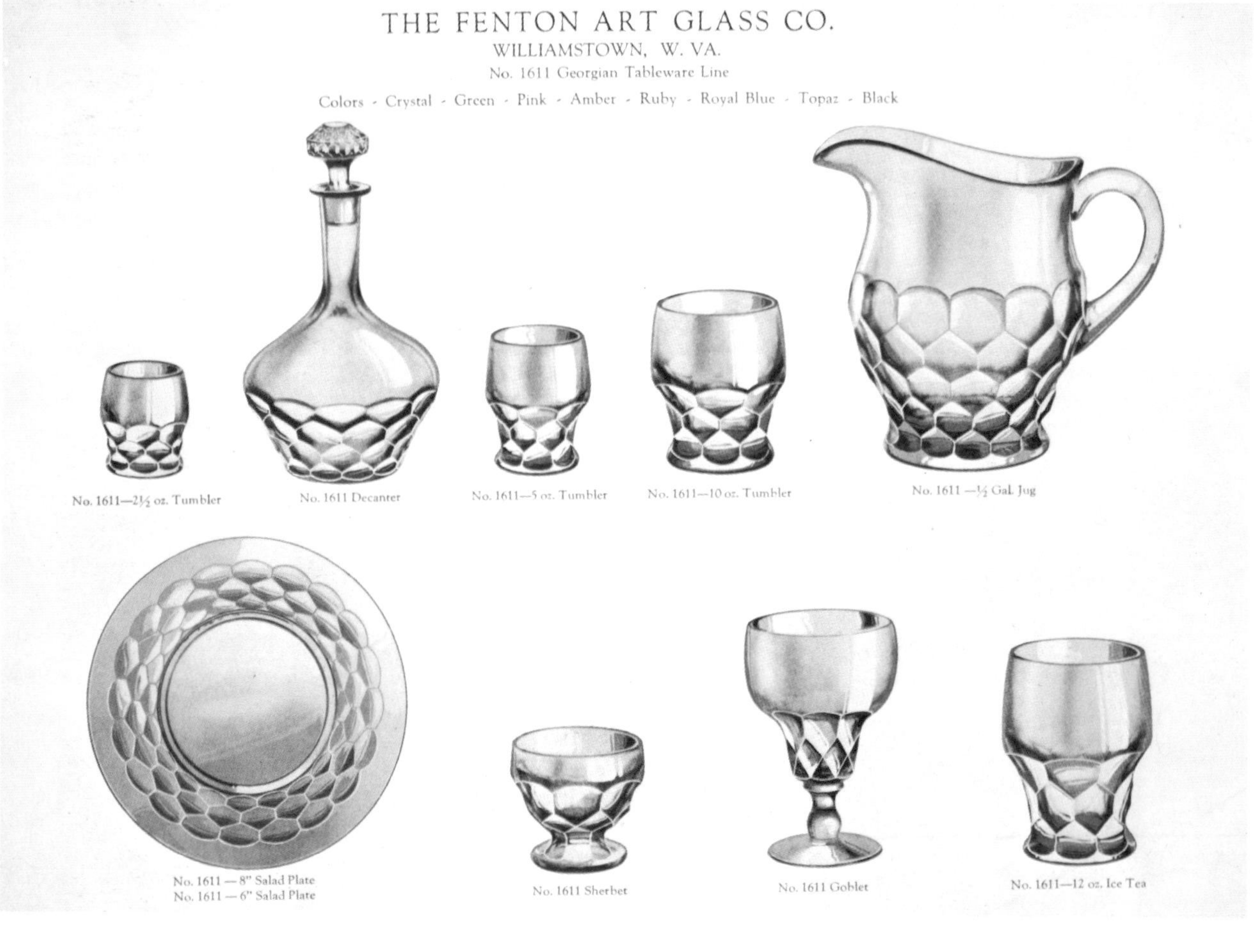
THE FENTON ART GLASS CO.
WILLIAMSTOWN, W. VA.
No. 1611 Georgian Tableware Line
Colors - Crystal - Green - Pink - Amber - Ruby - Royal Blue - Topaz - Black
No. 1611—2½ oz. Tumbler
No. 1611 Decanter
No. 1611—5 oz. Tumbler
No. 1611—10 oz. Tumbler
No. 1611 —½ Gal. Jug
No. 1611 — 8" Salad Plate
No. 1611 — 6" Salad Plate
No. 1611 Sherbet
No. 1611 Goblet
No. 1611—12 oz. Ice Tea

Circa 1933

(Above) Fenton's #1620 Plymouth pattern set in crystal—also made in color.
(Below) Fenton #1934 Liquor Sets with special frosted pattern tray—shown here in crystal, cobalt and ruby.

Circa 1935

Reprinted from LAMPS, February, 1932

1932 Advertisement

No. G-120 Dec. 2

No. B-20

No. B-30

No. G-135 Dec. 4

FENTON Art Glass Company PRESENTS

a group of its new and original designs in glass lamps emphasizing Early American motifs.

THESE lamps come in a wide range of colors, ornamentations, treatment, sizes and shapes. Equipped either with glass chimneys or parchment shades, they are completely harmonized units.

THE growing interest in glass lamps for ornamentation and utility to meet the prevailing period modes—the revival of things Colonial and Federal-make glass lamps in strong demand. Now is the time to feature them prominently in sales events.

VALUES are extraordinarily attractive. Throughout the range is popular priced.

FENTON lamps are now nationally sold through the salesforce of William R. Noe & Sons, New York, and are permanently displayed by that firm at 1 Park Avenue, New York, and space 319, American Furniture Mart, Chicago.

ON the facing page will be found complete details of the colors and decorative treatment of the eleven numbers illustrated.

Write today for circulars, price lists and complete information about the entire Fenton lamp lines.

THE FENTON ART GLASS COMPANY
WILLIAMSTOWN, W. VA.

No. G-70 Dec. 7

No. G-70 Dec. 8

No. G70 Dec. 9

No. B-10

No. G-80 Dec. 5

No. G-80 Dec. 4

No. G-80 Dec. 2

NEW YORK DISPLAY WITH WM. R. NOE & SONS 1 PARK AVE.

CHICAGO DISPLAY WITH WM. R. NOE & SONS SPACE 319 AMER. FURN. MART

Circa 1931

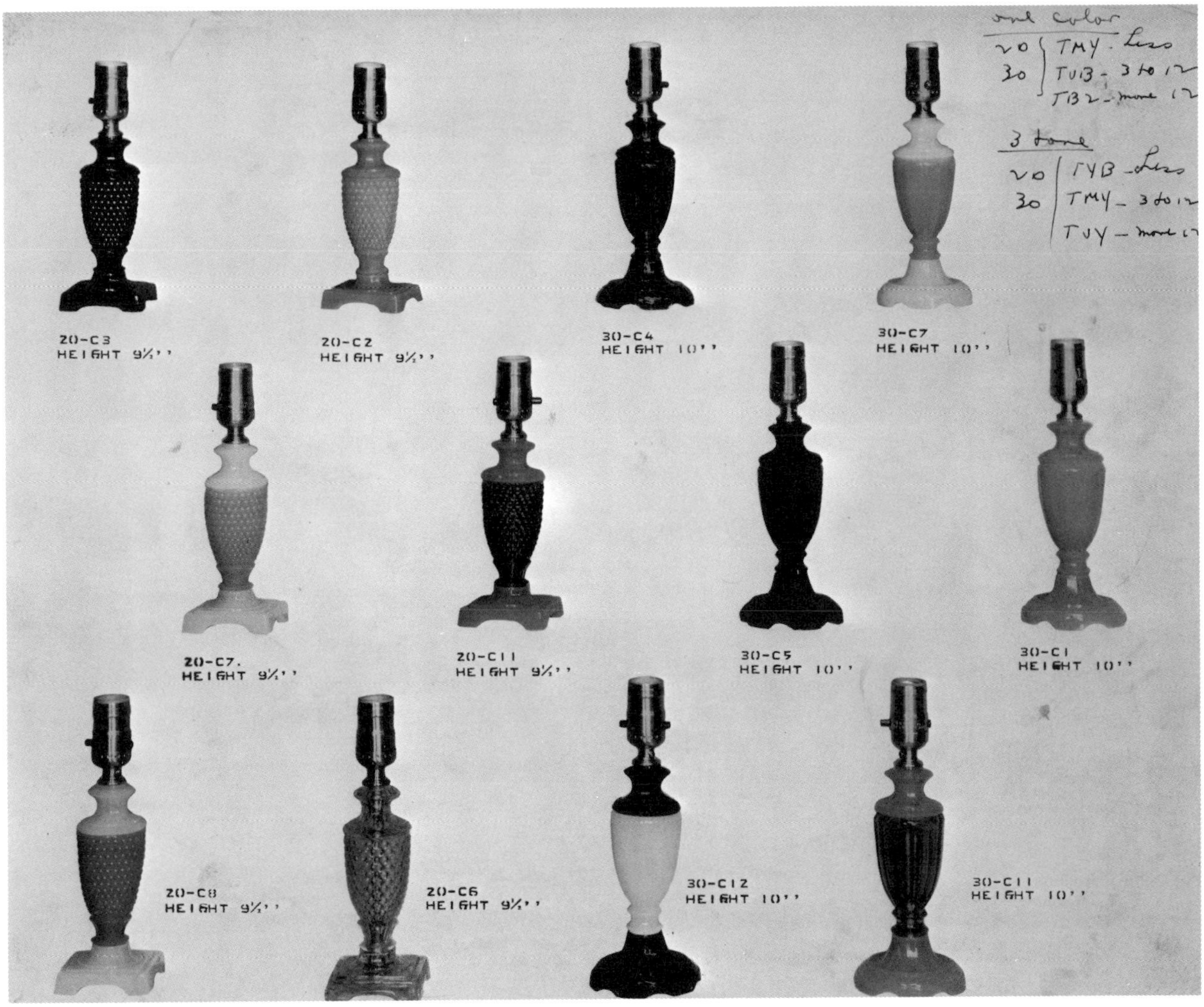

20-C3 HEIGHT 9½"
20-C2 HEIGHT 9½"
30-C4 HEIGHT 10"
30-C7 HEIGHT 10"

20-C7 HEIGHT 9½"
20-C11 HEIGHT 9½"
30-C5 HEIGHT 10"
30-C1 HEIGHT 10"

20-C8 HEIGHT 9½"
20-C6 HEIGHT 9½"
30-C12 HEIGHT 10"
30-C11 HEIGHT 10"

(Above and Below) Assortment of electric lamp bases.

Circa 1931

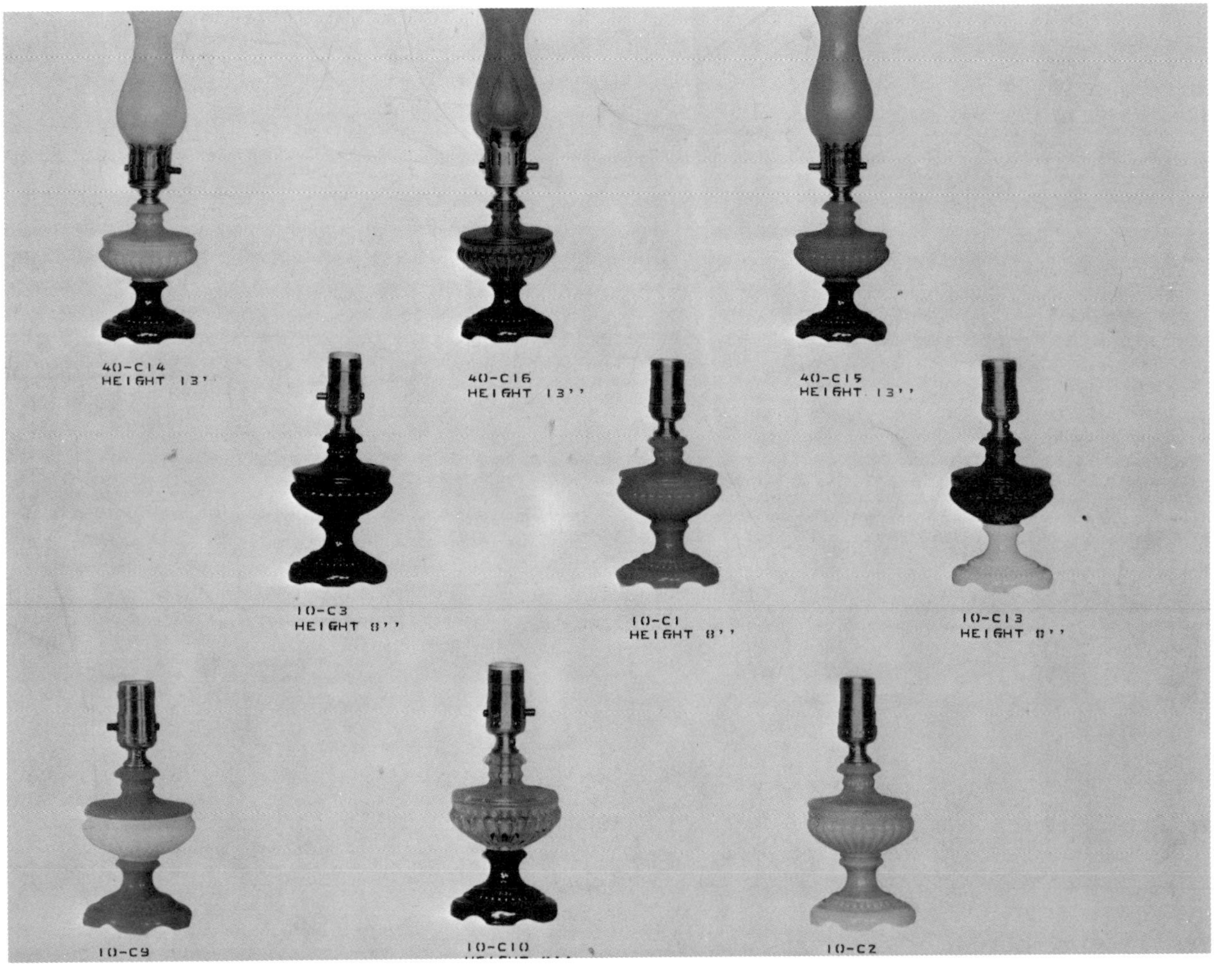

40-C14 HEIGHT 13"
40-C16 HEIGHT 13"
40-C15 HEIGHT 13"

10-C3 HEIGHT 8"
10-C1 HEIGHT 8"
10-C13 HEIGHT 8"

10-C9
10-C10
10-C2

85

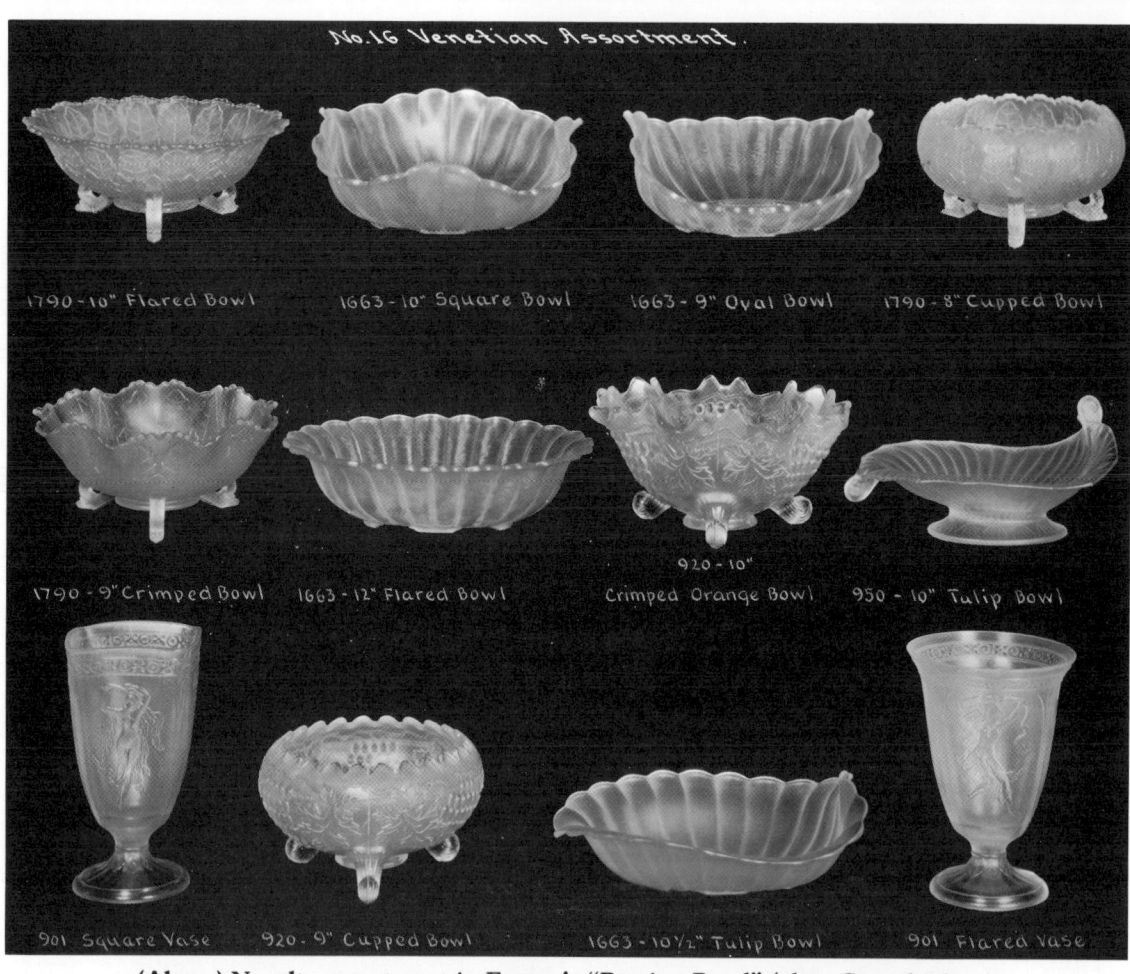

(Above) Novelty assortment in Fenton's "Persian Pearl" (clear Stretch glass).
(Below) Assortment of items in "Azure Blue" color (pale blue Stretch glass).

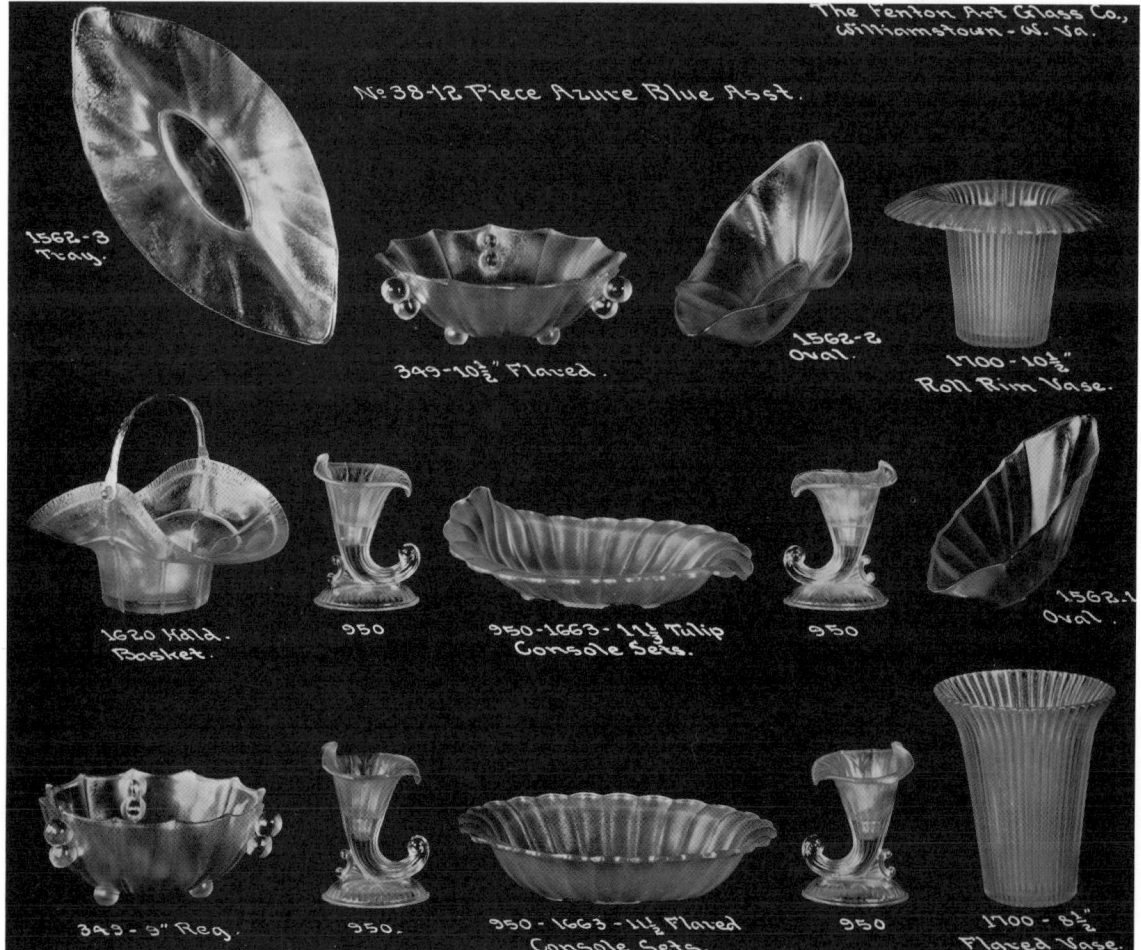

Circa 1933

(Above) Large assortment of items in Fenton's Ruby.
(Below) Additional offering of console sets in Ruby & Jade Green.

Circa 1933

87

Circa 1936

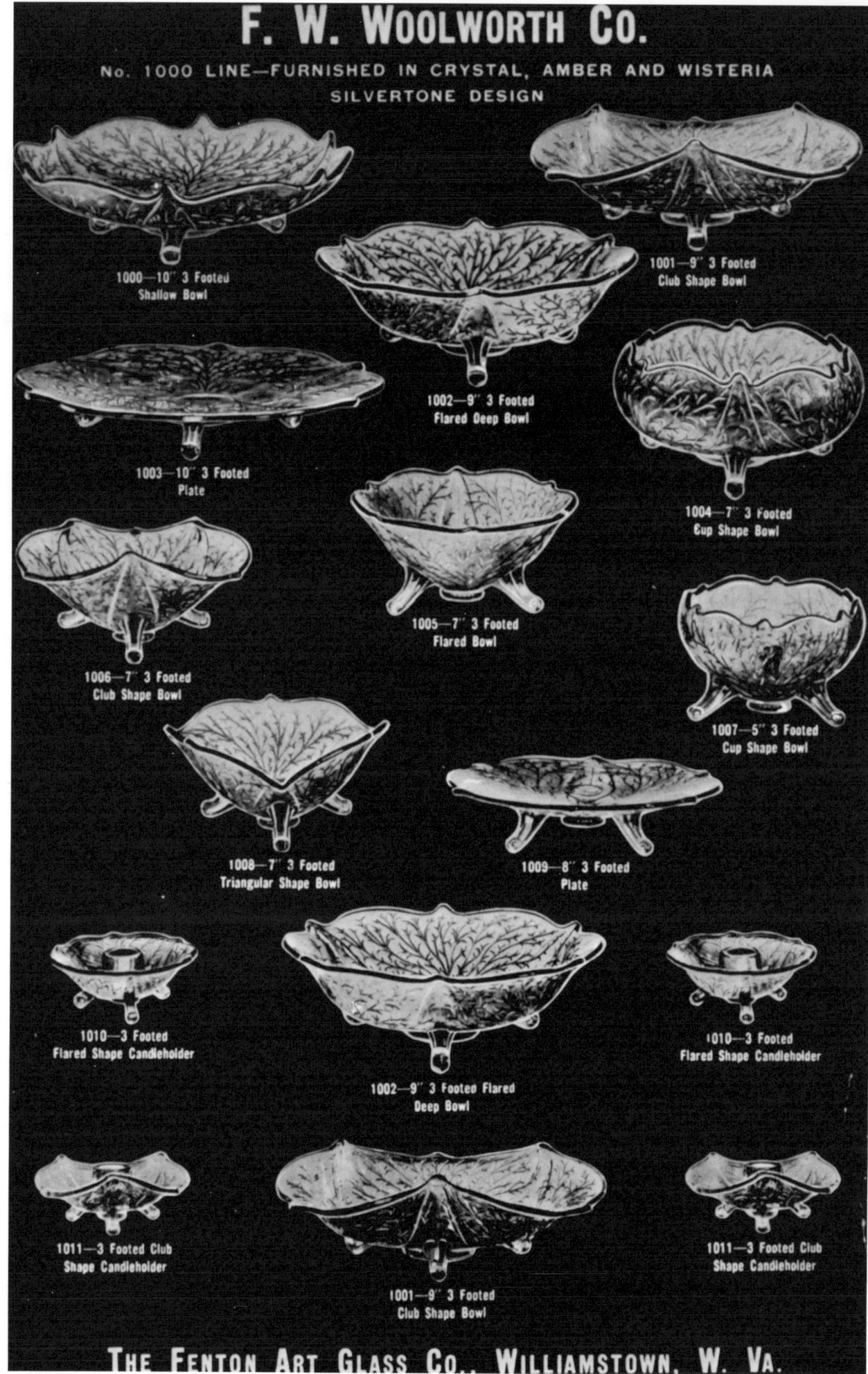

Early Woolworth ad featuring assortment of Silvertone design—not to be confused with the satin decoration of the same name.

DISPLAY THESE NOVEL GIFT ITEMS FOR QUICK PROFITABLE SALES
Authentic reproductions of the famous "Sandwich" designs

FAN VASE—No. 1900—10"
A Beautiful Vase
for
An Attractive Arrangement of Flowers —
Cry — Cape Cod Green — Colonial Blue
— Gold — Vaseline.

Hat, Slipper and Fan
Made in
Royal Blue — Colonial Blue — Crystal —
Wistaria — Amber — Cape Cod Green —
Gold — Vaseline.

SLIPPER — No. 1900
A NOVEL ASH TRAY
All Colors

FAN — No. 957 — 10"
This Item May Be Used as a Bon Bon —
Salad Plate — Dresser Tray — Or for an
Attractive Hors D'Oeuvre Tray.
All Colors

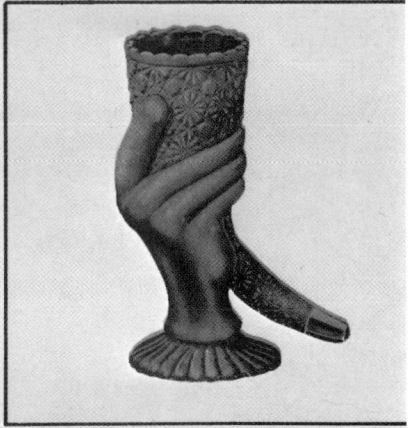

1900 — HAND CORNUCOPIA
or HORN OF PLENTY
For Small Flowers — Cry — Wistaria —
Colonial Blue — Vaseline

REPRODUCTIONS OF EARLY AMERICAN DAYS
Now We Bring Them to You
in Our Gorgeous Assortment of Color.
Practical . . . Beautiful and Useful Items
for Every Home.

BE ONE OF THE FIRST IN YOUR COMMUNITY TO ORDER THESE SPECIAL ITEMS
Order Now — Use the Convenient Order Card Enclosed

FIVE PIECE HI-HAT CIGARETTE SET

1900 — HI-HAT
Here We Have a Practical Match or Toothpick Holder — And Something Different for Serving, Crabmeat, Shrimp or Fruit Cocktails.
All Colors

1900 — Ash Trays — And With the Ash Trays a Beautiful Cigarette Set.
All Colors

Use the Convenient Order Card —
NO STAMP NECESSARY

GLASSWARE THAT SELLS!
by
FENTON

All Items Illustrated
are in the
Daisy and Button Design

REPRESENTATIVES

Chicago, Ill.
  Martin M. Simpson & Co.
  1562 Merchandise Mart

New York, N. Y.
  Horace C. Gray Co.
  200 Fifth Ave.

Boston, Mass.
  H. P. & H. F. Hunt Co.
  93 Summer St.

Philadelphia, Pa.
  T. Downs, Jr.
  Burd Bldg.

San Francisco, Calif.
  Baker Smith Co.
  728 S. Hill St.

Los Angeles, Calif.
  Baker Smith Co.
  728 S. Hill St.

Seattle, Wash.
  Baker Smith Co.
  403 Lowman Bldg.

Denver, Colo.
  Mercer & Mercer
  Commonwealth Bldg.

Dallas, Texas
  Gilbert J. Lehman
  The Ervington

Baltimore, Md.
  W. R. Neal
  Hanover Bldg.
  110 W. Fayette St.

St. Louis, Mo.
  Harry W. Becker
  515 Kinloch Bldg.

Detroit, Mich.
  Amory B. Swift
  1346 Broadway

"Hi-Hat"
A SURE FIRE SALES PRODUCER

by
FENTON ART GLASS CO.
Williamstown, W. Va.

Specialists in Colored Glass
For - 32 - Years

Circa 1936-37

No. 1800
12 pc. Assortment

List prices per dz. (Individual prices)

1 pc. each following items in each assortment

1800-6¼" Fld. Vase	$5.00
1800-6¼" Crpd Vase	5.00
1800-6¼" Tulip Vase	5.00
1800-6¼" Cupd Vase	5.00
1800-6½" Reg. Vase	5.00
1800-3 ftd-7" fld. Bon Bon	4.00
1800-3 ftd-7½" shal. BonBon	4.00
1800-3 ftd-8¼" plate	4.00
1800-3 ftd-6½" Club BonBon	4.00
1800-3 ftd Tria Bon Bons-6¾"	4.00
1800-3 ftd Cupd Bon Bon-5½"	4.00
1800-3 ftd Covd Bon Bon-6"	7.20

Asst. Price, ea. $4.00
In gross lots, ea. 3.50

Less 50%

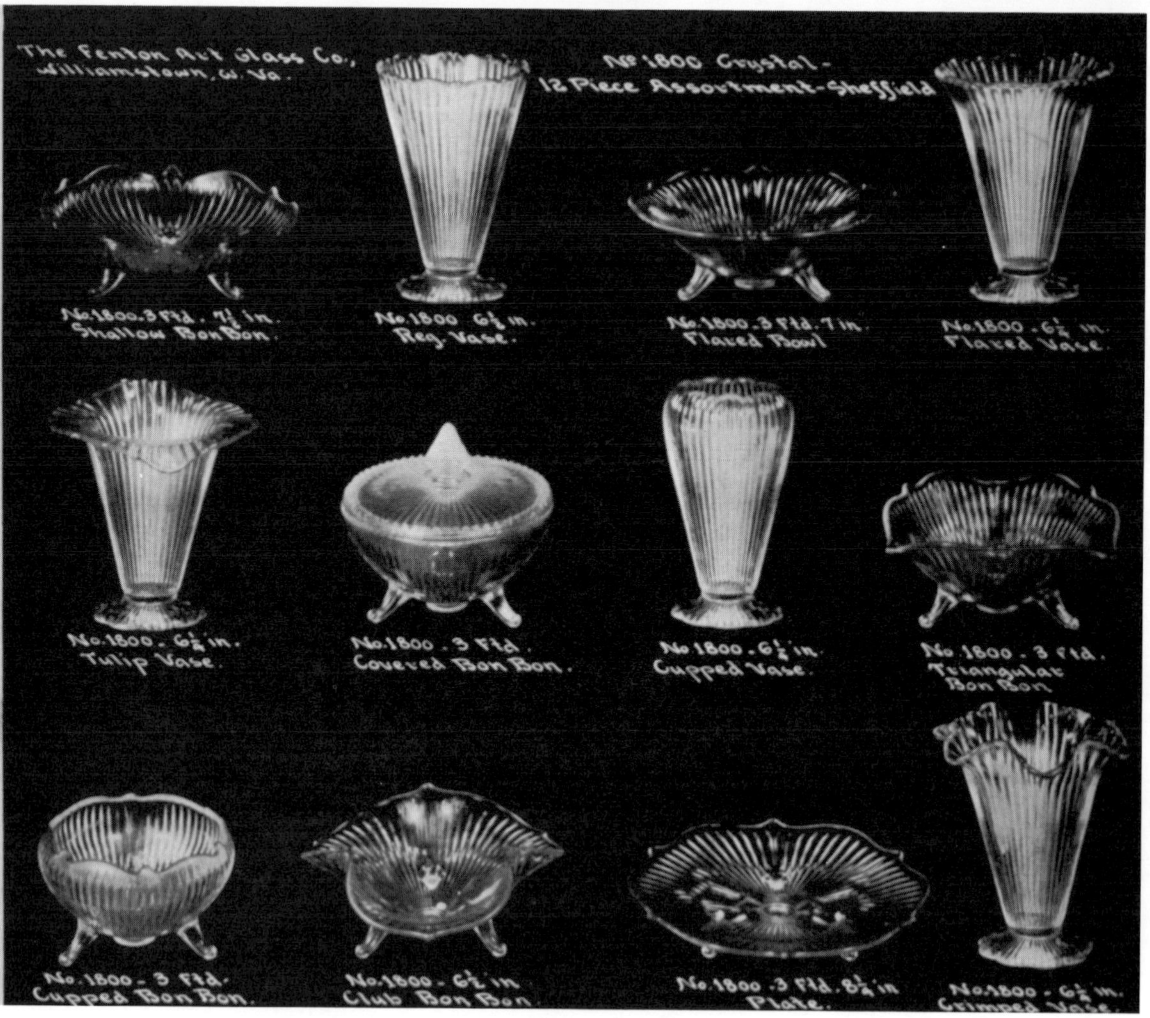

Assortments of *Sheffield* pattern—below with *Silvertone* decoration.

Circa 1937

90

Circa 1937

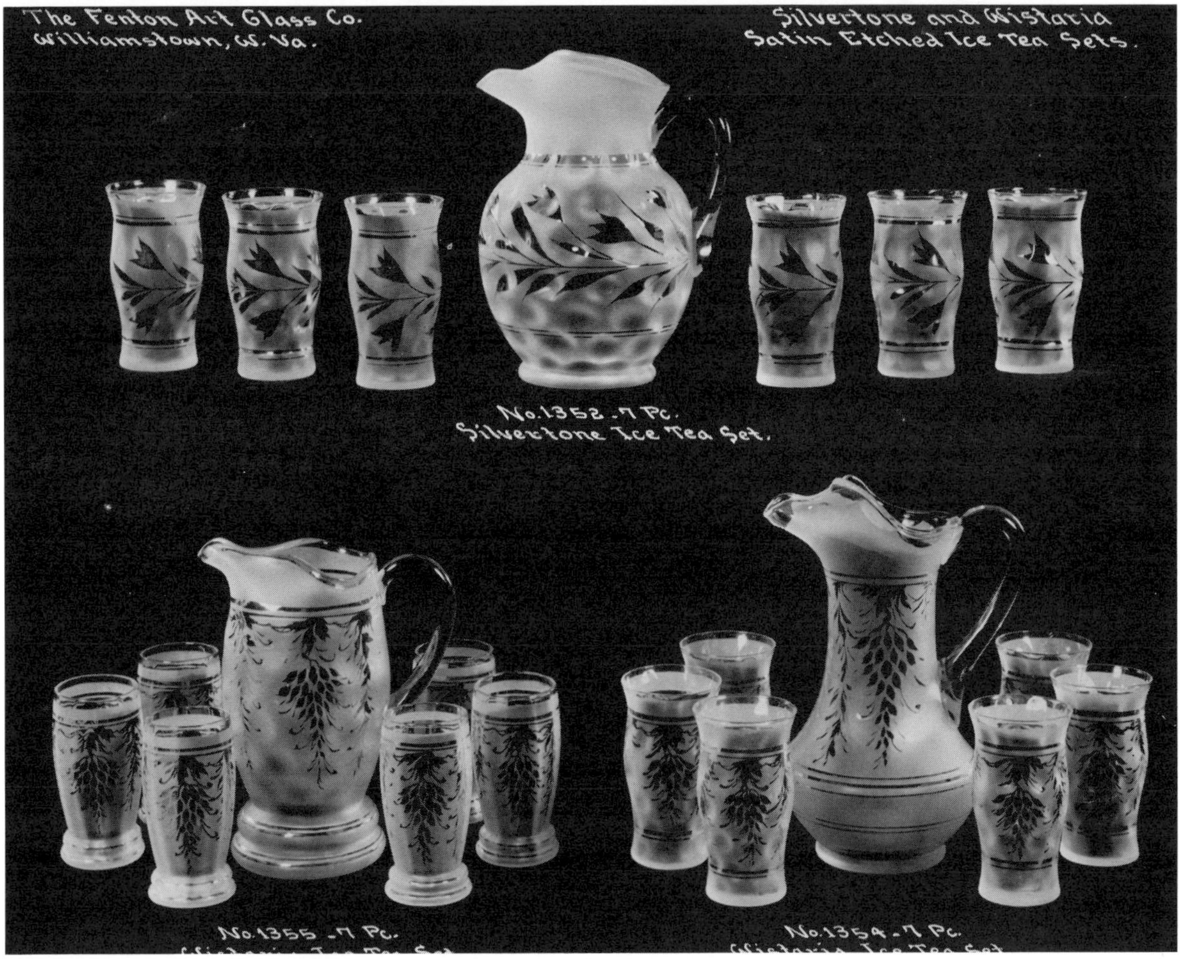

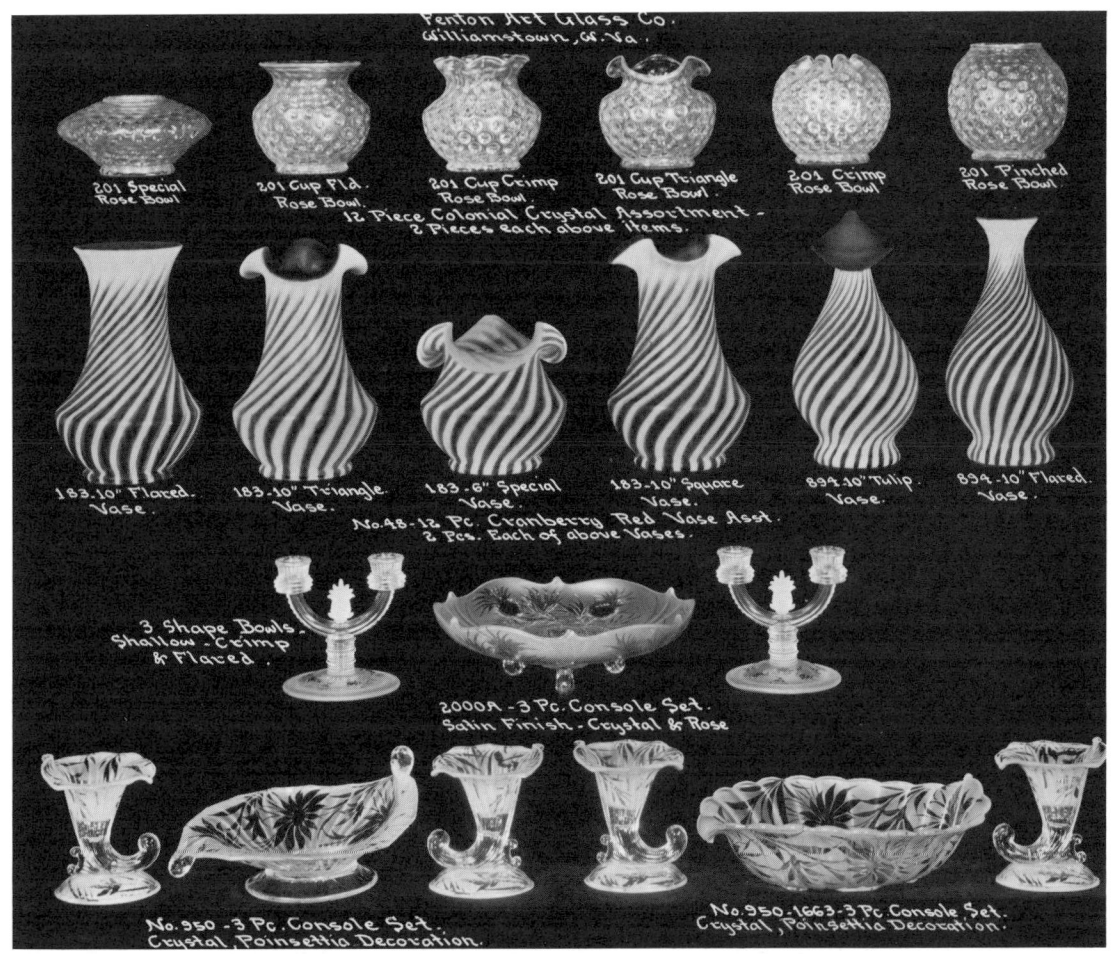

(Above) Assorted Satin-etched ice tea sets, circa 1937.
(Below) Varied assortment; note the unusual crystal rose bowls on top row.

Circa 1938-39

Circa 1936

No. 33 — San Toy Crystal Assortment

	Indiv. Price Per Dozen
184-8″ Vase	$15.00
950 Candlesticks (1 pair) doz. pair	12.00
950 Oval Bowl	12.00
180 Hyacinth Vase	5.00
847-6″ Cupd BonBon	12.00
847-6″ Crimped Vase	12.00
847-7½″ Flared Bowl	12.00
847-6″ Regular Bowl	12.00
847-6″ Fan Vase	12.00
705 Flower Ball & Base	12.00
847-8½″ Shal Crpd Bowl	12.00

Regular Pkg. Chg.

Assortment price $10.00

Wide assortment of satin etched crystal in *San-Toy* (above) and *Wistaria* patterns (below).

Circa 1938

No. 39 — 12 pc. Wistaria Assortment

1 pc. ea. following items:

	Indiv. Price Per Dozen
857-8″ Fan Vase	$18.00
857 Flared Bowl	18.00
893 Ginger Jar, Base & Cover	24.00
183 Vase	18.00
184-10″ Vase	18.00
844 Cov'd BonBon	18.00
231 Plate	18.00
349-11″ Fld Bowl	18.00
621 Vase & Base	18.00
184-12″ Vase	24.00
1616 Ice Pail	18.00

Asst. Price $18.00 each

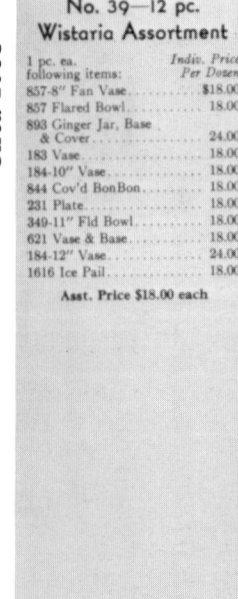

Circa 1937

(Above) Console sets and bowls in rare satin-etched pattern I am naming "Snow Fern".
(Below) Wide assortment of *Satin Ming,* made in crystal, green and rose.

Circa 1935-36

**No. 30
Ming Assortment
Crystal, Rose & Green**

	Indiv. Price Per Dozen
184-10" Vase	$15.00
184-12" Vase	18.00
621-8" Fld Vase & Base	14.40
249-10" Deep Fld Bowl	15.00
249-11½" Fld Bowl	15.00
249-10½" Shal Bowl	15.00
249-10½" Crpd Bowl	15.00
857-8" Fan Vase	14.40
1684-9" Hld Basket	12.00
846-6" Cupd Bowl & Base	14.40
846-8½" Fld Bowl & Base	14.40
893 Ginger Jar, Base & Cover	18.00
Regular Pkg. Chg.	

Asst. Price $14.40 doz.

93

Circa 1938

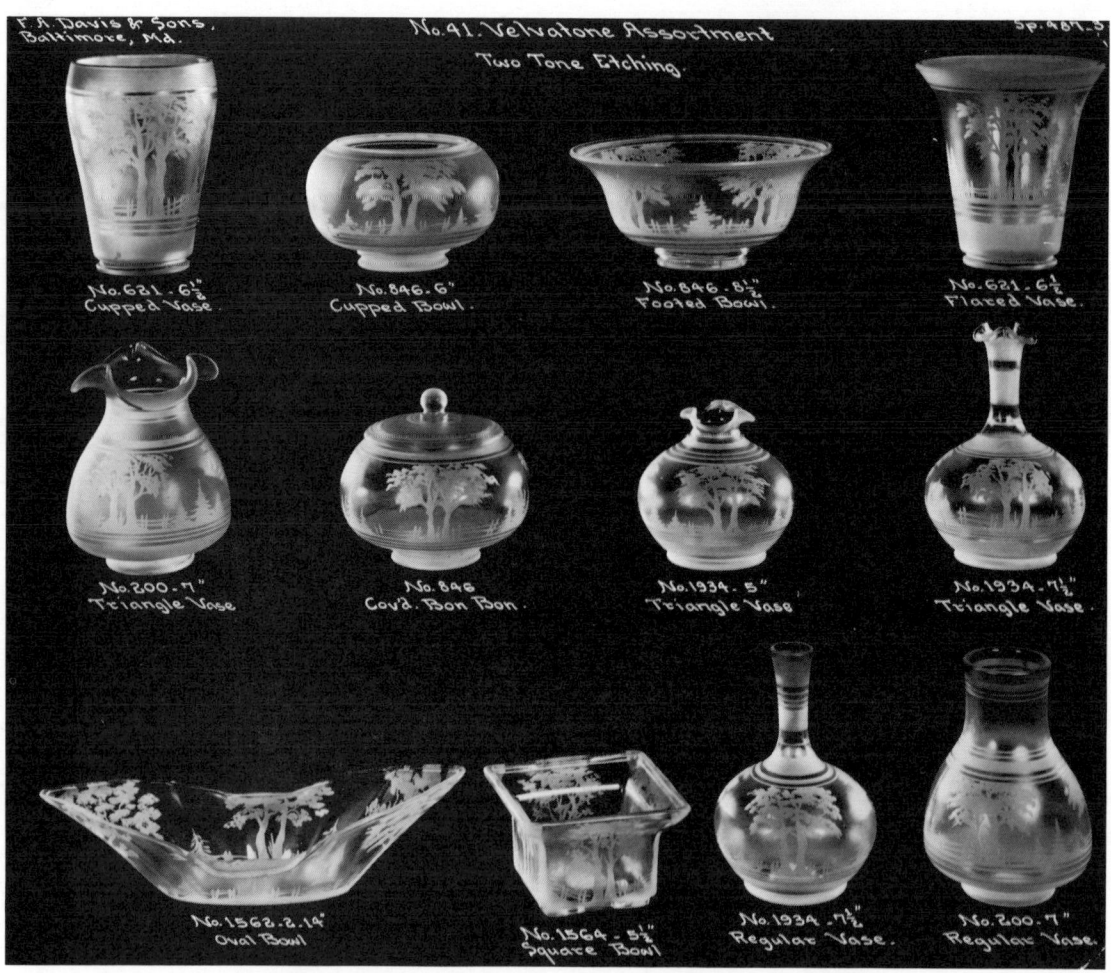

(Above) Lovely scenic *Velvatone* assortment, circa 1938.
(Below) Satin etched *Poinsettia* assortment, circa 1939.

Circa 1939

Circa 1938

No. 2000-A
Bon Bon Assortment

	List Price Per Dozen
2000-6½" Fld Bon Bon, S.F.	$6.00
2000-7" Salver Bon Bon, S.F.	6.00
2000-5½" Reg Bon Bon, S.F.	6.00
2000-6½" Crimped Bon Bon, S.F.	6.00
2000-5½" Cupd Bon Bon, S.F.	6.00
2000-6½" Club Bon Bon, S.F.	6.00
2000-6½" Ftd Fld Bon Bon, S.F.	9.00
2000-6½" Ftd Club Bon Bon, S.F.	9.00
2000-6½" Ftd Salver Bon Bon, S.F.	9.00
2000-5½" Ftd Reg Bon Bon, S.F.	9.00
2000-6½" Ftd Crimped Bon Bon, S.F.	9.00
2000-5½" Ftd Cupd Bon Bon, S.F.	9.00

Assortment Price $7.20
Less 50%
Regular Package Charge

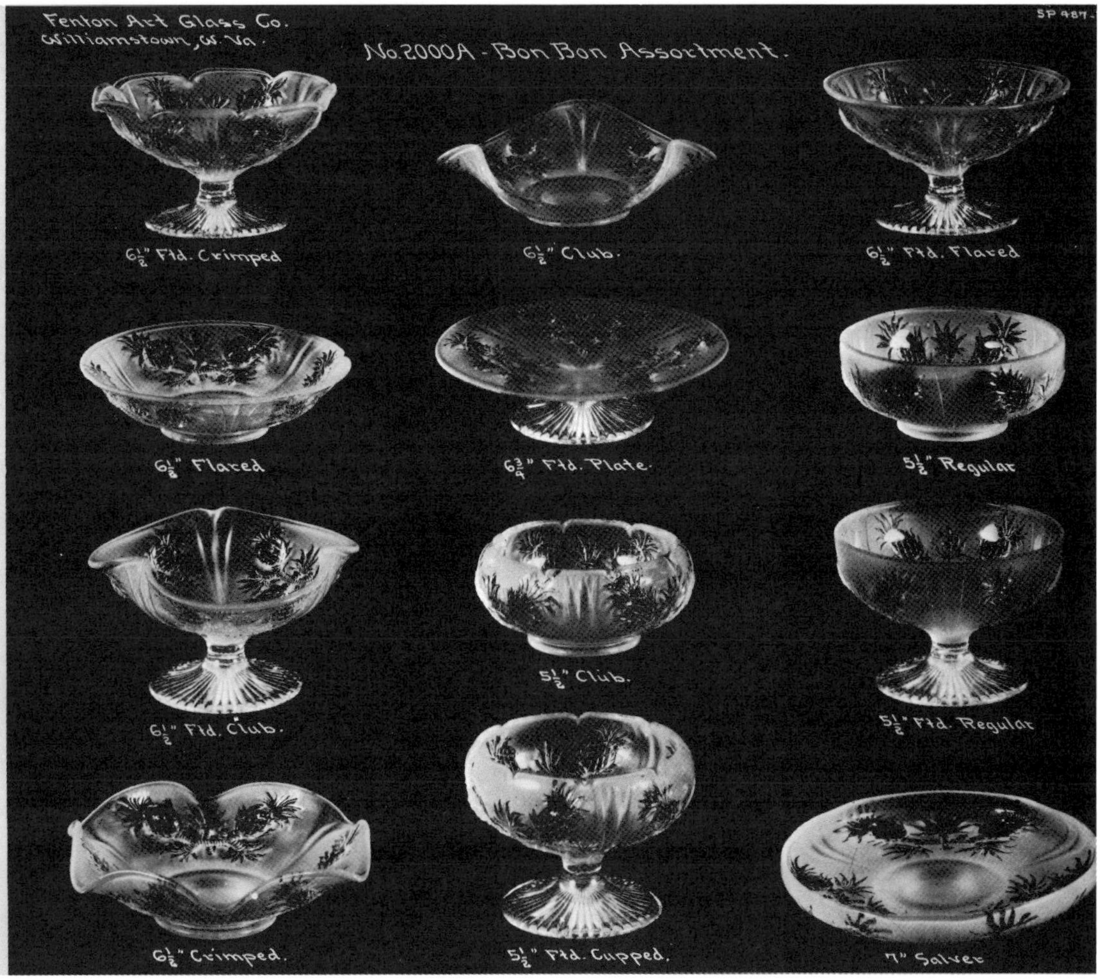

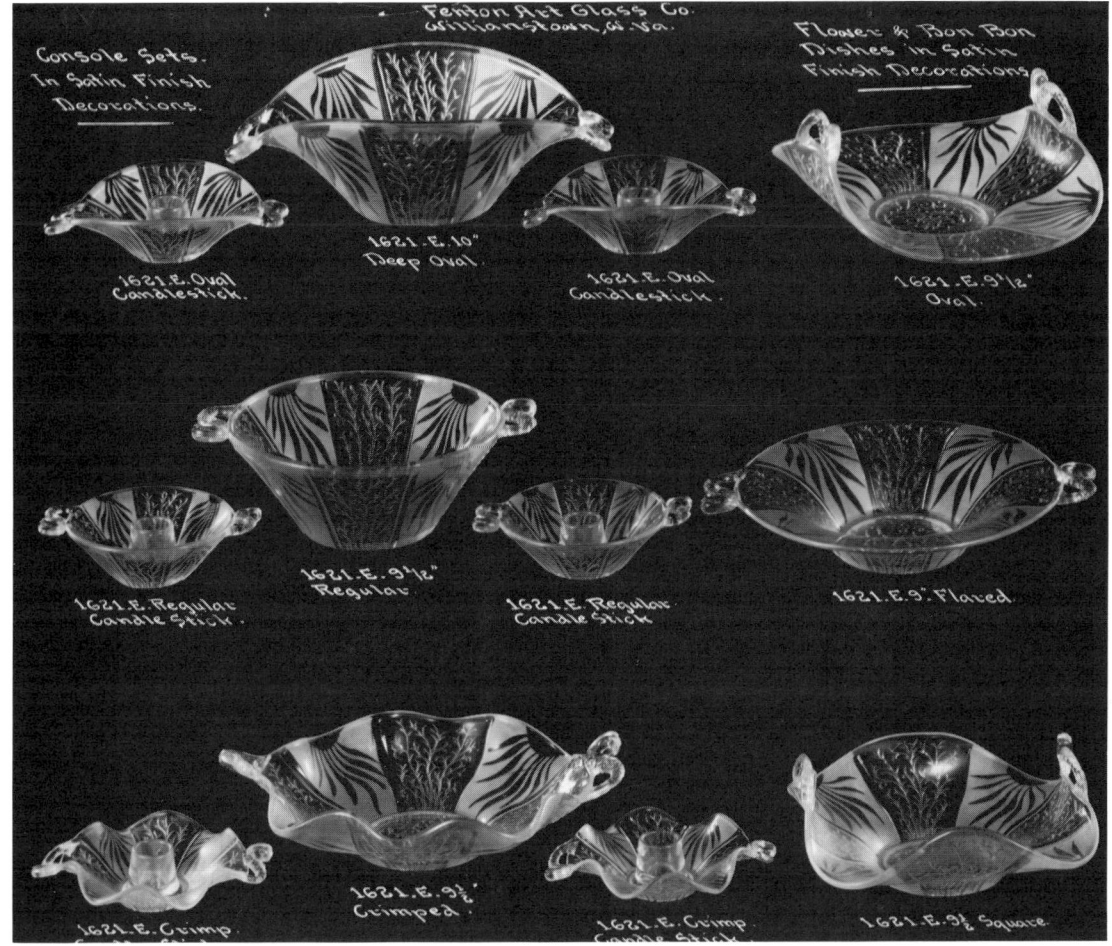

(Above) Assortment of "Fenton's Pineapple", crystal with satin finish.
(Below) Assorted console sets & bon-bons with satin decoration.

Circa 1936

Circa 1937-38

No. 1900 Cape Cod Crystal Line

List per dz.

1900-7″ Rose Bowl	$12.00
1900-9½″ Flared Bowl	12.00
1900-13½″ Plate	12.00
1900-7½″ Reg. Bowl	12.00
1900 Candelabra, dz. pr.	18.00
1900 Hdld. Clover Leaf Bowl	12.00
1900-12″ Flared Bowl-Hdld.	12.00
1900-12″ Boat Bowl-Hdld.	12.00
1900-11″ Square Hdld. Bowl	12.00

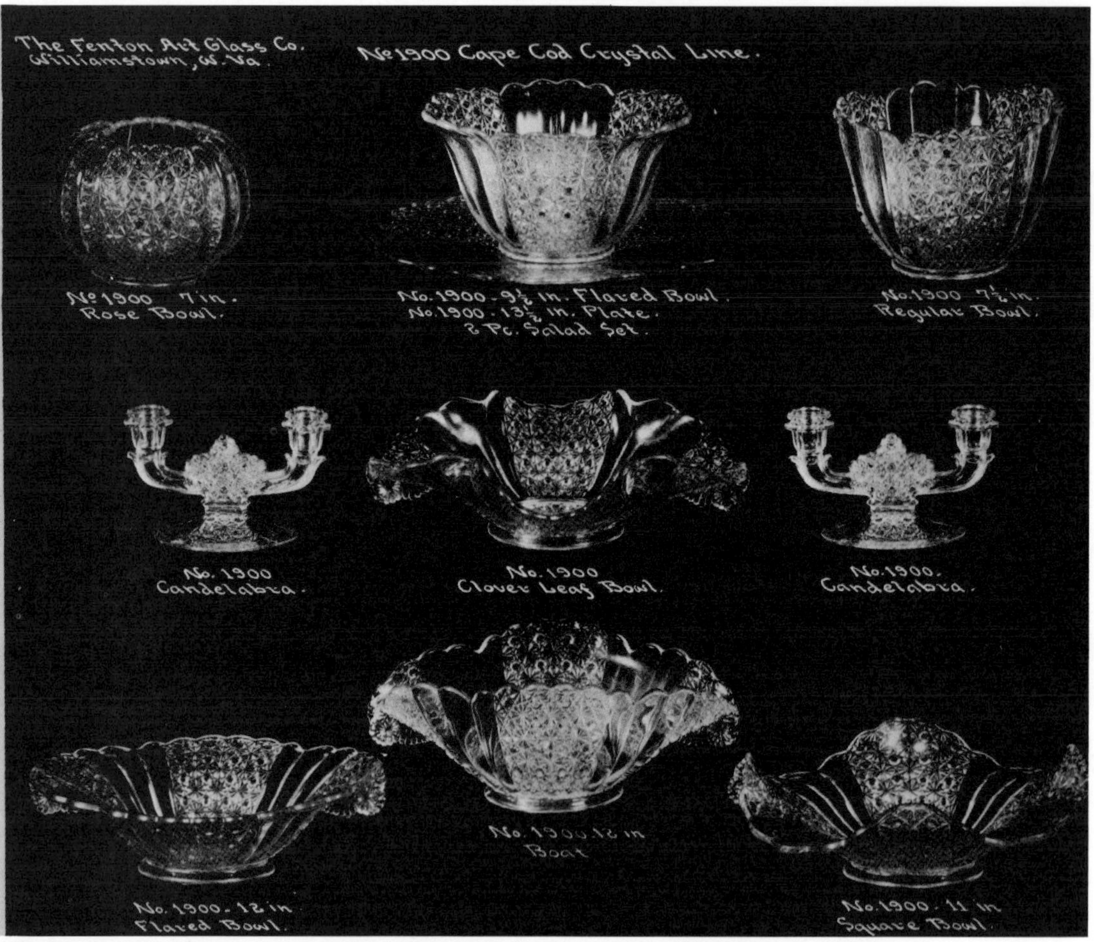

(Above) Assortment of *Cape Cod* line in crystal—revived in 1953 in opaque colors.
(Below) Varied milk glass assortment in several popular Fenton designs.

Circa 1933

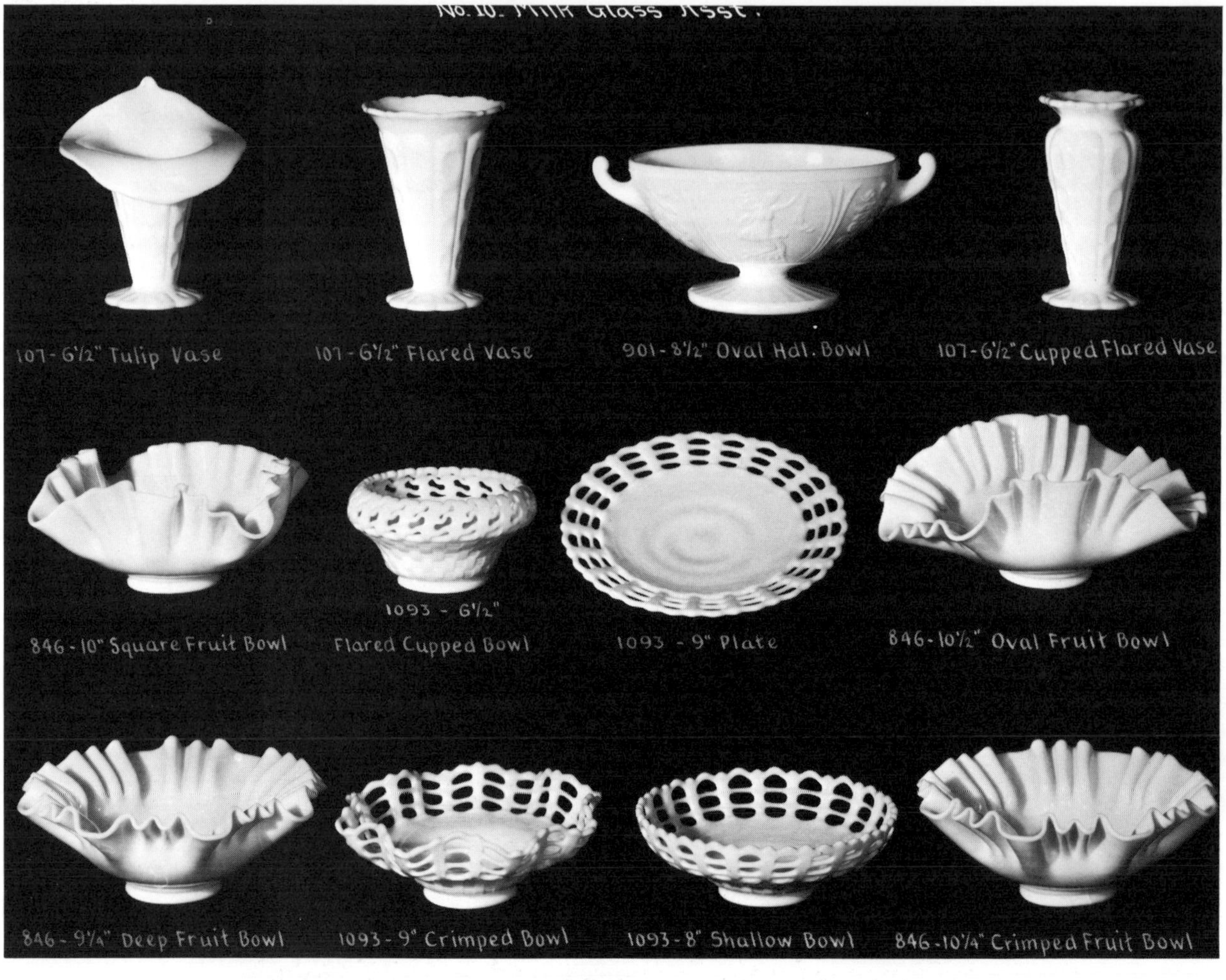

No. 42 Special
ertone Assortment

List Price
Per Dozen

0" Vase.........$14.40
loverleaf Bowl... 14.40
" Vase........ 14.40
1" Crimped Bowl 14.40
1¾" Cake Plate. 14.40
2-13" Oval Bowl. 14.40
Ice Pail........ 14.40
/1-13½" Oval
wl............ 14.40
ovd Bon Bon.... 14.40
" Fan Vase...... 14.40
½" Fld Bowl &
se............. 14.40
11" Hdld Basket. 14.40
ortment Price $14.40

Less 50%

gular Package Charge

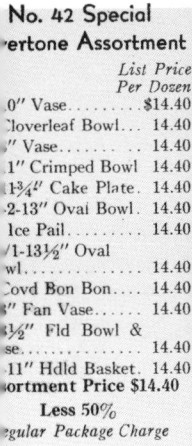

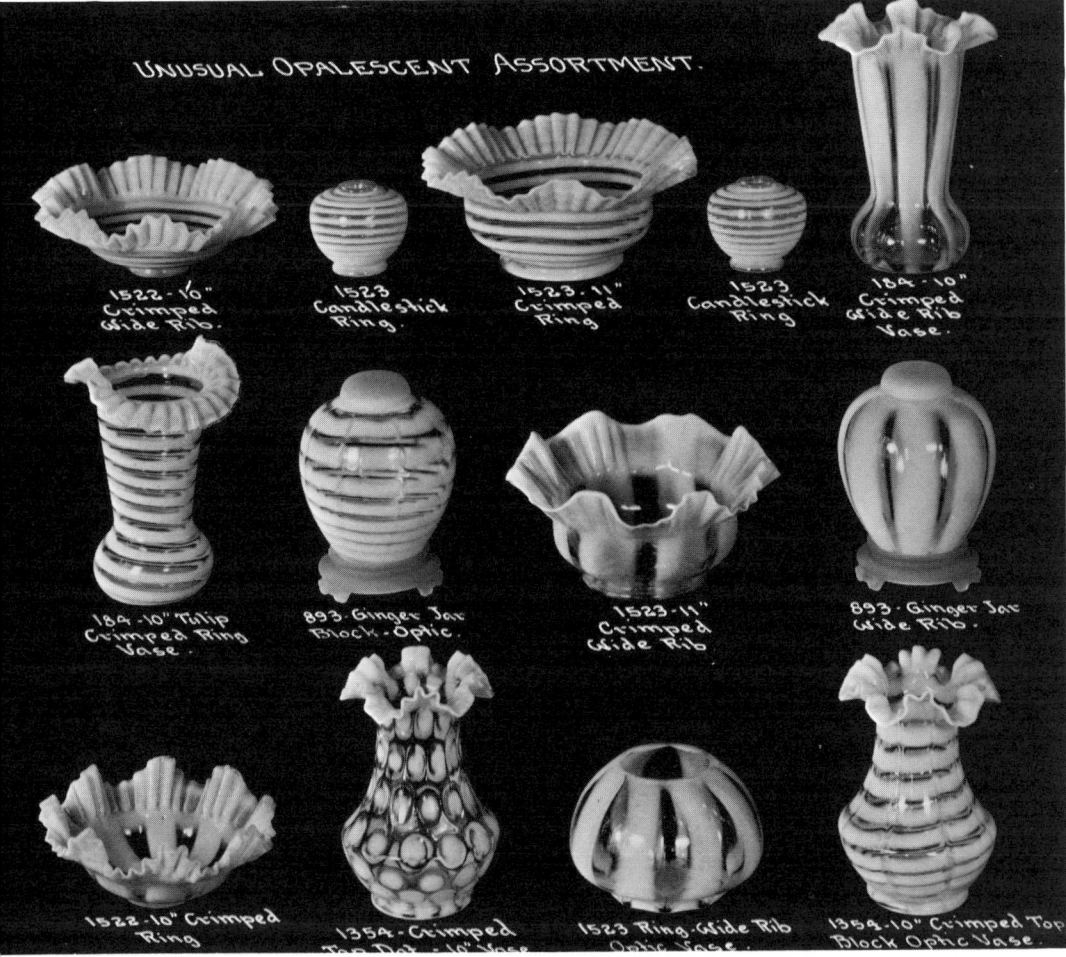

(Above) Assortment of *Silvertone* satin-etched crystal.

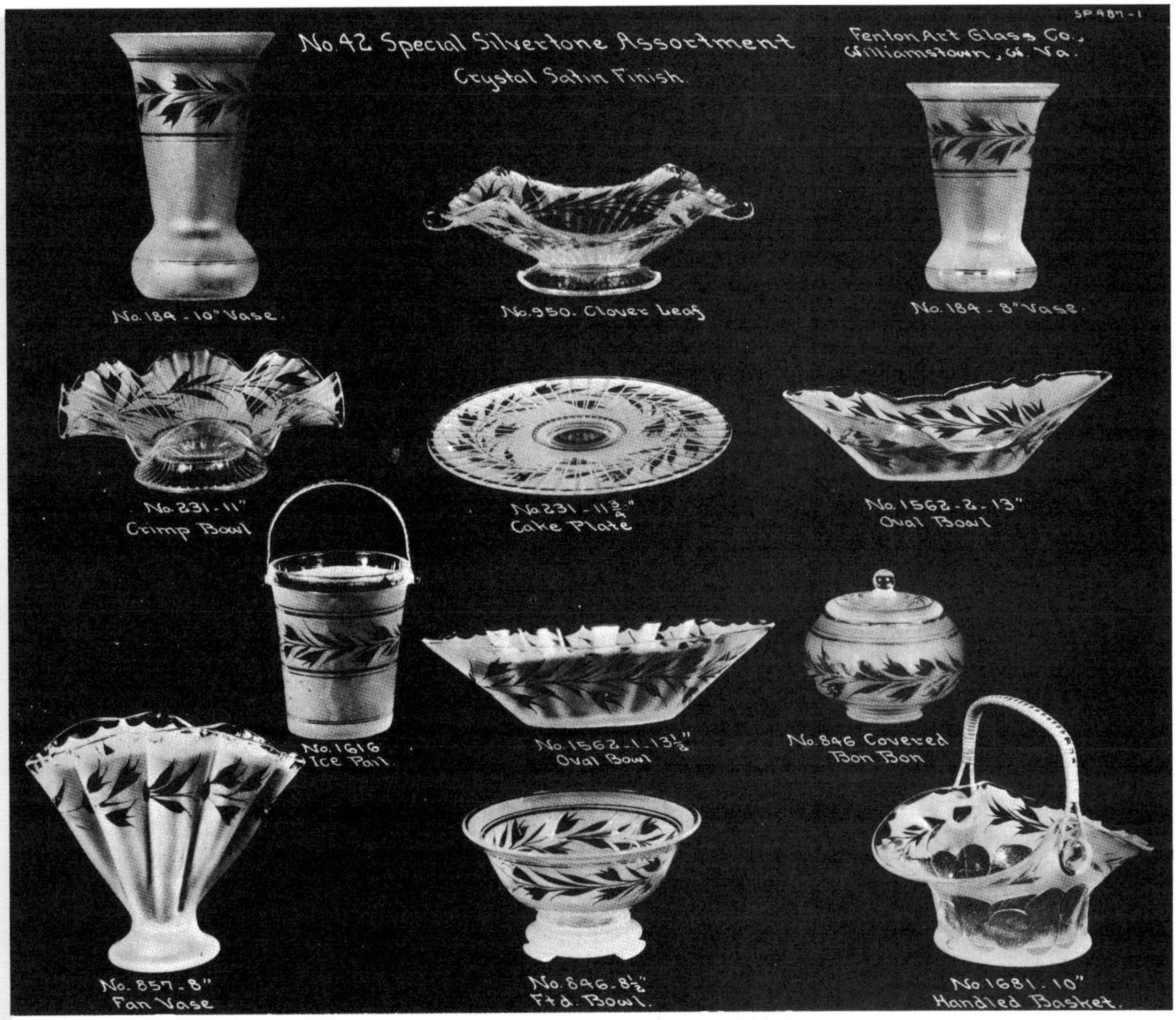

(Below) The title says "unusual", and this is indisputable — most items shown are very rare today.

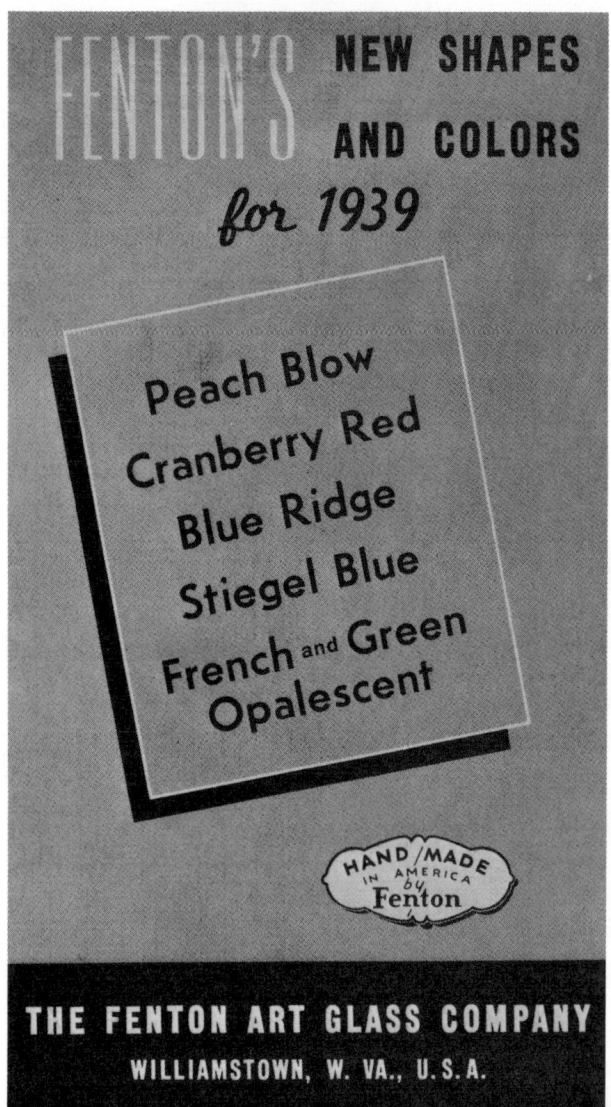

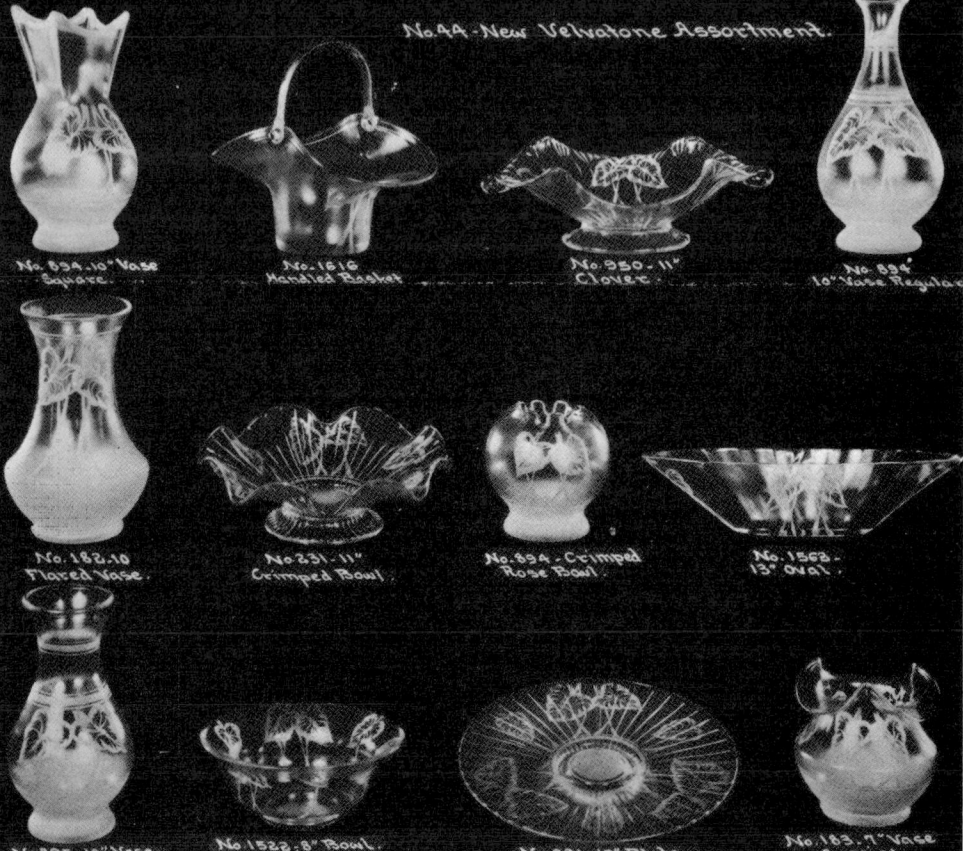

(Above) Three items in *SPIRAL OPTIC* made in several colors.

(Below) Assortment of satin-etched design I am naming *TWIN IVY*, very rare today.

1939 Brochure

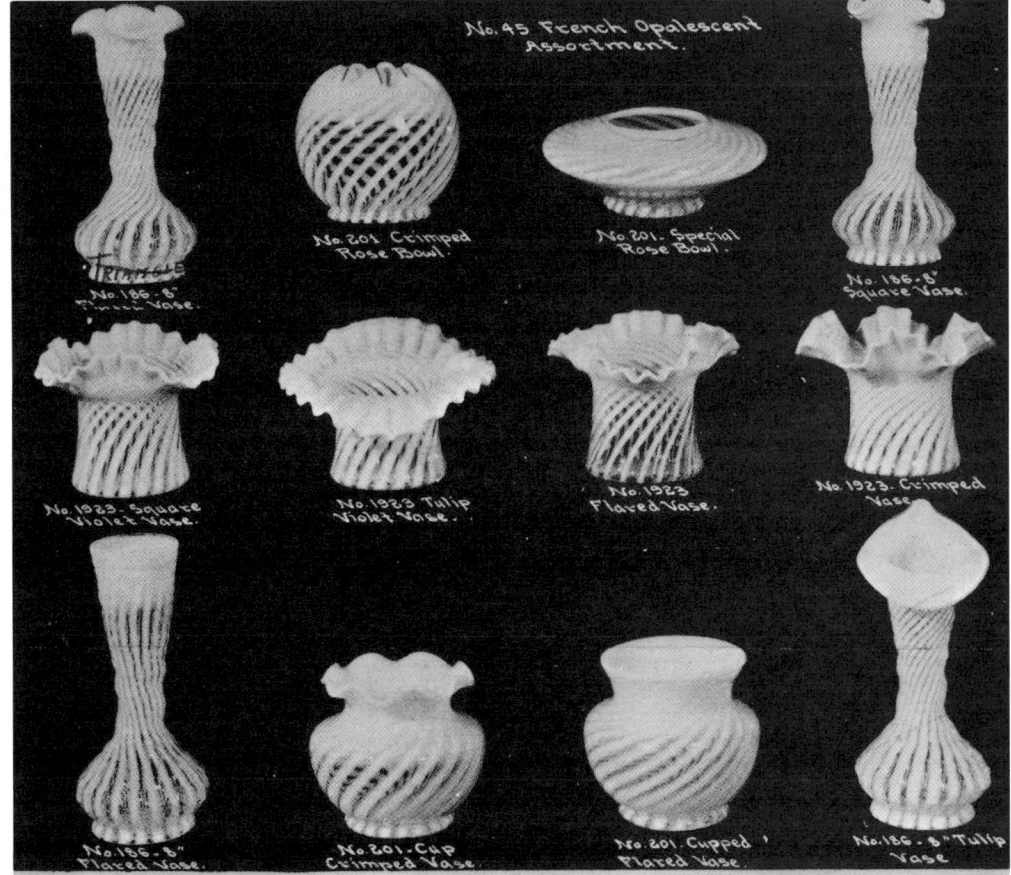

No. 45 French Opalescent Assortment

THE ABOVE ASSORTMENT ALSO MADE AS FOLLOWS:

No. 46 Blue Ridge No. 50 Opalescent Green
No. 47 Cranberry Red No. 51 Small Cranberry Red Asst.
No. 48 Stiegel Blue No. 52 Small Peach Blow Asst.
No. 49 Peach Blow

(Above) This assortment of shapes made in eight different colors listed here, including Stiegel blue (blue opalescent).

(Below) More shapes in Peach Blow, also made in Spiral Optic, Cranberry and Blue Ridge.

1939 Brochure

Peach Blow, Cranberry Red, and Blue Ridge

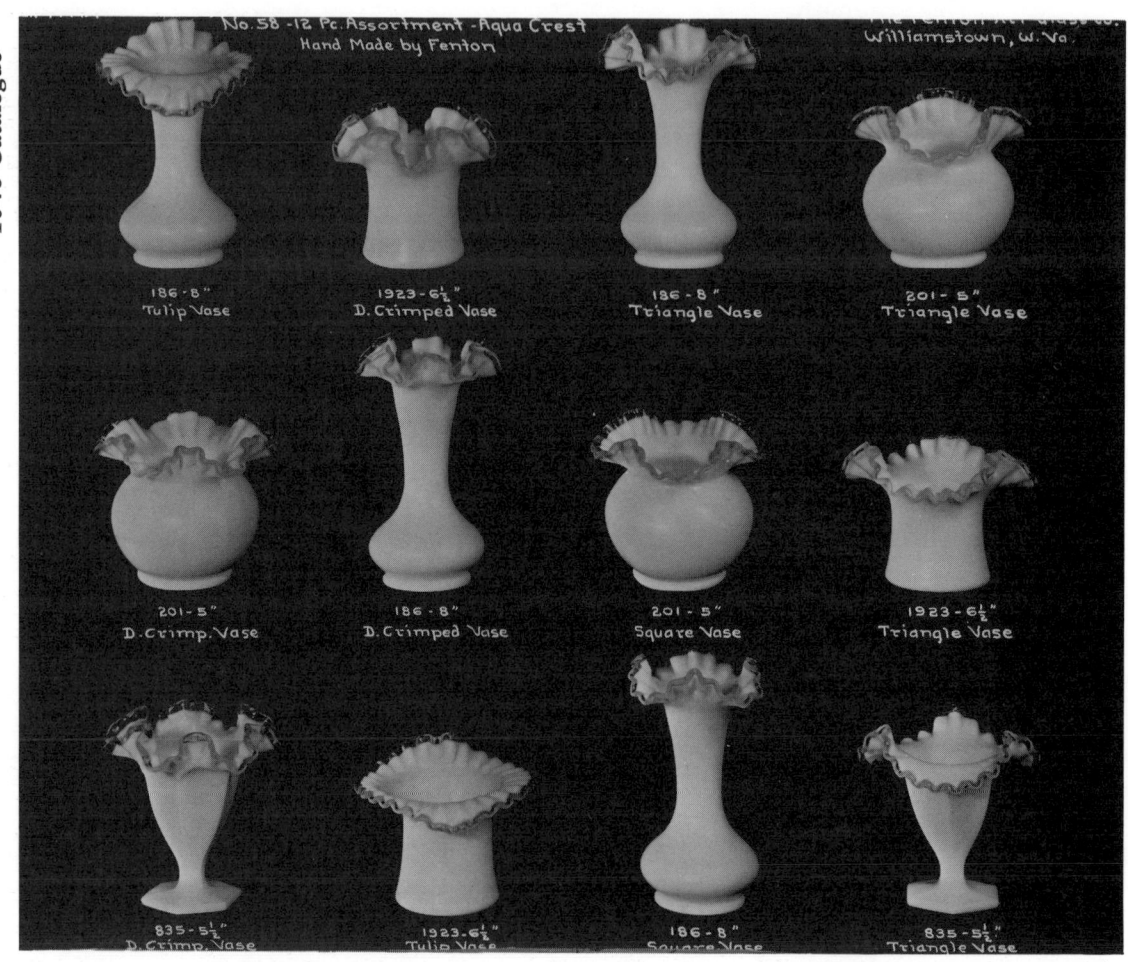

(Above & Below) Wide assortment of early shapes in *Aqua Crest*.

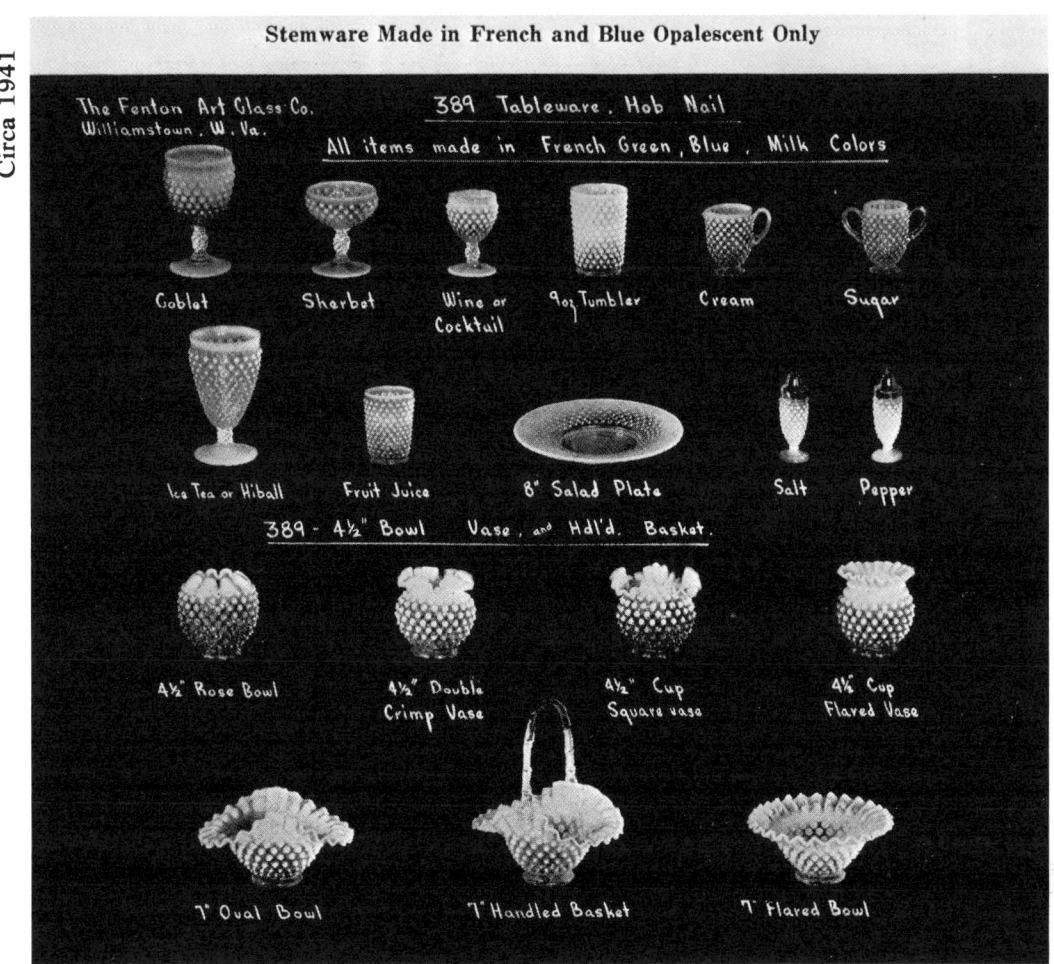

No. 389—Hobnail Items Open Stock

(Above & Below) Many of the earliest shapes in Hobnail, some continued successfully into later years.

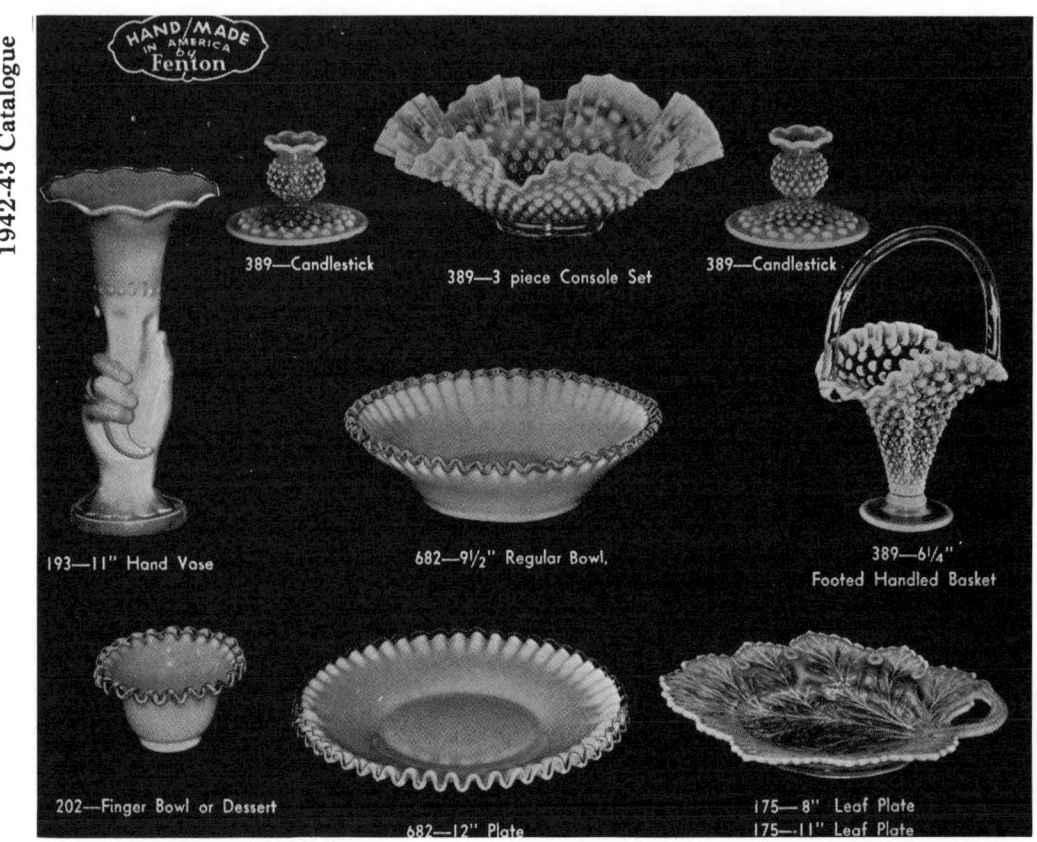

(Above) This assortment appeared in the 1943 catalogue.
(Below) This assortment was offered in both 1942 & 1943 catalogues.

1940-41 Catalogue

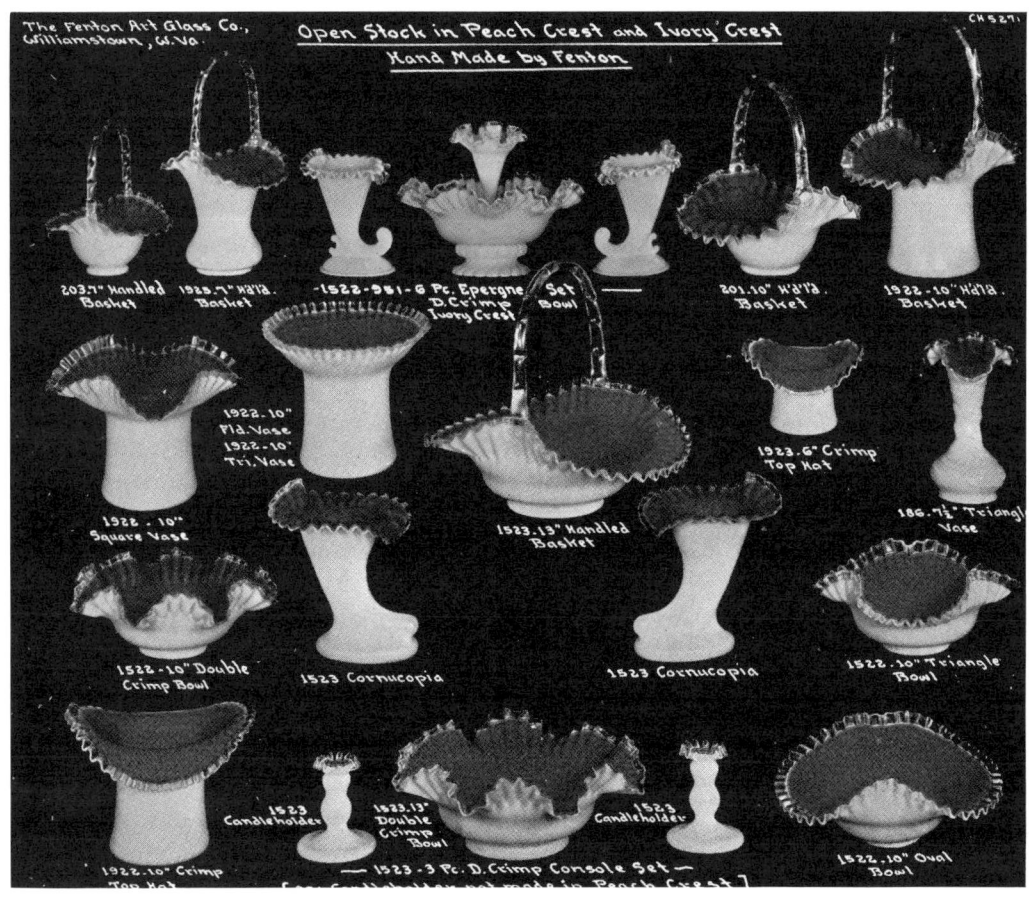

(Above) All of these items except #951 candleholder were offered in both Peach Crest and Ivory Crest.

(Below) This assortment appeared in both 1942 and 1943 catalogues.

1942-43 Catalogue

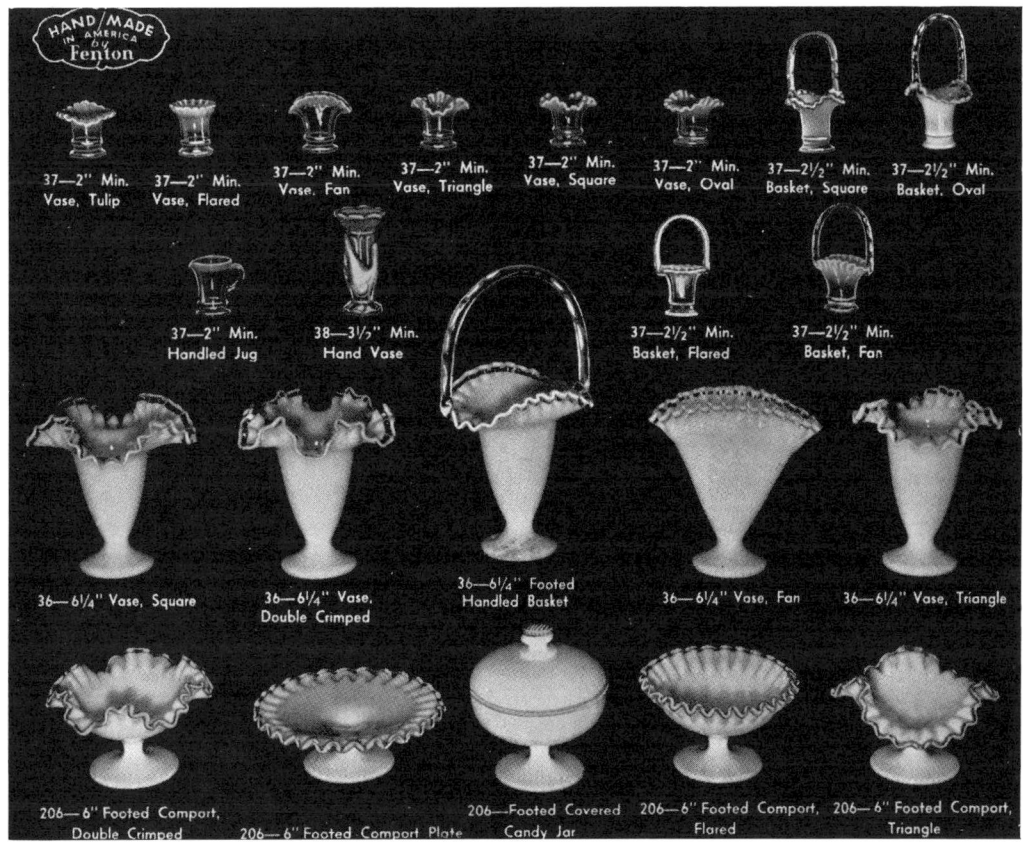

103

1947
Coin Dot Catalogue

Fenton's COIN DOT line was first introduced in 1947. It is a copy of a Victorian glass pattern called POLKA DOT, yet all the Fenton shapes are different from the molds used at the turn-of-the-century. The vast majority of the early glass has a polished pontil at the base, whereas the Fenton pieces do not.

No. 894
10-Inch Vase
Colors: Blue Opalescent
Cranberry Red
French Opalescent

No. 194
13-Inch Double Crimp Vase
Colors: Cranberry Red
French Opalescent
Blue Opalescent

This shape is also available in an 11-inch Vase.

Coin Dot by Fenton

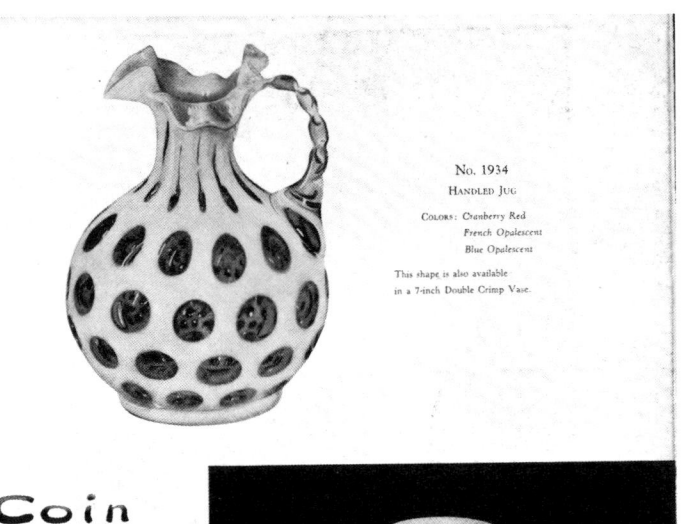

No. 1934
HANDLED JUG
COLORS: Cranberry Red
French Opalescent
Blue Opalescent

This shape is also available in a 7-inch Double Crimp Vase.

No. 893
ROSE JAR
COLORS: French Opalescent
Cranberry Red
Blue Opalescent

No. 1522
COVERED CANDY JAR
COLORS: Cranberry Red
Blue Opalescent
French Opalescent

No. 1522
10-INCH DOUBLE CRIMP BOWL
COLORS: Blue Opalescent
Cranberry Red
French Opalescent

No. 1522
10-INCH HANDLED BASKET
COLORS: Blue Opalescent
Cranberry Red
French Opalescent

No. 203
7-INCH BOWL
COLORS: Blue Opalescent
French Opalescent
Blue Opalescent

No. 203
7-INCH HANDLED BASKET
COLORS: Blue Opalescent
Cranberry Red
French Opalescent

No. 1353
12-INCH HANDLED BASKET
COLORS: Cranberry Red
French Opalescent
Blue Opalescent

No. 201
SQUAT JUG
COLORS: Blue Opalescent
Cranberry Red
French Opalescent

No. 194
11-INCH 2-HANDLED VASE
COLORS: Blue Opalescent
Cranberry Red
French Opalescent

No. 189
10-INCH VASE
COLORS: Cranberry Red
French Opalescent
Blue Opalescent

by Fenton

1947 COIN DOT

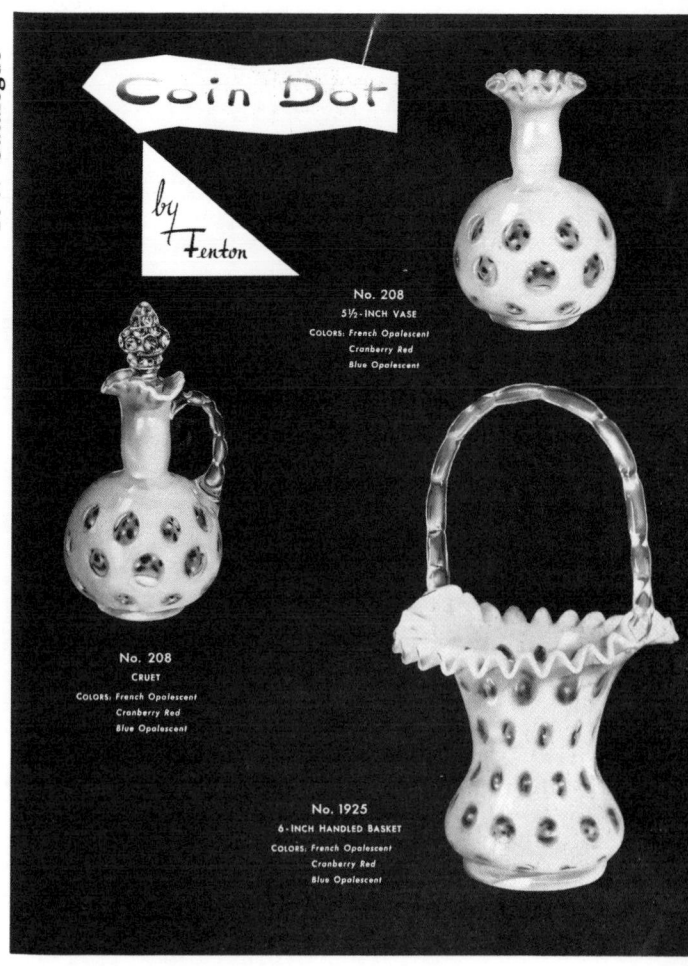

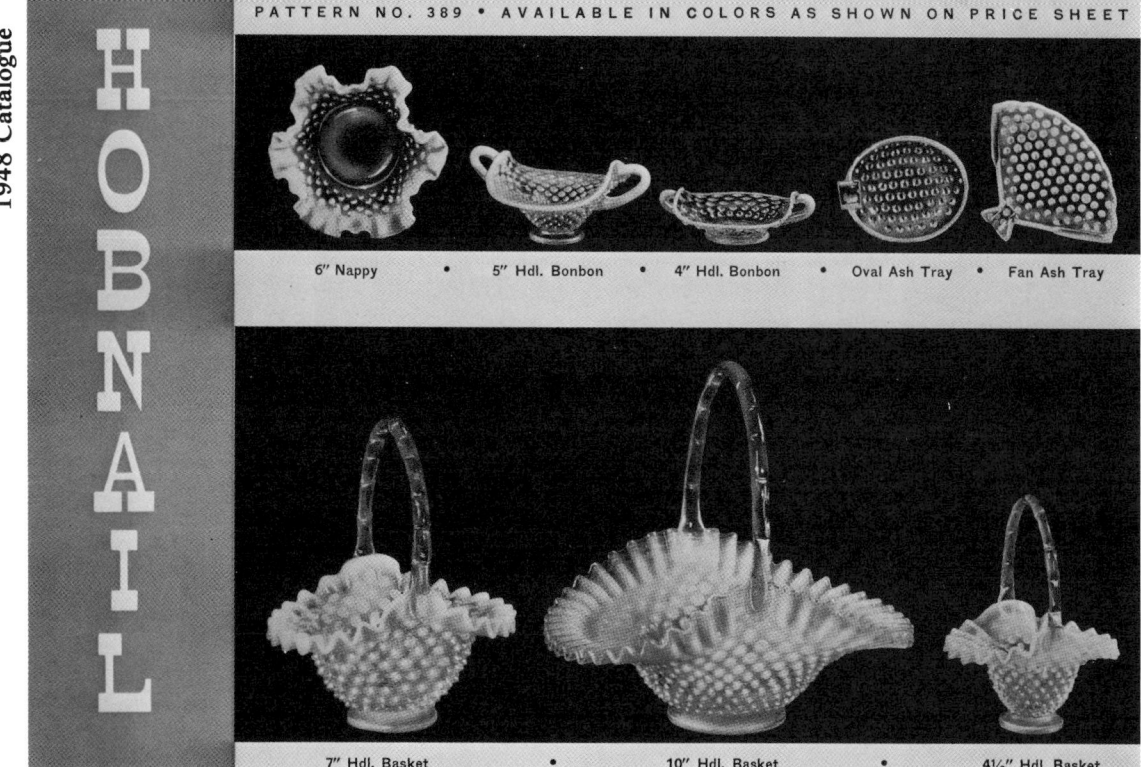

1948
Fenton Catalogue

The 1948 catalogue is reprinted here almost in its entirety. Two pages of COIN DOT were passed over, since the same items appeared in the 1947 catalogue. The popular HOBNAIL was produced in French, blue and cranberry opalescent. The cranberry opalescent is a color which cannot be pressed with regulated success, so this line was generally limited to mold-blown items, like baskets, vases and pitchers—among others.

(Above) Several new items appeared in HOBNAIL in 1948. All of the pieces shown here were available in French and blue opalescent. The mayonnaise and jam set were also made in cranberry.

(Below) All items shown here were available only in French and blue opalescent.

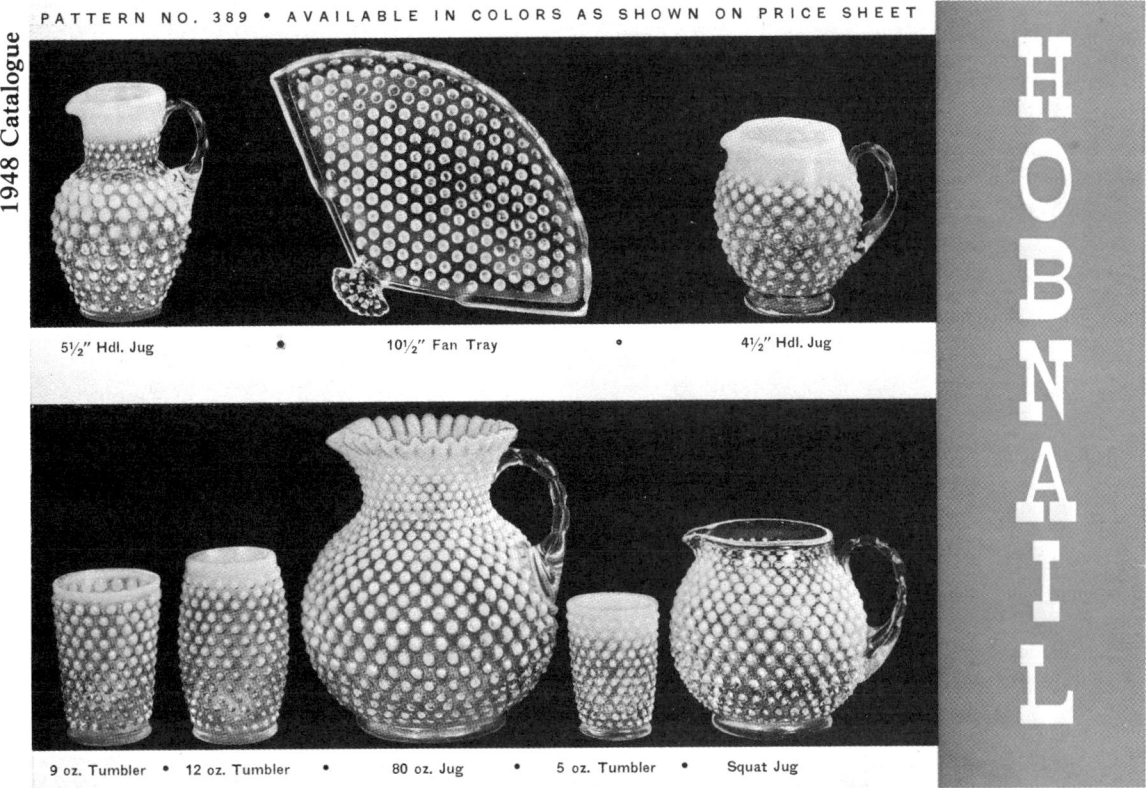

(Above) All of the above were made in French, blue and—except for the fan tray, and 5 and 9 oz. tumblers—cranberry opalescent.

(Below) The console set on the top row was made only in French and blue opalescent; the items on the bottom row were also made in cranberry.

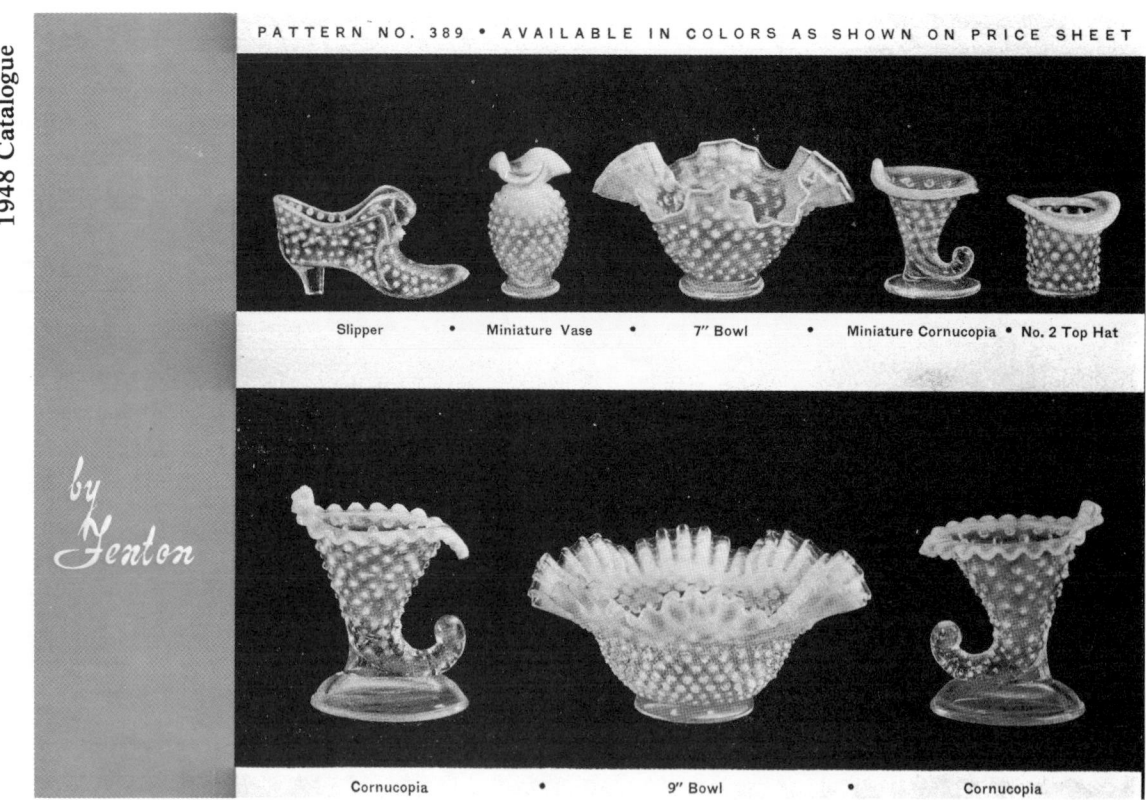

(Above) In 1948, all of the above were made in French and blue opalescent; the 7" and 9" bowls and miniature vase were also made in cranberry.

(Below) Assortment of Fenton's Diamond Lace, also shown in 1950 catalogue. This line is a copy of the Victorian HOBNAIL-IN-SQUARE or VESTA pattern made in Fenton shapes. In 1948, the only colors available were French and blue opalescent.

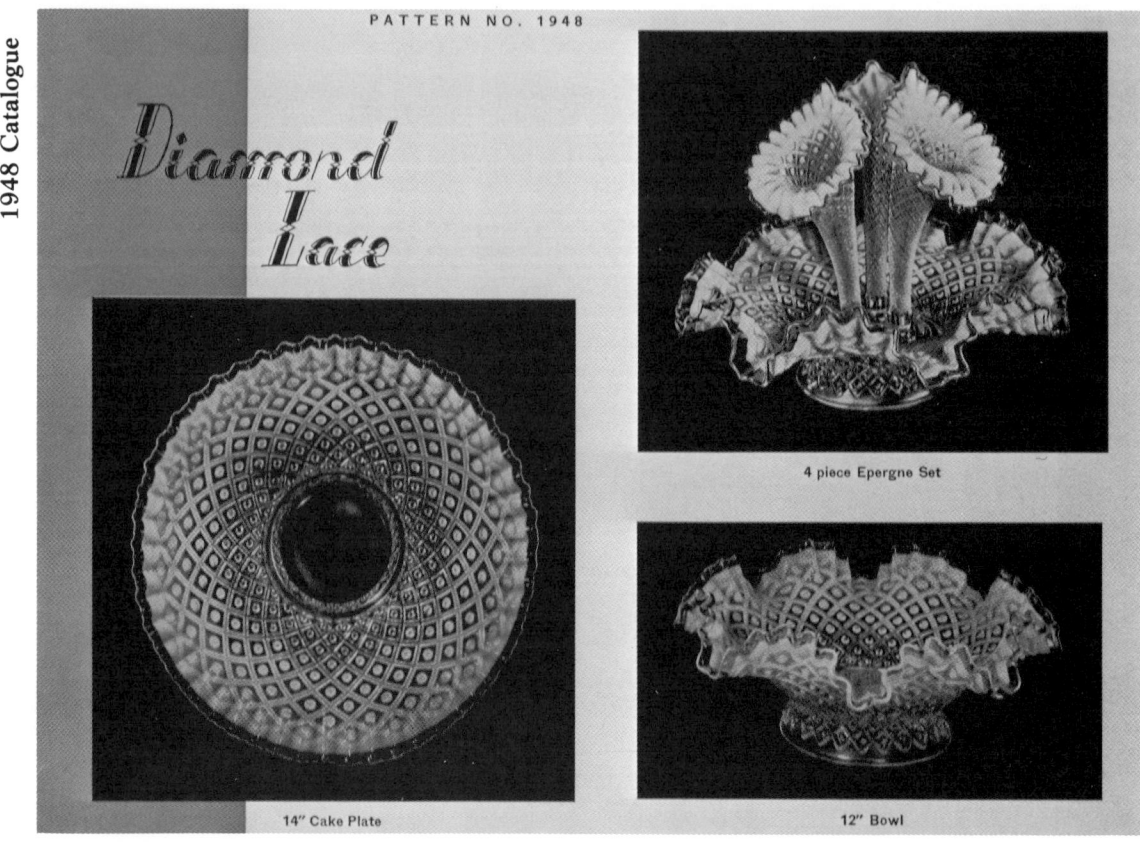

NEW ITEMS IN

Silver Crest
Green Crest
Aqua Crest . . . . . . and *Diam*

(Above) Several new shapes in the "Crest" lines and DIAMOND LACE shown here.

(Below) All items in DIAMOND LACE shown on these pages were also shown in 1950 catalogue. In 1948, these items were made only in French and blue opalescent.

ond Lace . . . .

1948 Catalogue

Crests and Overlays

AVAILABLE IN COLORS AS SHOWN ON PRICE LIST

| No. 192 6" Vase | No. 192 5½" Vase | No. 192 5" Vase | No. 192 5½" Hdl. Jug | No. 192 6" Hdl. Jug |

| No. 192A 9" Vase | No. 192A 9" Hdl. Jug | No. 192 8" Vase | No. 192 8" Hdl. Jug |

(Above) All items shown here were made in ruby, rose and blue overlay in 1948.
(Below) These items were available only in Silver Crest and Aqua Crest in 1948.

1948 Catalogue

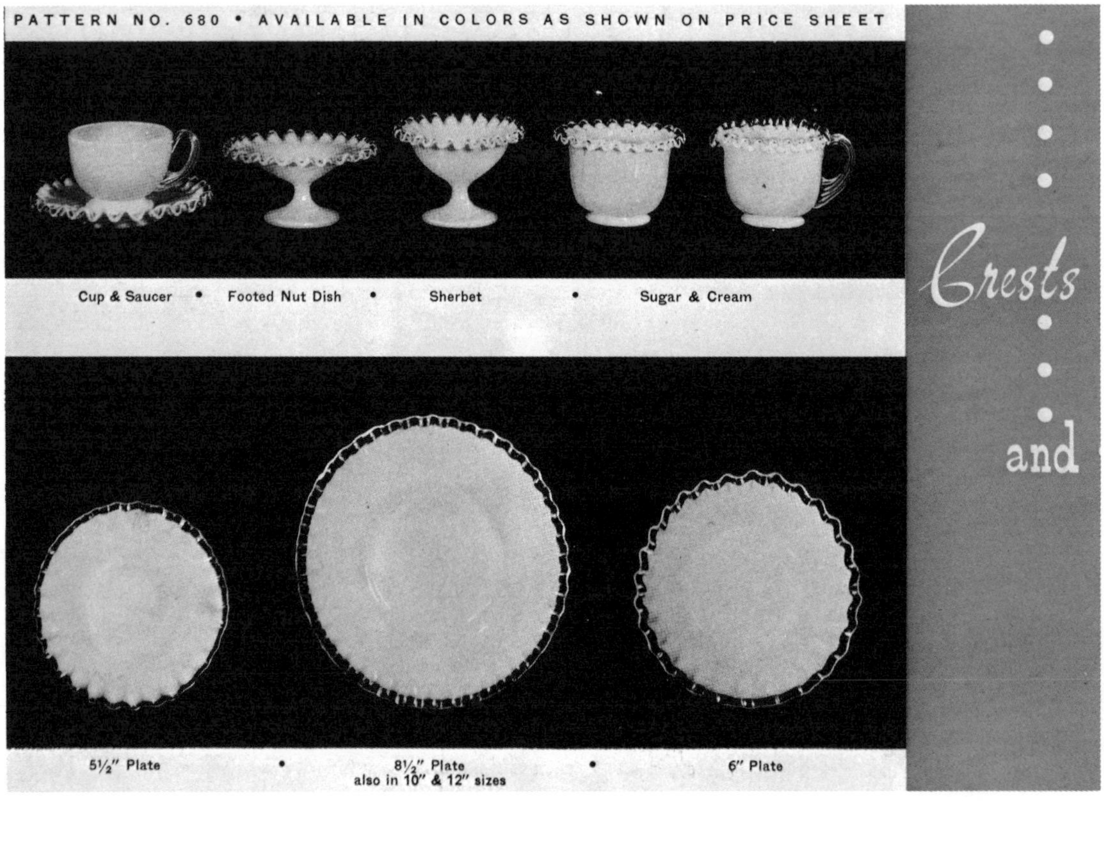

Crests and

PATTERN NO. 680 • AVAILABLE IN COLORS AS SHOWN ON PRICE SHEET

| Cup & Saucer | Footed Nut Dish | Sherbet | Sugar & Cream |

| 5½" Plate | 8½" Plate also in 10" & 12" sizes | 6" Plate |

112

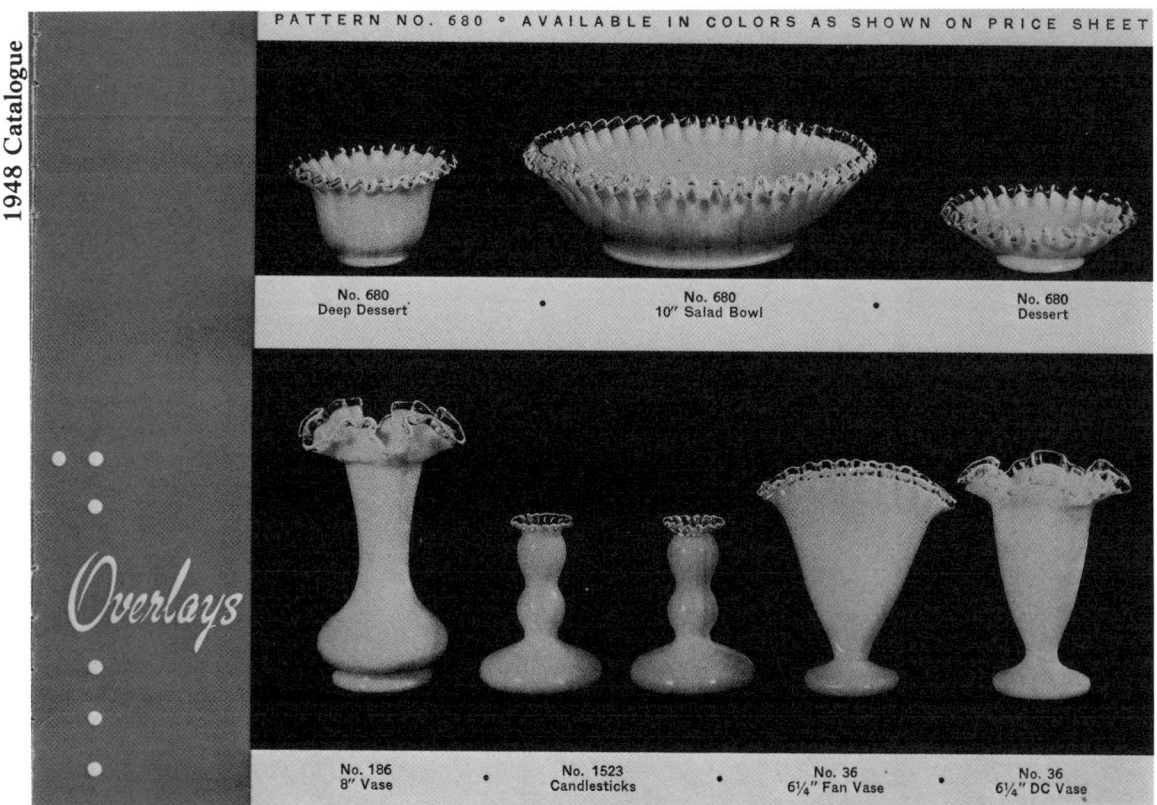

(Above) The items on the top row were made only in Silver Crest and Aqua Crest in 1948; all items on the bottom row were made in Silver Crest. The 8" vase and the candlesticks were available also in Peach Crest. The only items on this page made in Aqua Crest were the candlesticks.

(Below) The items shown below were available in several combinations. The No. 187 vase was made only in Peach Crest. The other items on the top row only in Silver and Aqua Crest. The pitcher and tumbler were made only in Ruby Overlay, whereas the bowl and basket were also made in Rose and Blue Overlay and in Peach Crest.

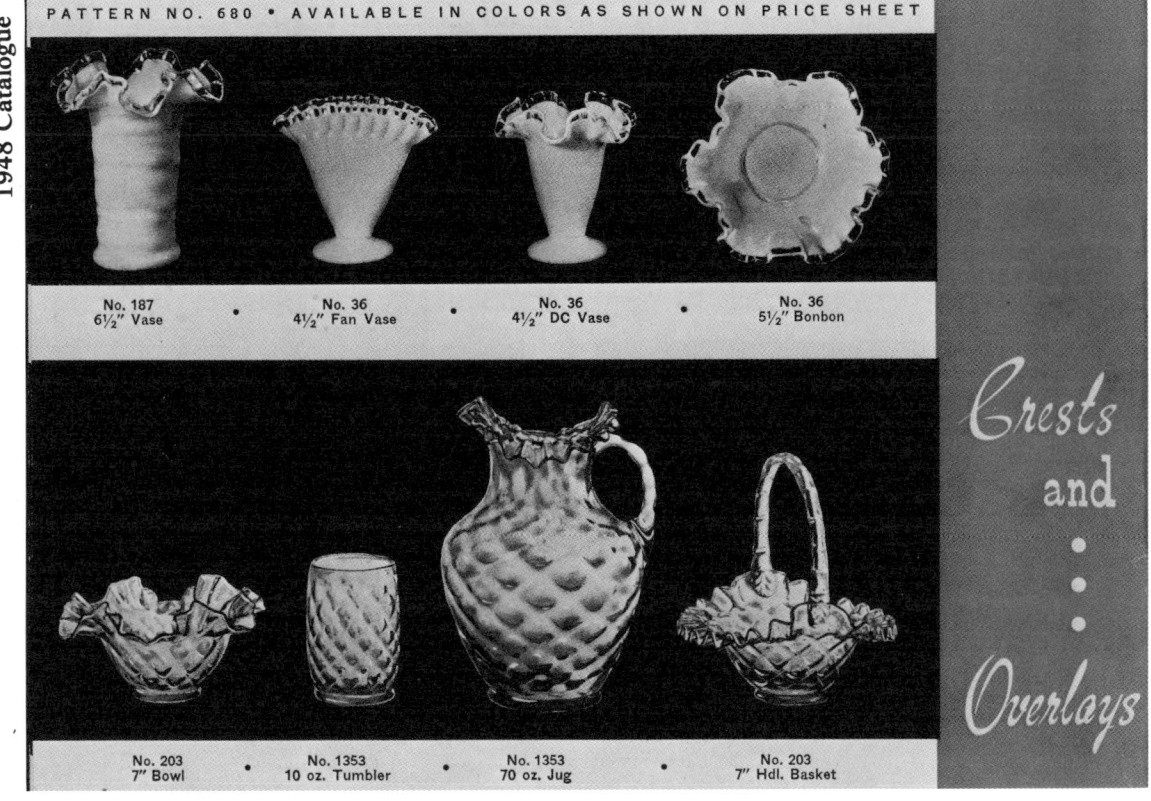

113

HOBNAIL by Fenton

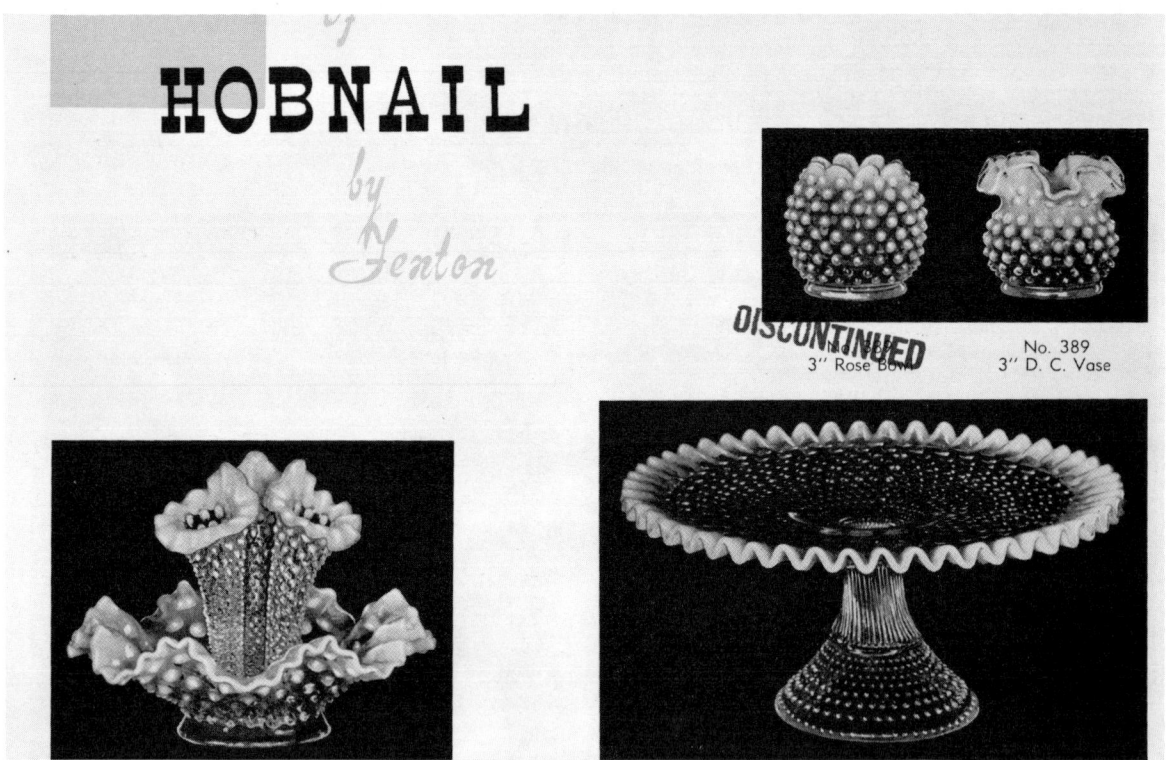

1950 Fenton Catalogue

(Above & Below) Among the new Hobnail items offered in 1950 were a rose bowl, a sugar & cream set with crimped top, and a salt and pepper in a different shape.

1950 Catalogue

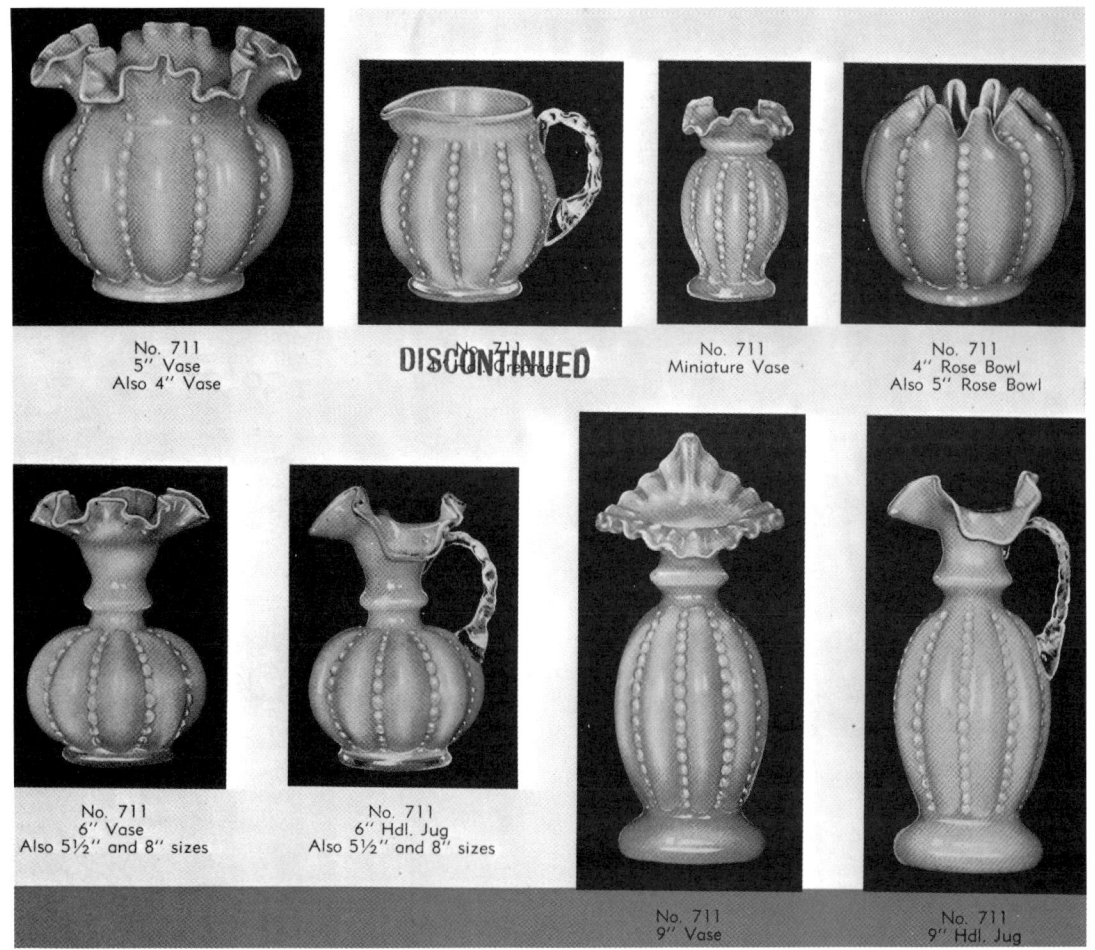

(Above and Below) Assortment of BEADED MELON (No. 711).

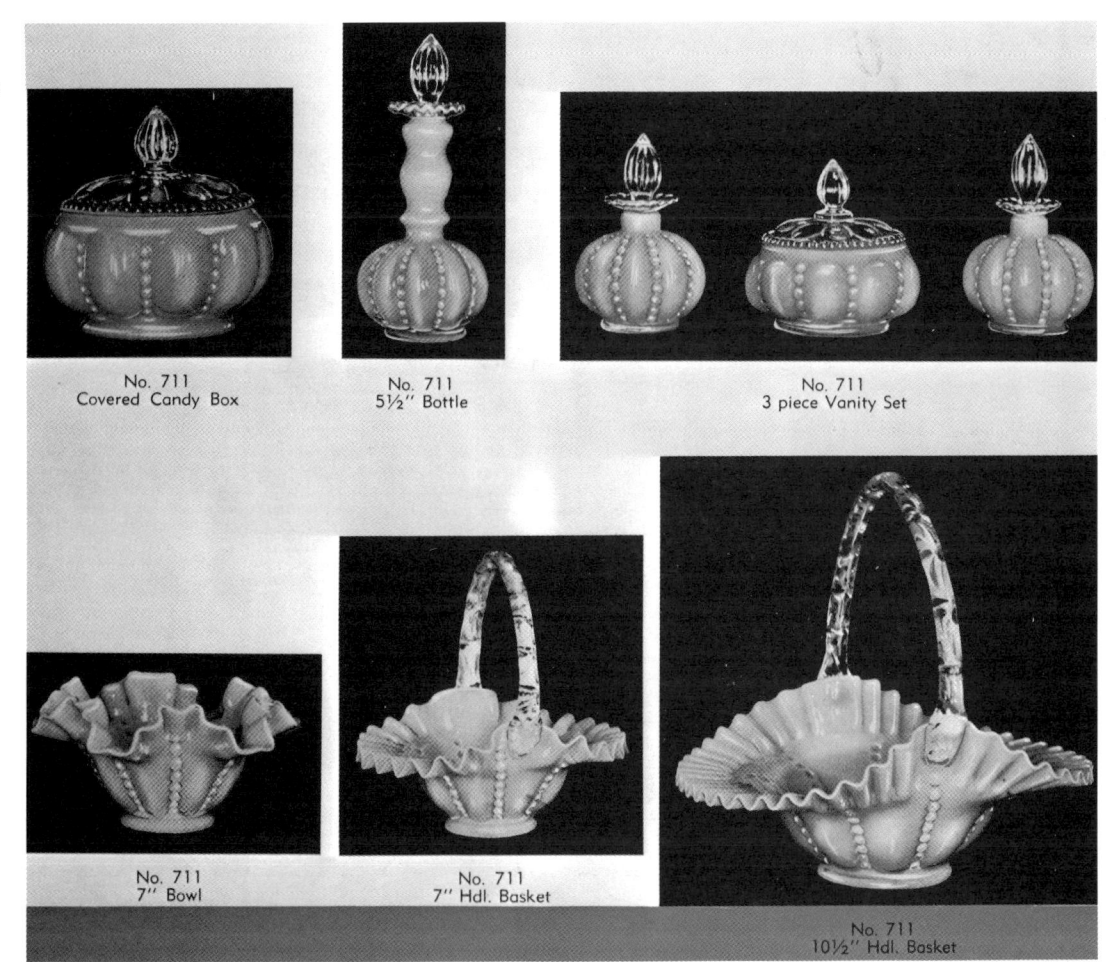

115

(Above) The tid-bit trays were offered this year in two and three-tier sizes; note also the reproduction goblet & sherbet in "New England Pineapple" pattern.
(Below) Varied assortment, including cased IVY vases and basket.

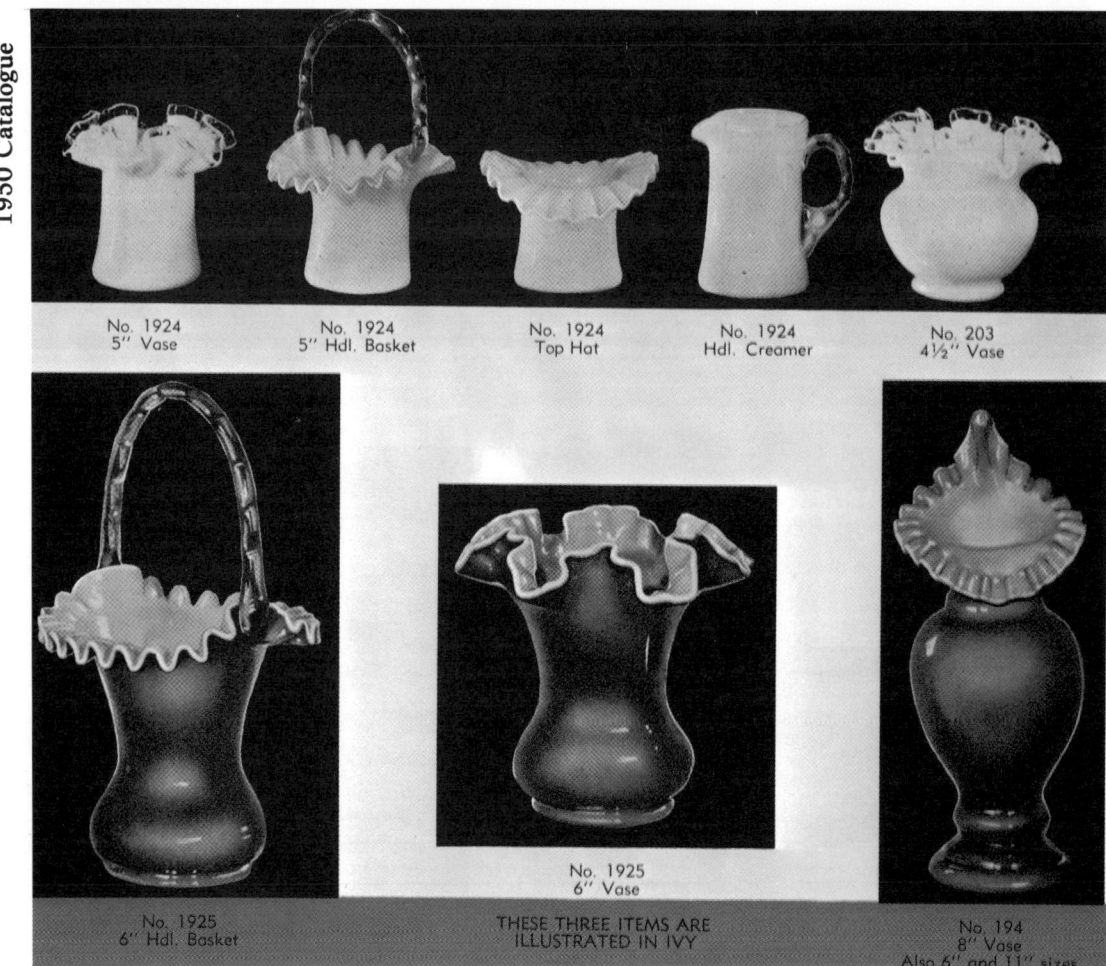

1950 Catalogue

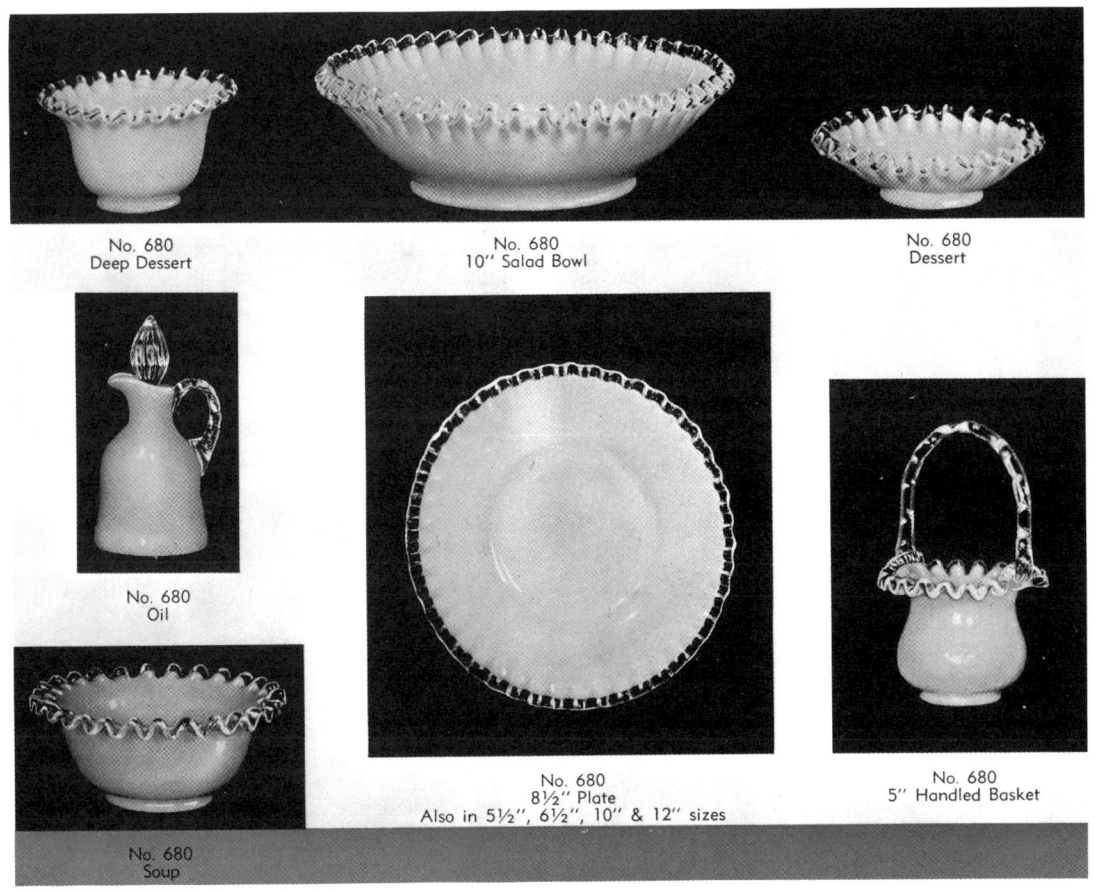

No. 680
Deep Dessert

No. 680
10" Salad Bowl

No. 680
Dessert

No. 680
Oil

No. 680
8½" Plate
Also in 5½", 6½", 10" & 12" sizes

No. 680
5" Handled Basket

No. 680
Soup

(Above and Below) A wide assortment of items, offered in 1950 in Silver Crest.

1950 Catalogue

No. 951
Cornucopia

No. 1522/951
6 pc. Epergne Set
(Includes Candlesticks)

No. 1522
4 pc. Epergne Set
(Does not include Candlesticks)

No. 951
Cornucopia

No. 680
Candleholder

No. 680
8½" Flared Bowl

No. 680
Candleholder

117

1951 Brochure

Priscilla

No. 1890
Cocktail

No. 1890
Wine

No. 1890
Sherbet

No. 1890
Goblet

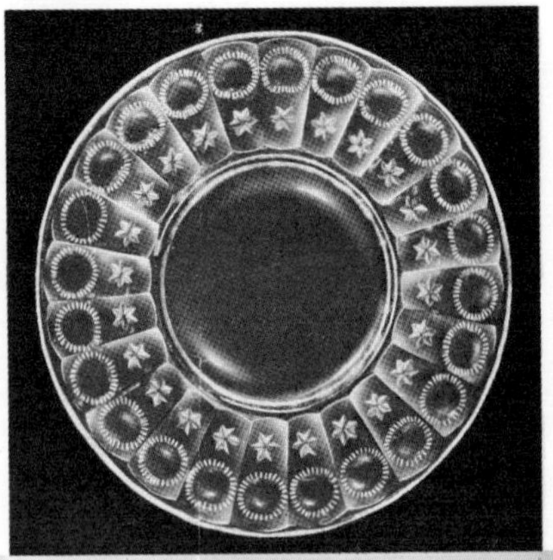

No. 1890
8" Plate
Also in 6" Size

(Above and Below) Complete assortment of Priscilla pattern, shown in a 1951 brochure.

1951 Brochure

No. 1890
Sugar and Cream Set

No. 1890
6" Hdl. Bonbon

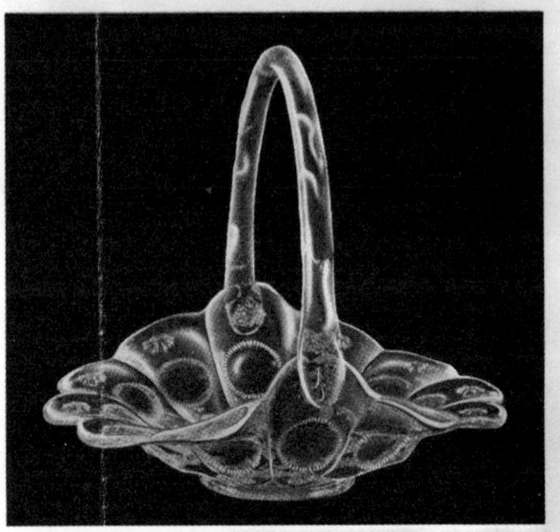

No. 1890
12" Hdl. Basket

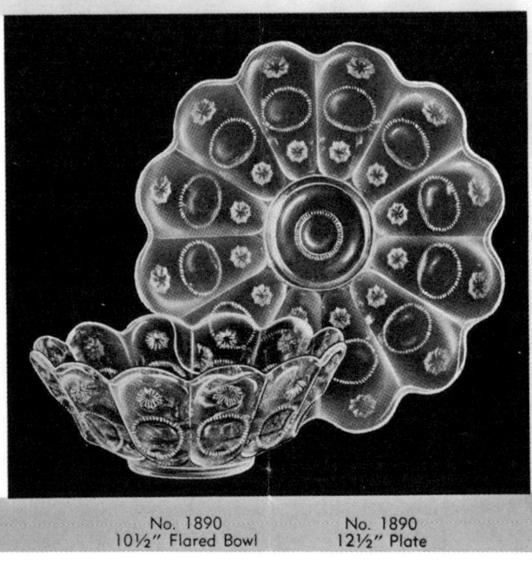

No. 1890
10½" Flared Bowl

No. 1890
12½" Plate

No. 1890
9" Cupped Bowl

No. 1890
11" Rolled Edge Plate

1951
Catalogue Supplement

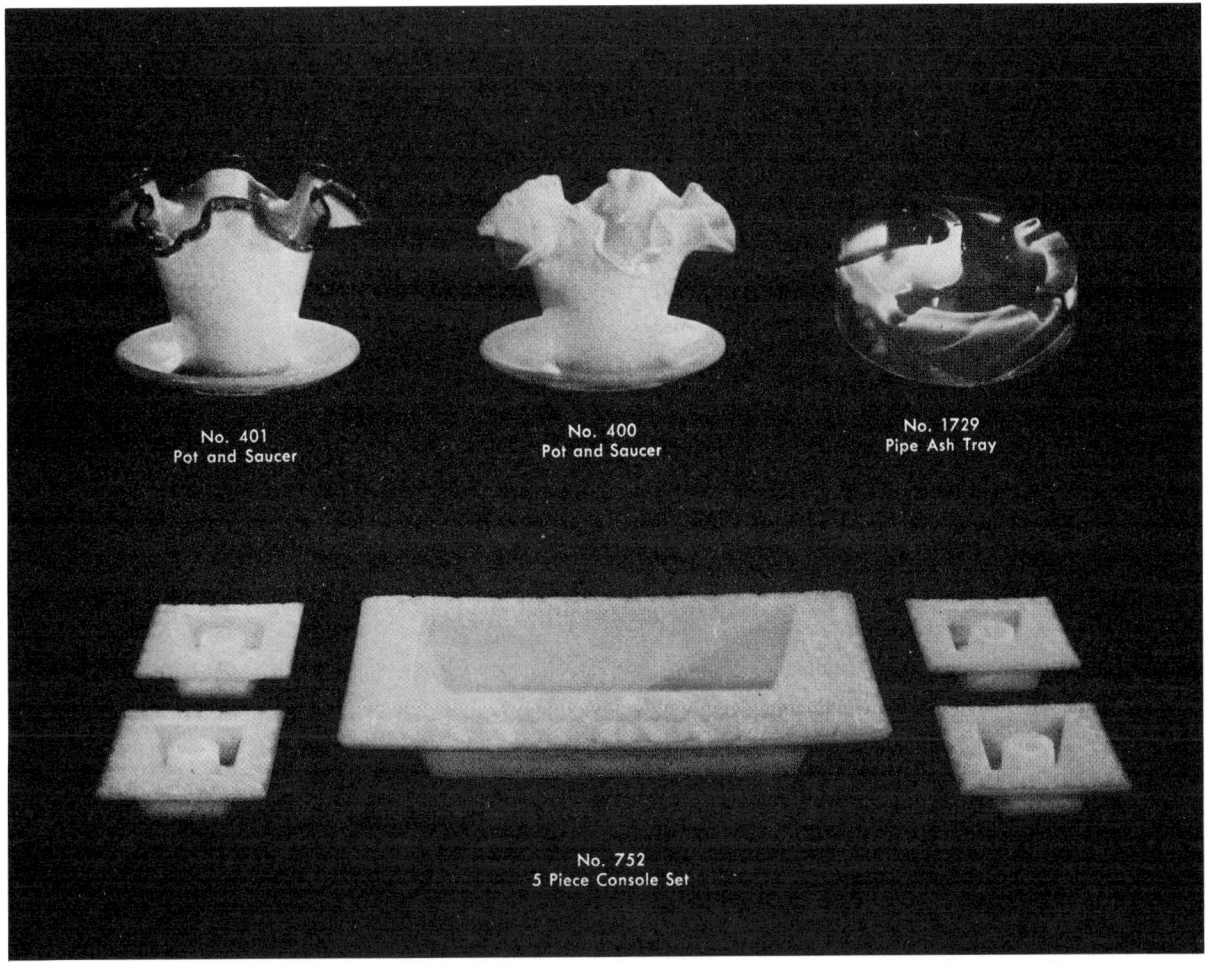

New items in milk and "marble" glass shown in 1951 supplement.

(Above) The square shaped Hobnail made its first appearance in the 1951 supplement, made in blue and French opalescent only.
(Below) Assorted items in Snow Crest and satin glass.

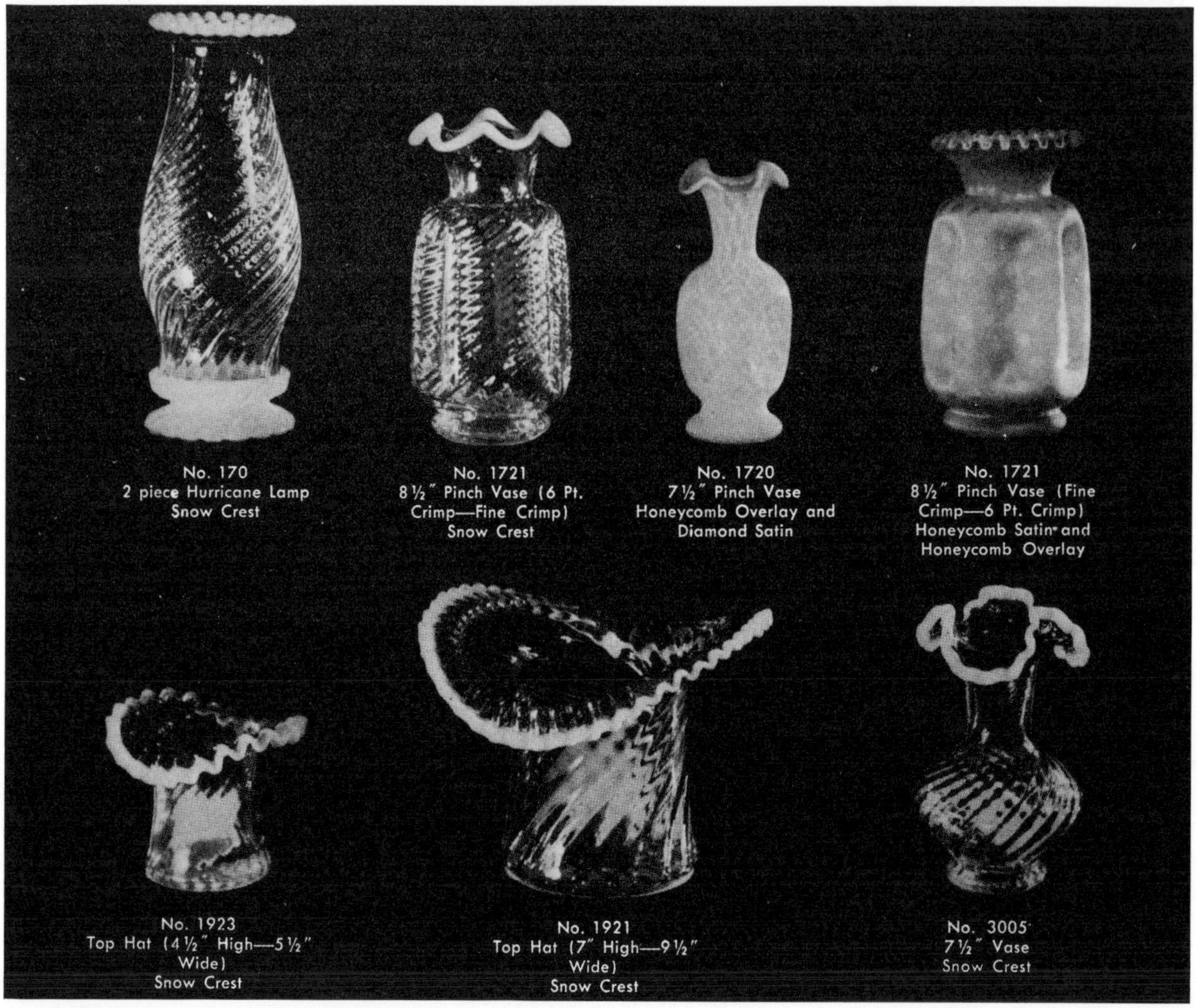

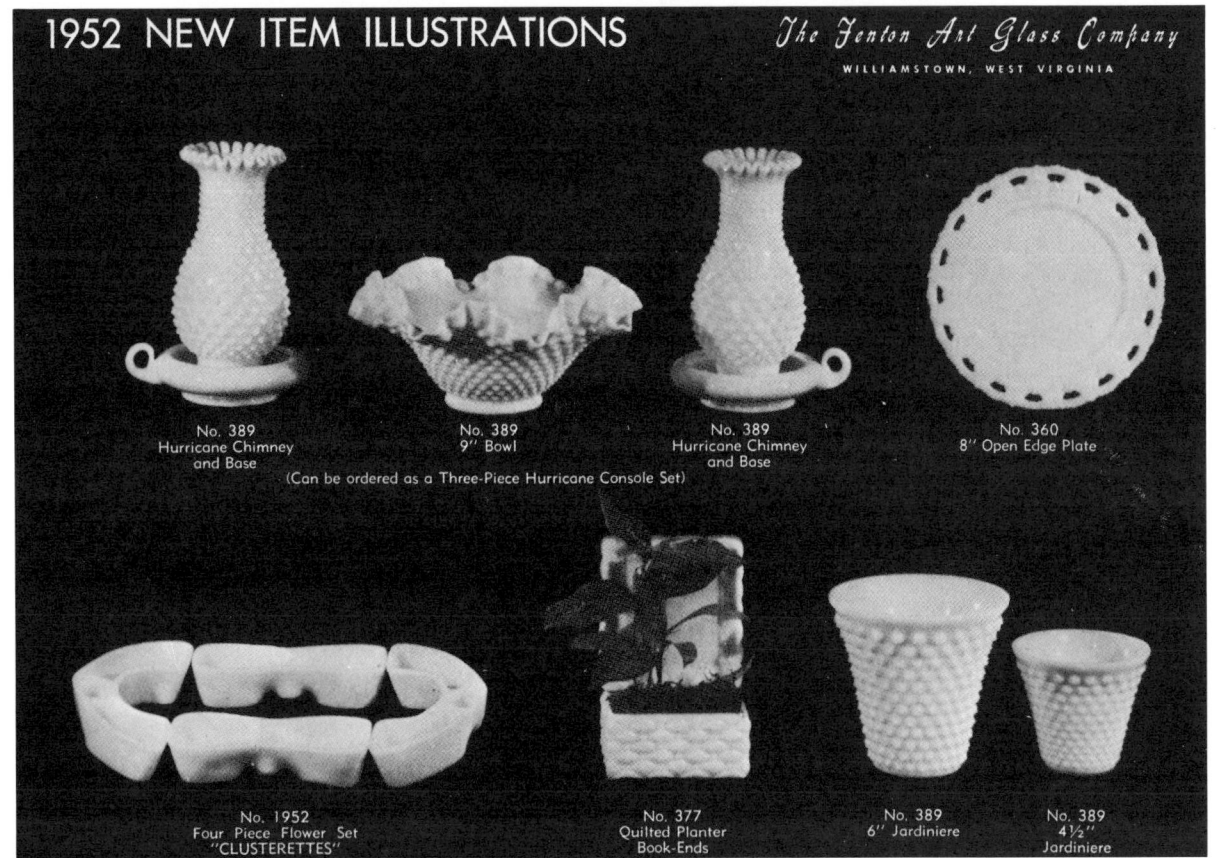

1952
Catalogue Supplement

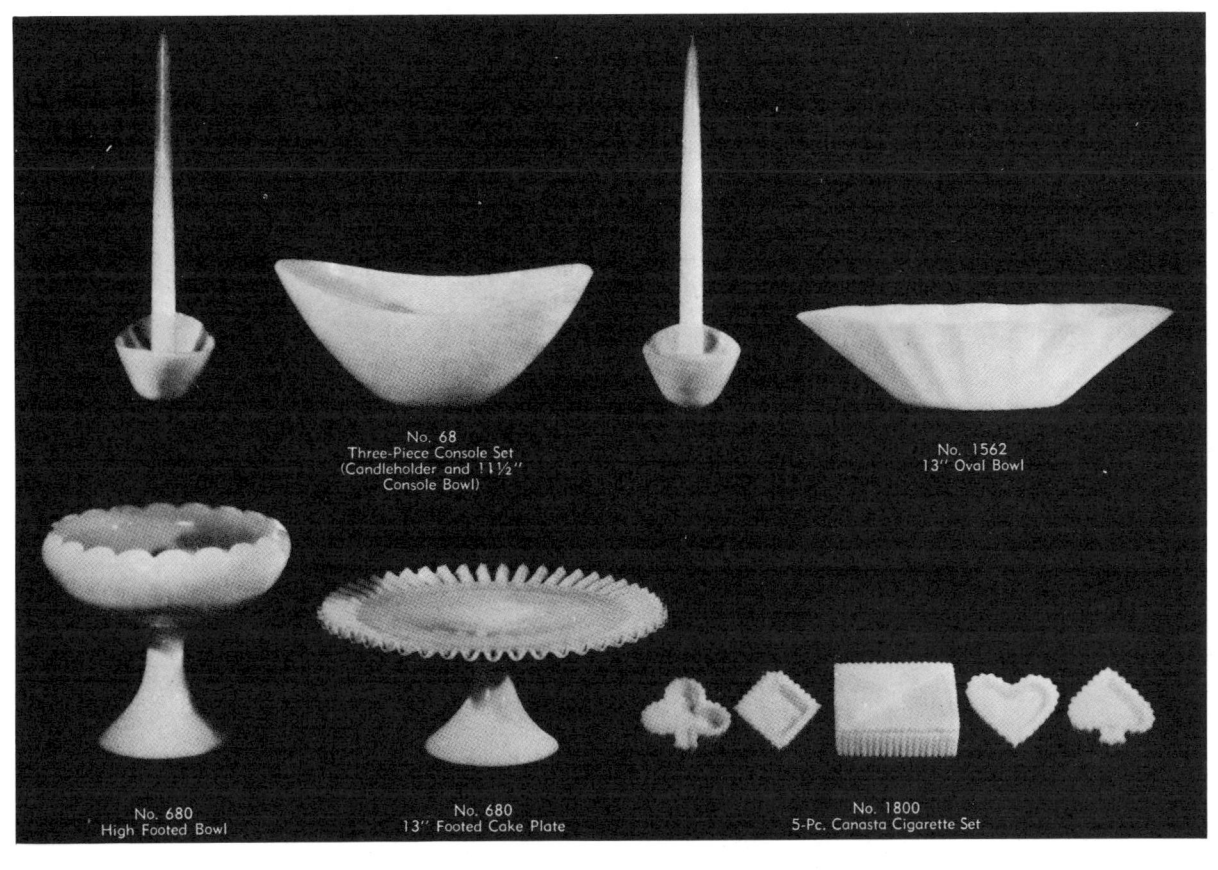

1952 Supplement

1952 Supplement

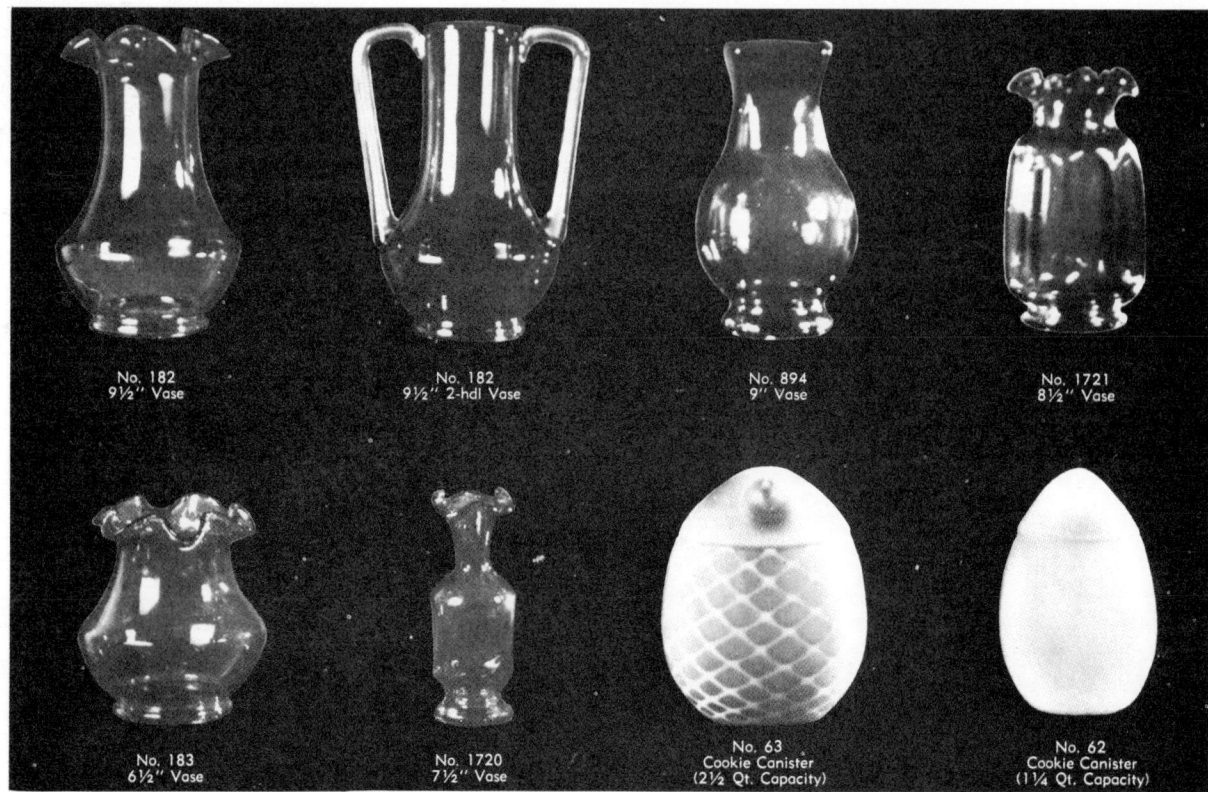

122

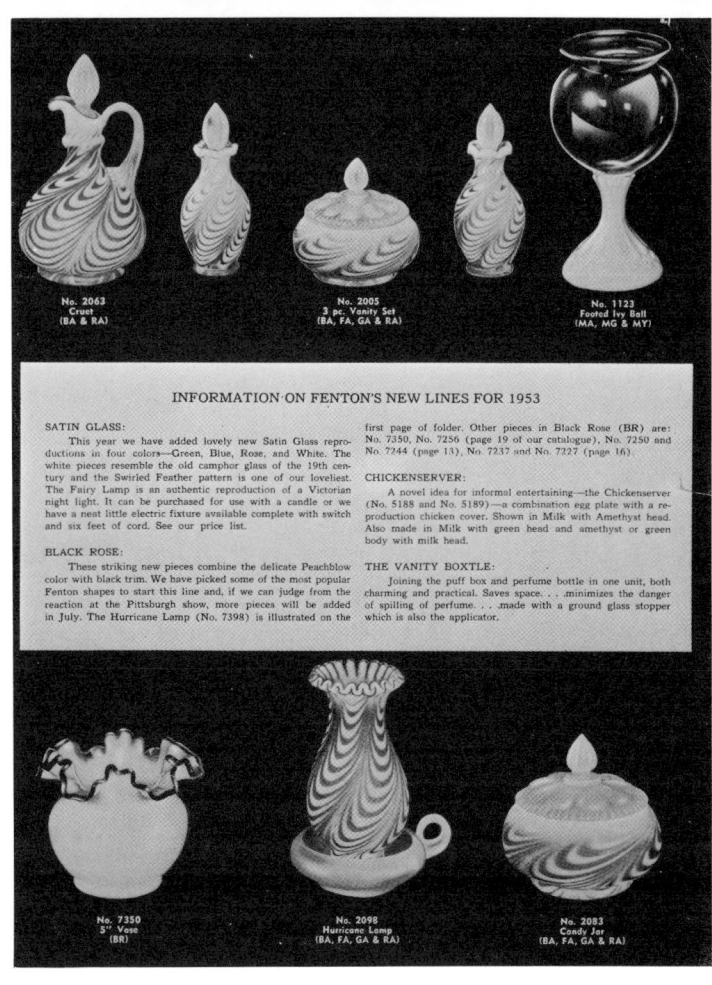

January 1953 Supplement

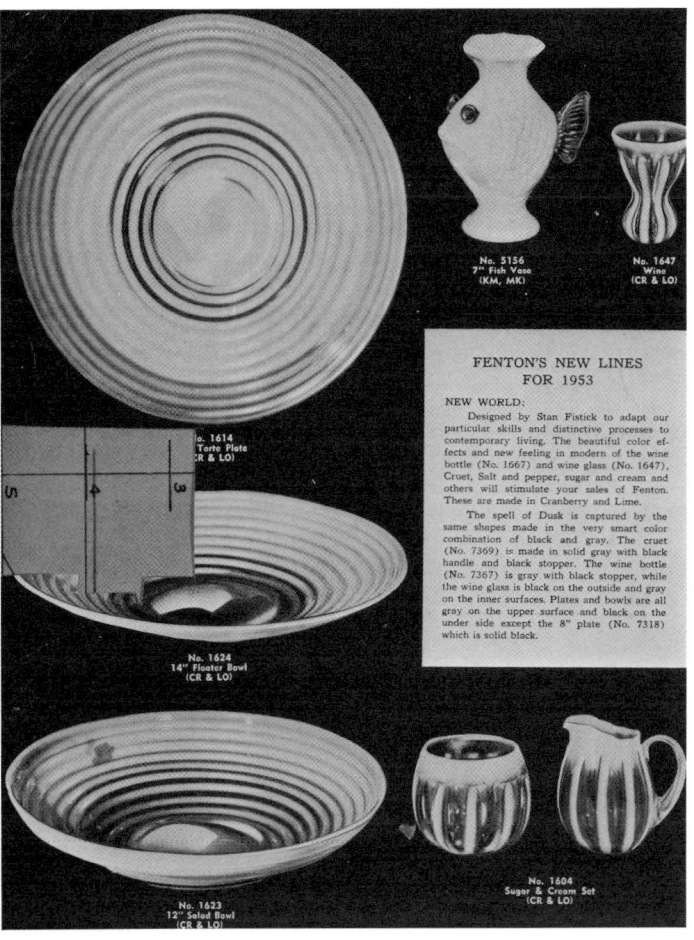
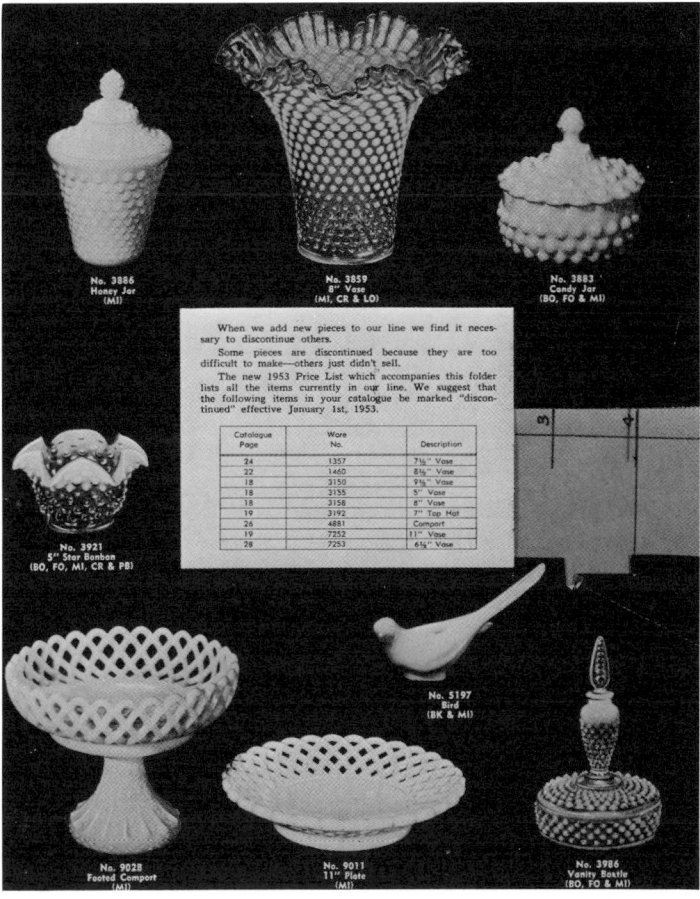

HOW IT'S MADE

To make Hobnail pieces, the glass is blown or pressed into a mold like the one in the sketch. Each "hobnail" shows in the mold as a deep dimple, which becomes the raised part of the finished glass.

The picture shows the blower placing the gather into the mold which stands on the floor at the edge of his platform. An apprentice will close the mold around the blob of glass, the blower will judge the exact amount of air pressure needed to fill the mold. Here again is a skill hard to analyse. Too much glass in the mold would make a thick, clumsy piece.

Hobnail, like Coin Dot, uses two different processes, depending on the colors. French Opalescent, Blue Opalescent, and Milk Glass are single layers of glass. Skillful cooling and re-warming brings out the opacity of the edges and the hobs in French and Blue Opalescent. Cranberry and Lime Hobnail are cased glass, using a layer of French Opalescent outside, and colored glass inside. Peach Blow uses gold ruby glass inside, Milk Glass outside . . . Crimped edges are made with the foot operated crimper this finisher is using.

Hobnail

5

No. 3887 Footed Covered Comport
No. 3886 Honey Jar
No. 3883 Candy Jar
No. 3986 Vanity Bottle

No. 3921 5" Star Bonbon
No. 3859 8" Vase
No. 3870 Candleholder

No. 3840 Punch Cup
No. 3820 Punch Bowl
No. 9520 Punch Ladle
No. 3908 10 pc. Punch Set
No. 3911 14 pc. Punch Set

12

1953-54 Fenton Catalogue

1953-54 Catalogue

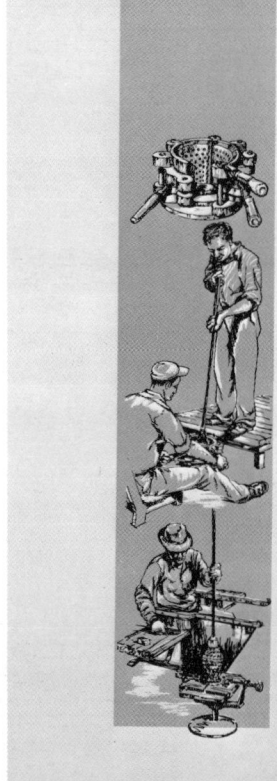

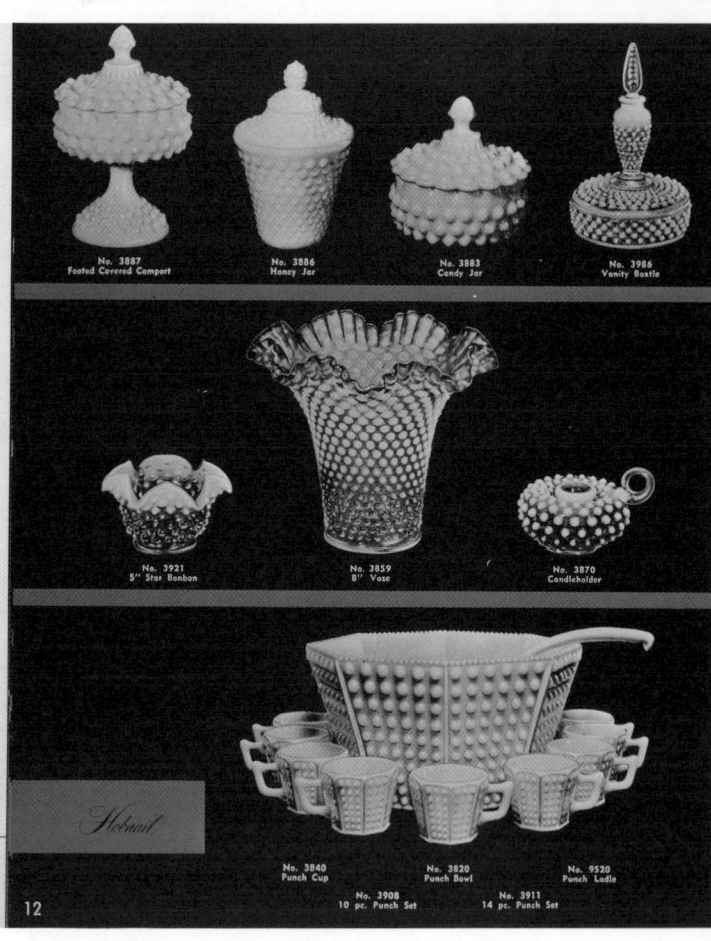

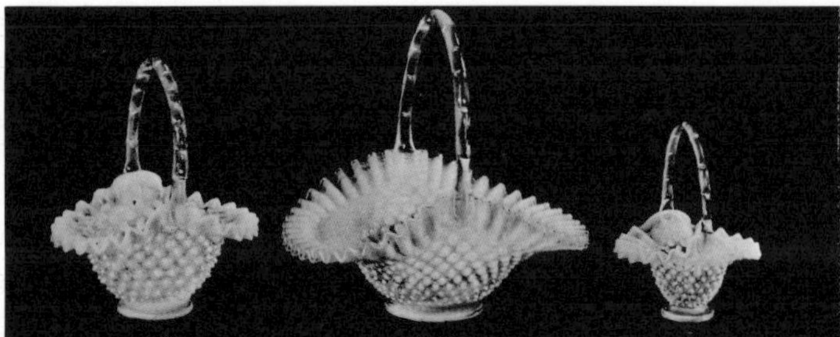

No. 3837 7" Basket
No. 3830 10" Basket
No. 3834 4½" Basket

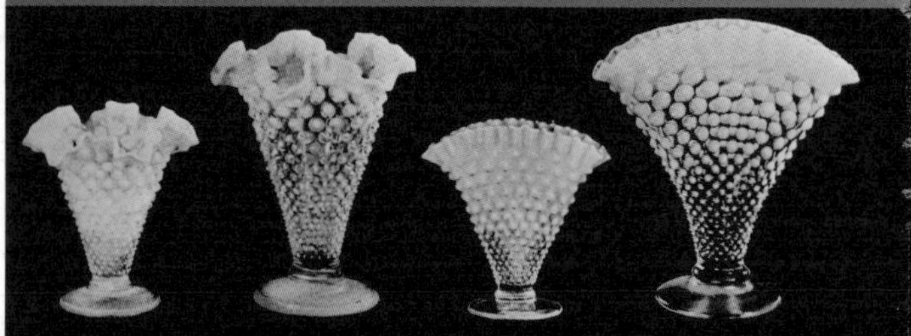

No. 3956 6¼" D.C. Vase
No. 3958 8" D.C. Vase
No. 3957 6¼" Fan Vase
No. 3959 8" Fan Vase

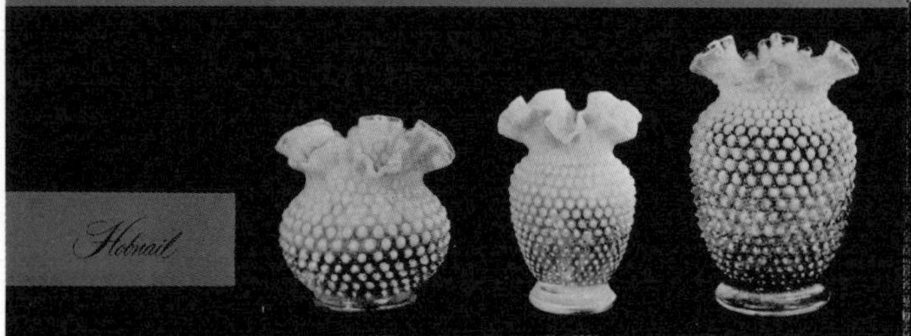

No. 3850 5" Vase
No. 3856 6" Vase
No. 3858 8" Vase

10

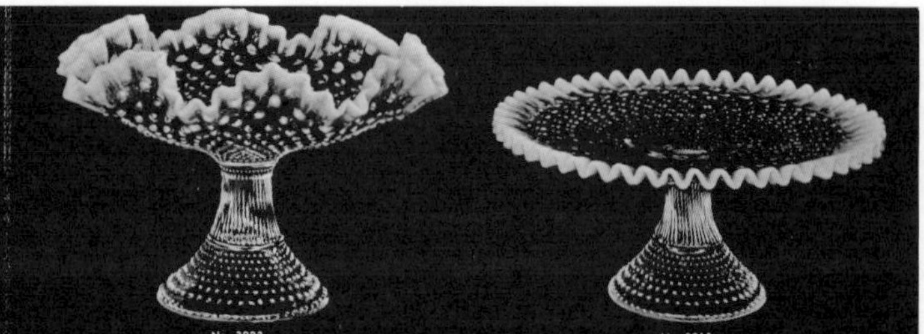

No. 3923 11" Footed Bowl
No. 3913 13" Footed Cake Plate

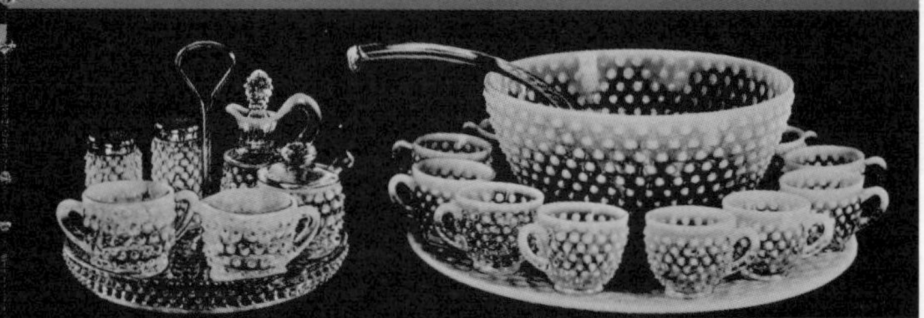

No. 3879 Chrome Handled Tray
No. 3809 Condiment Set
No. 3847 Punch Cup
No. 3827 Punch Bowl
No. 9527 Punch Ladle
No. 3807 15 pc. Punch Set
No. 3817 16" Torte Plate

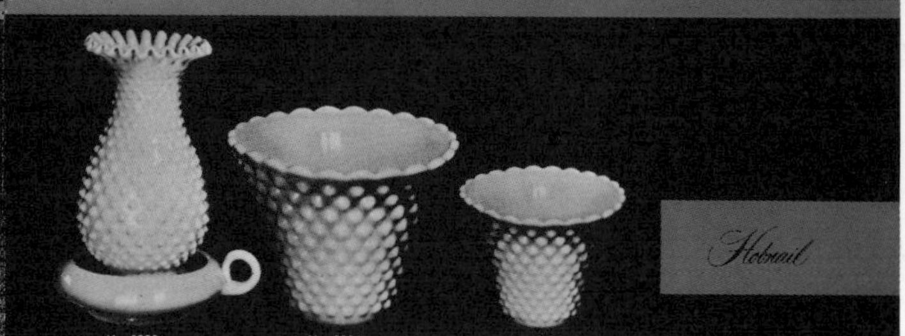

No. 3998 Hurricane Lamp
No. 3996 6" Jardiniere
No. 3994 4½" Jardiniere

11

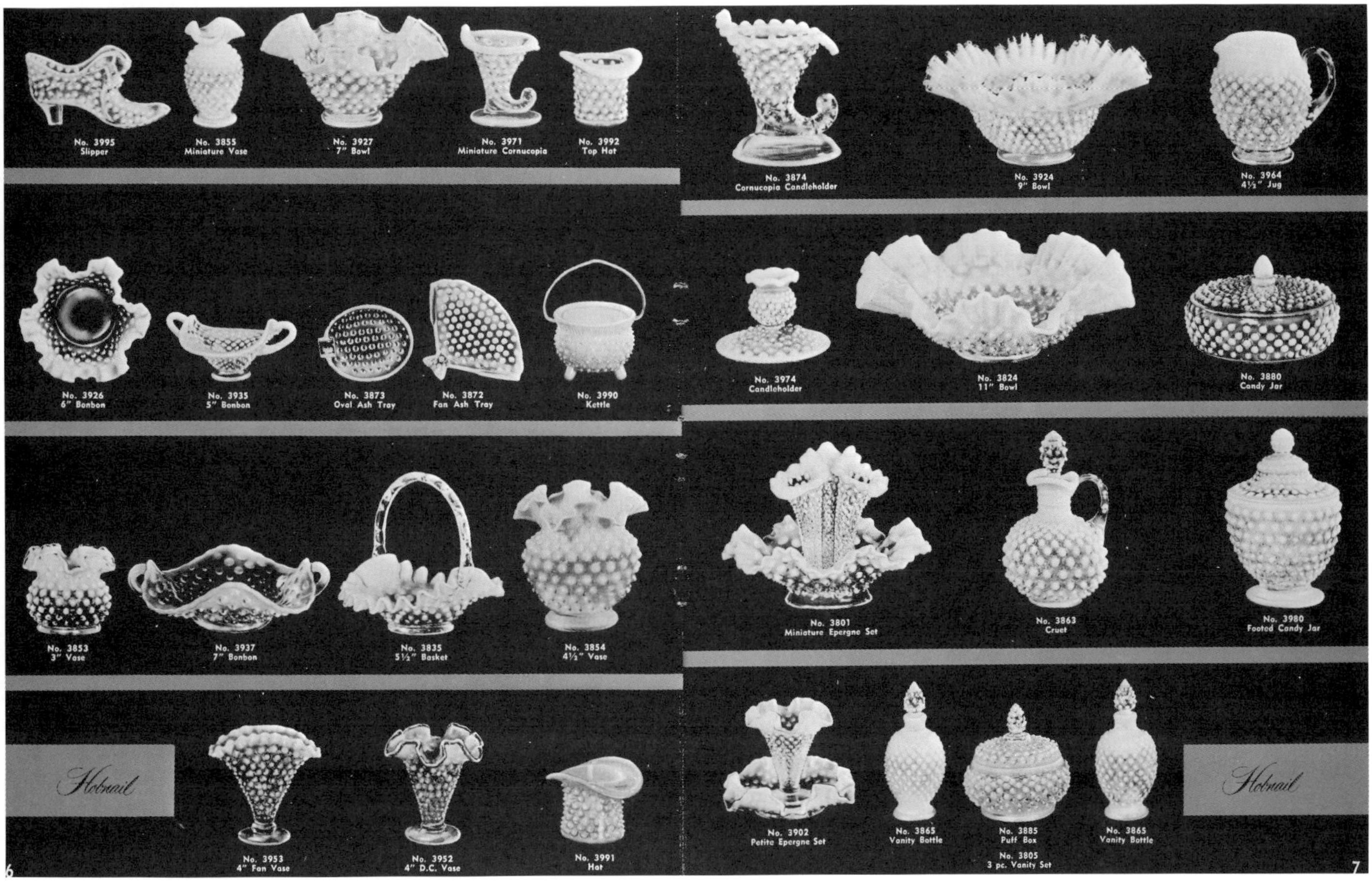

Hobnail

No.	Item
3995	Slipper
3855	Miniature Vase
3927	7" Bowl
2971	Miniature Cornucopia
3992	Top Hat
3874	Cornucopia Candleholder
3924	9" Bowl
3964	4½" Jug
3926	6" Bonbon
3935	5" Bonbon
3873	Oval Ash Tray
3872	Fan Ash Tray
3990	Kettle
3974	Candleholder
3824	11" Bowl
3880	Candy Jar
3853	3" Vase
3937	7" Bonbon
3835	5½" Basket
3854	4½" Vase
3801	Miniature Epergne Set
3863	Cruet
3980	Footed Candy Jar
3953	4" Fan Vase
3952	4" D.C. Vase
3991	Hat
3902	Petite Epergne Set
3865	Vanity Bottle
3885	Puff Box
3865	Vanity Bottle
3805	3 pc. Vanity Set

Hobnail

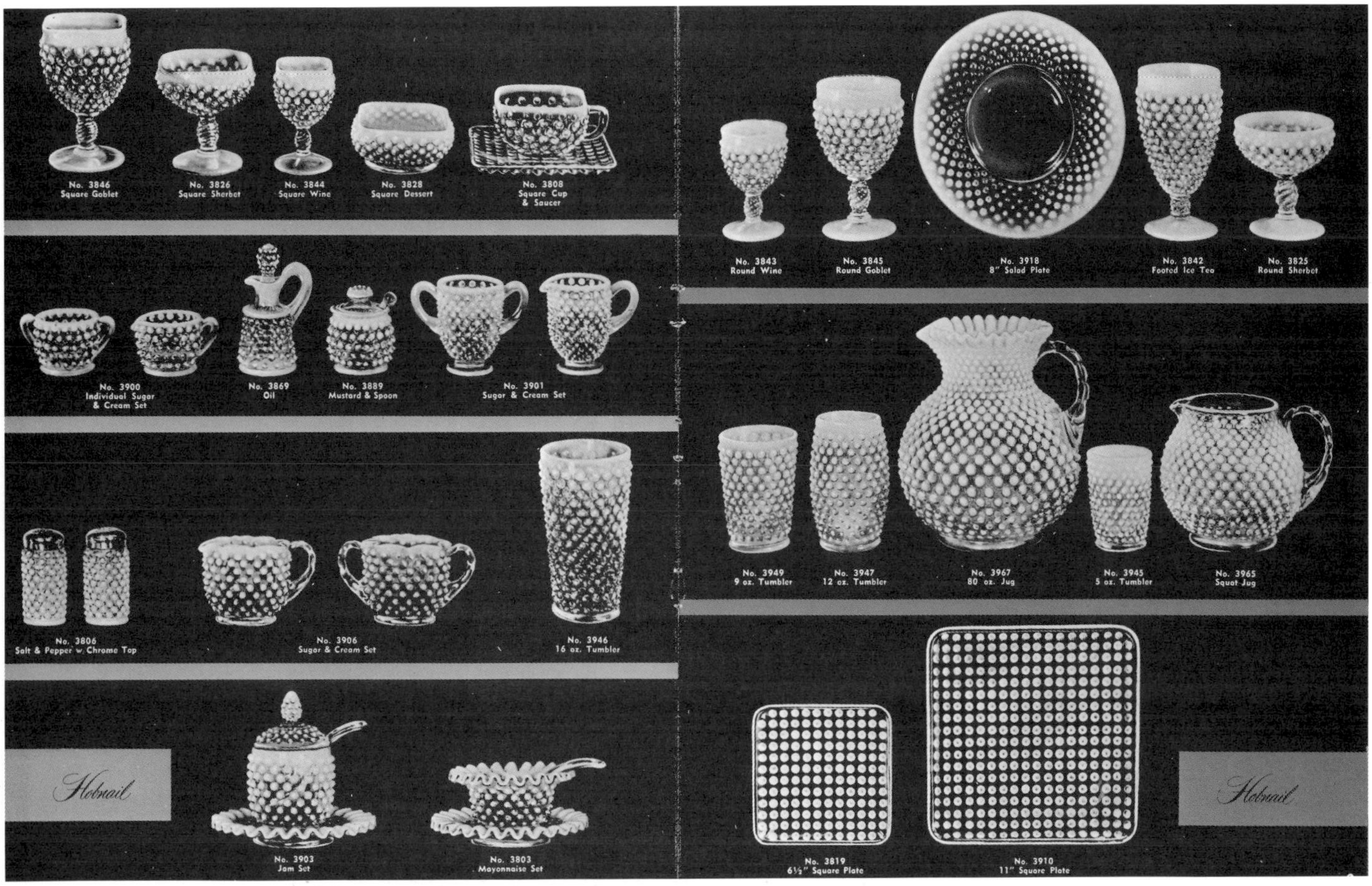 No.	Item
3846	Square Goblet
3826	Square Sherbet
3844	Square Wine
3828	Square Dessert
3808	Square Cup & Saucer
3843	Round Wine
3845	Round Goblet
3918	8" Salad Plate
3842	Footed Ice Tea
3825	Round Sherbet
3900	Individual Sugar & Cream Set
3869	Oil
3889	Mustard & Spoon
3901	Sugar & Cream Set
3806	Salt & Pepper w. Chrome Top
3906	Sugar & Cream Set
3946	16 oz. Tumbler
3949	9 oz. Tumbler
3947	12 oz. Tumbler
3967	80 oz. Jug
3945	5 oz. Tumbler
3965	Squat Jug
3903	Jam Set
3803	Mayonnaise Set
2819	6½" Square Plate
3910	11" Square Plate

125

HOW IT'S MADE

Crest ware is that glass which has an edging of a different color. The edge is put on the basic form by a very skilled craftsman, whose ticklish job requires that he apply an equal amount of glass all the way around the edge, using only his sure hand and eye.

Overlays are cased glass. First, a small blob of colored glass is gathered on the end of the blowpipe. Then, a layer of another kind of glass is gathered over this. The blower forces a "puff" into the gather, and the two kinds of glass are fused together and worked as one piece from there on.

On a handled piece, a small gob of molten glass is gathered from the furnace, warmed in a glory hole, and carried to the handler to be applied to a glass piece. The handler presses one end of it to the body of the piece, cuts off the desired length, loops it deftly until the other end is in its proper place, then swiftly shapes it until it is hard enough to hold its graceful curve.

Crests and Overlays

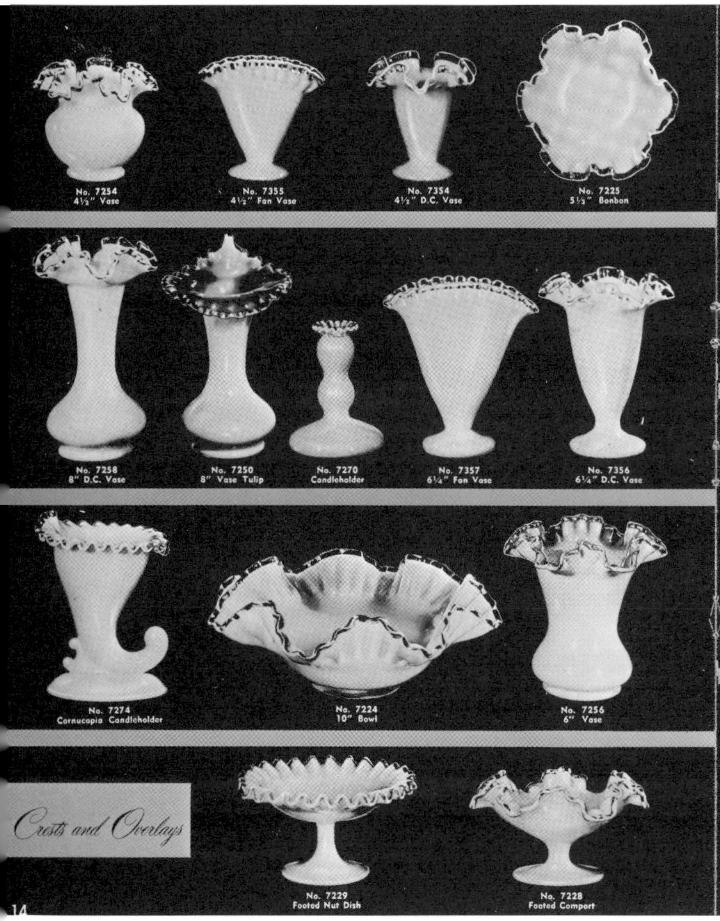

No. 7254
4½" Vase

No. 7355
4½" Fan Vase

No. 7354
4½" D.C. Vase

No. 7225
5½" Bonbon

No. 7258
8" D.C. Vase

No. 7250
8" Vase Tulip

No. 7270
Candleholder

No. 7357
6¼" Fan Vase

No. 7356
6¼" D.C. Vase

No. 7274
Cornucopia Candleholder

No. 7224
10" Bowl

No. 7256
6" Vase

Crests and Overlays

No. 7229
Footed Nut Dish

No. 7228
Footed Comport

14

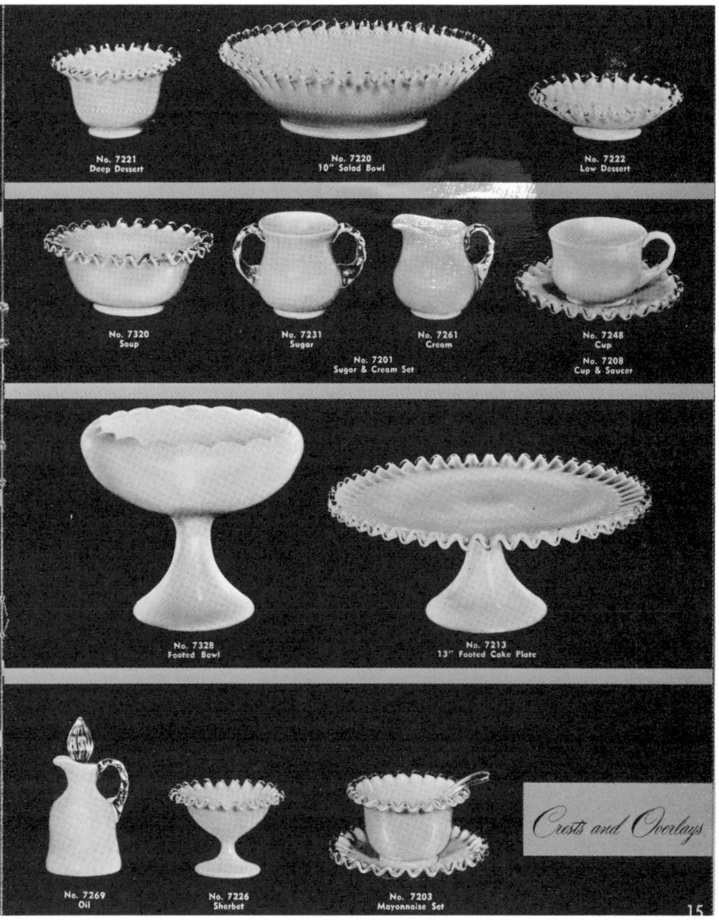

No. 7221
Deep Dessert

No. 7220
10" Salad Bowl

No. 7222
Low Dessert

No. 7320
Soup

No. 7231
Sugar

No. 7261
Cream

No. 7201
Sugar & Cream Set

No. 7248
Cup

No. 7208
Cup & Saucer

No. 7328
Footed Bowl

No. 7213
13" Footed Cake Plate

No. 7269
Oil

No. 7226
Sherbet

No. 7203
Mayonnaise Set

Crests and Overlays

15

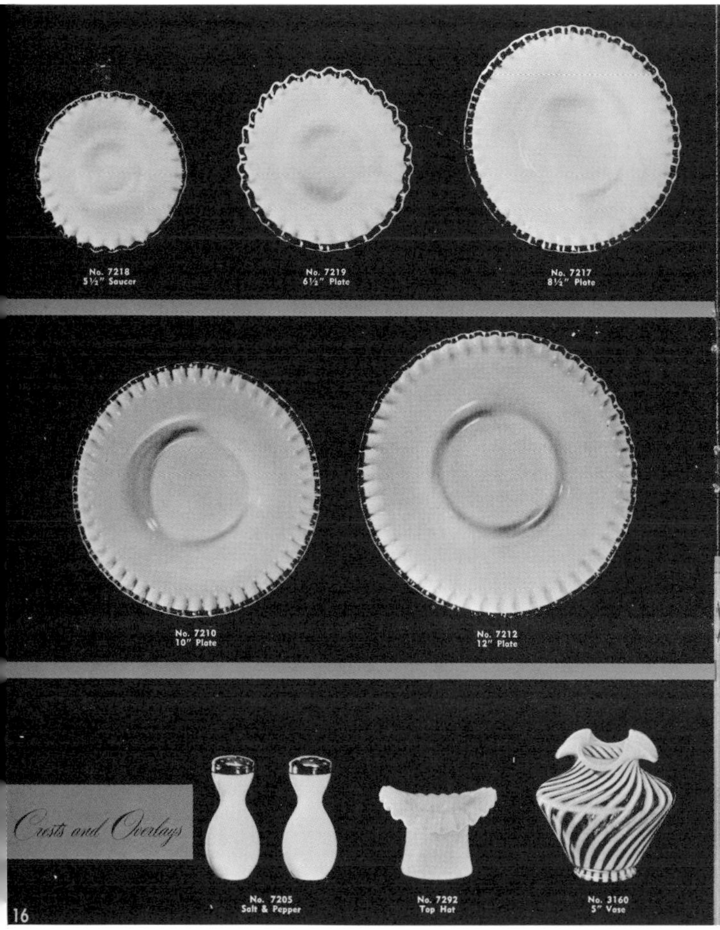

No. 7218
5½" Saucer

No. 7219
6½" Plate

No. 7217
8½" Plate

No. 7210
10" Plate

No. 7212
12" Plate

Crests and Overlays

No. 7205
Salt & Pepper

No. 7292
Top Hat

No. 3160
5" Vase

16

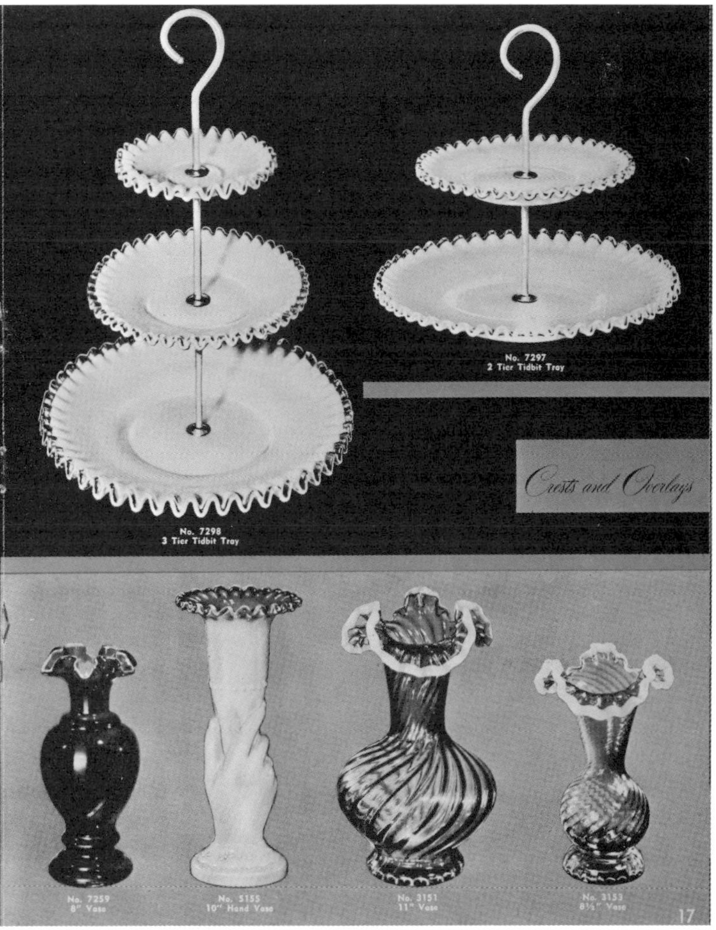

No. 7298
3 Tier Tidbit Tray

No. 7297
2 Tier Tidbit Tray

Crests and Overlays

No. 7259
8" Vase

No. 5155
10" Hand Vase

No. 3151
11" Vase

No. 3153
8½" Vase

17

1953-54 Catalogue

HOW IT'S MADE

The basic pattern mold for all Coin Dot pieces is called a spot mold. By skillful construction of this mold, the pattern is formed in the glass. Feel the inside of a Coin Dot piece, and you will find there is a hollow at each transparent area. Look through it, and you'll see an interesting optical effect—six dots on the far side making a daisy pattern inside each near dot.

Certain kinds of glass, when allowed to cool slightly, will turn white or cloudy if reheated. This is the "secret" of Coin Dot—the parts which you see as white are cooled briefly and warmed again at the "glory hole" in an operation requiring about as much instinctive skill and judgment as anything you can imagine.

French Opalescent and Blue Opalescent glass can be made to turn Opaque. To make Cranberry and Lime Coin Dot, a colored bubble of Gold Ruby or Green is blown inside a gather of French Opalescent, giving you a piece that is actually two layers of glass fused together—clear glass on the inside, opaque glass on the outside. This is called cased ware.

Fenton is the only manufacturer in America making gold ruby glass. This is the glass used on the inside of all Cranberry pieces, and it requires the addition of coin gold to the glass batch. When first made, gold ruby glass is a pale green in color—like magic, reheating turns it to a rich ruby red. Blowing stretches it thin, until it takes on the soft glow you see in Cranberry and Peach Crest.

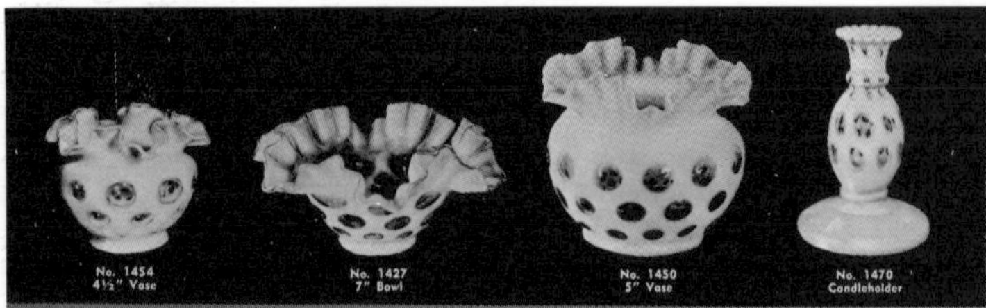

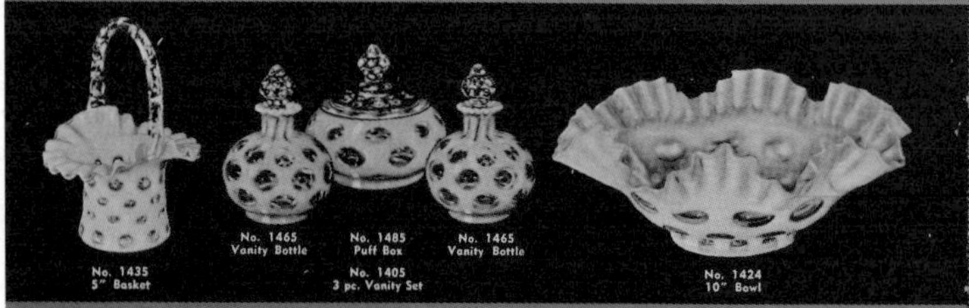

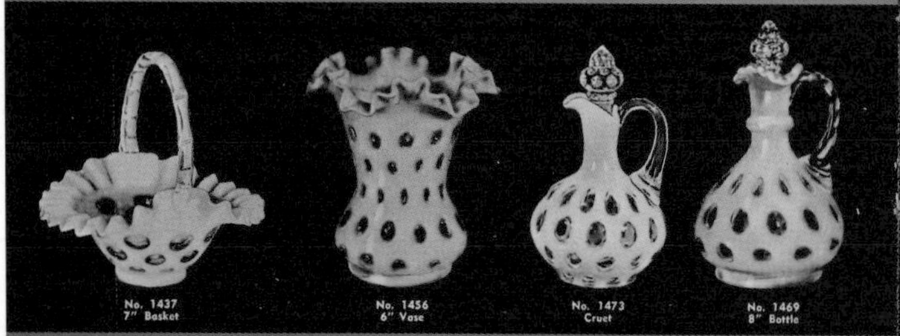

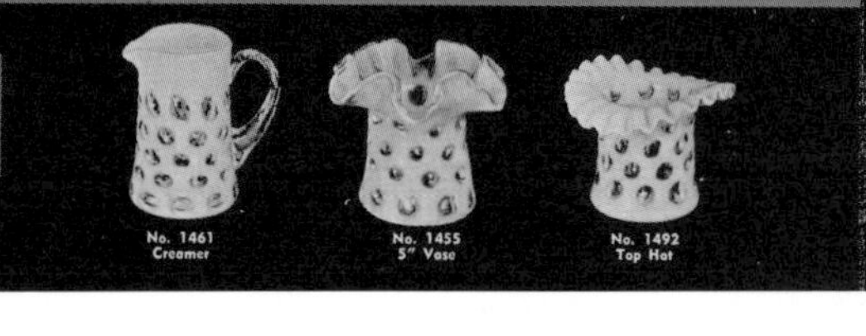

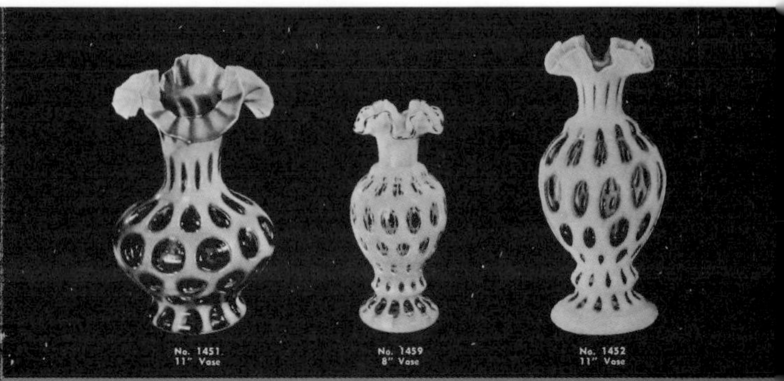

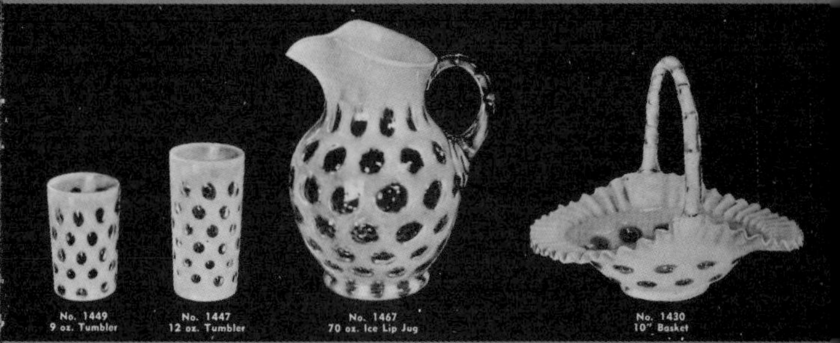

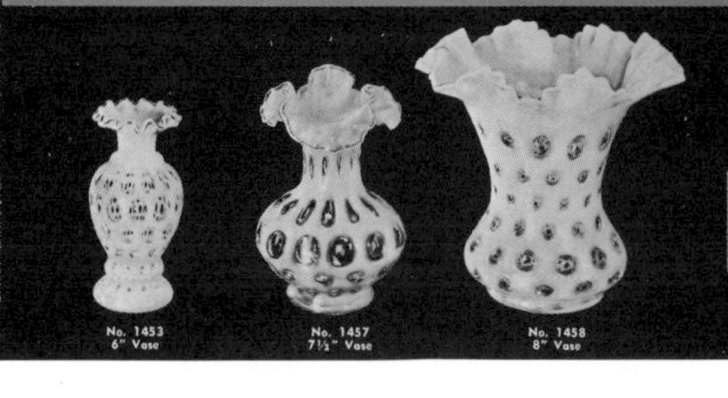

Coin Dot

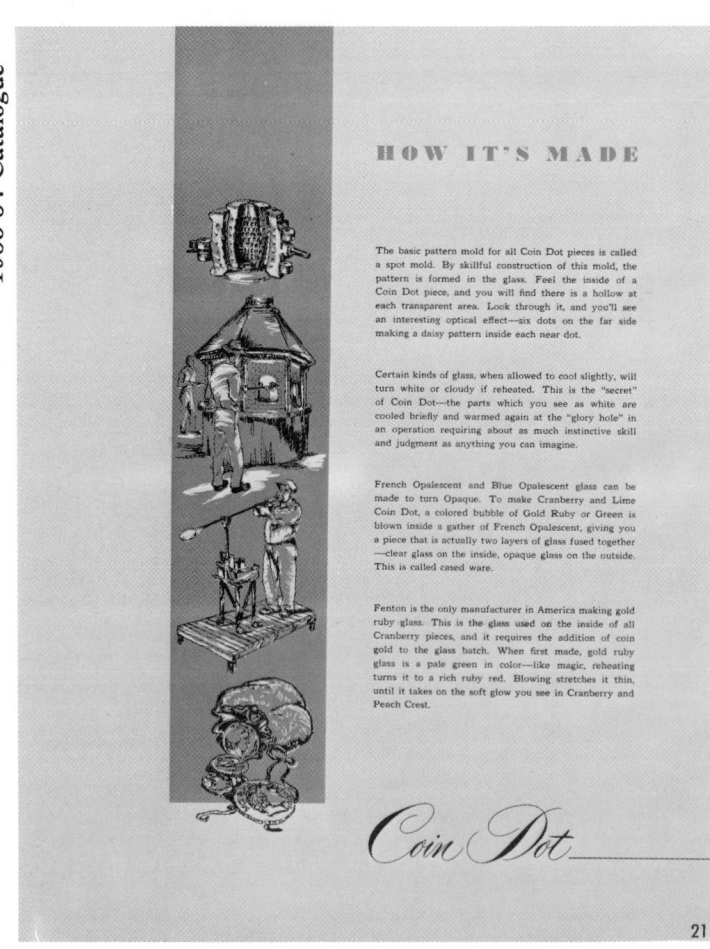

HOW IT'S MADE

The drawing at the left shows the cast iron mold used in making Fenton's lacy edge "Backward C" plate. It took a skilled mold-maker hundreds of hours to cut the intricate and delicate pattern into the mold. The upper half of the mold is called the "Ring" and must fit and match the lower half of the mold exactly.

With a snip of his shears the "Presser" cuts the right amount of glass from the gather. He pushes the mold beneath the plunger in the background and pulls the lever on his press, applying just enough pressure to force the glass throughout every part of the mold into the "Backward C" pattern.

The "Presser" is an expert with years of glassmaking knowledge. No machine could match his knowledge. He knows, by the feel, that this glass filled mold may require more pressure than the last one. Just enough glass—just enough pressure—and just enough time—is the secret of fine Fenton Handmade Glass.

After a few seconds cooling while still in the mold, the mold is turned over—permitting the finished piece of glass to drop out of the mold onto an asbestos paddle.

Every step in making this beautiful Fenton plate has been by hand . . . Handmade all the way!

This 'n That

No. 1858 8" Vase — No. 1658 8" Vase — No. 1758 8" Vase — No. 9020 10" Shell Bowl

No. 2063 Cruet — No. 1857 7½" Vase — No. 1657 7½" Vase — No. 1757 7½" Vase — No. 1352 8½" Vase

No. 1863 Cruet — No. 1663 Cruet — No. 1763 Cruet

Satin

25

No. 1656 6" Vase — No. 1756 6" Vase — No. 5508 Cigarette Set

No. 9078 Ash Tray — No. 5875 Club Ash Tray — No. 5876 Diamond Ash Tray — No. 5889 Cigarette Box, No. 5808 5 pc. Canasta Ciggrette Set — No. 5877 Heart Ash Tray — No. 5878 Spade Ash Tray

No. 2098 Hurricane Lamp — No. 2083 Candy Jar — No. 9002 Clusterettes

This 'n That

No. 2090 Electrified, No. 2092 With Candleholder Fairy Lamp — No. 2005 3 pc. Vanity Set

No. 4808 Epergne Set — No. 4801 Epergne Set

No. 5197 Bird — No. 7299 Pot and Saucer

No. 9029 Footed Comport — No. 4802 Epergne Set — No. 9013 Footed Plate

This 'n That

No. 4825 Comport — No. 4874 Low Candleholder — No. 4824 9½" Bowl, No. 4804 3 pc. Console Set — No. 4874 Low Candleholder

27

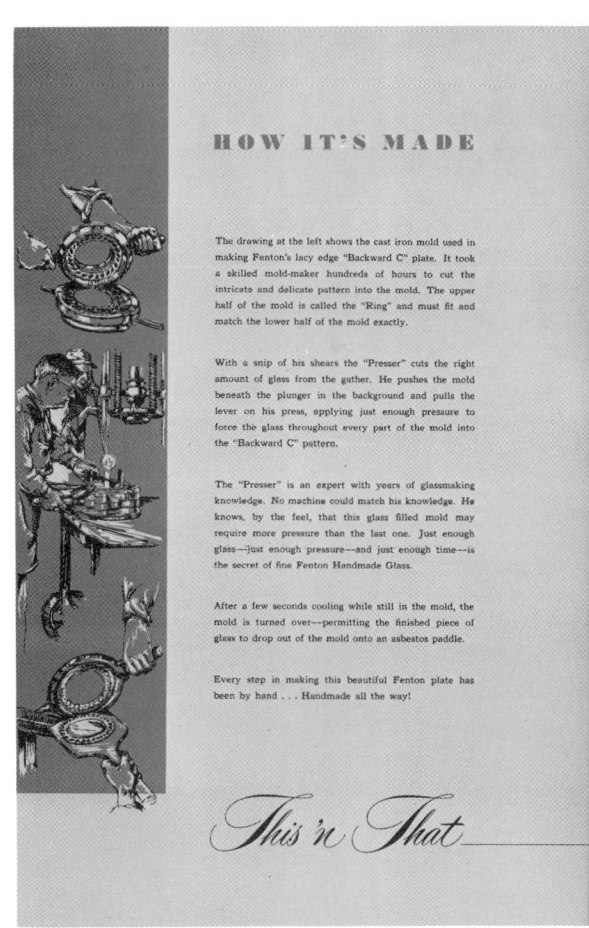

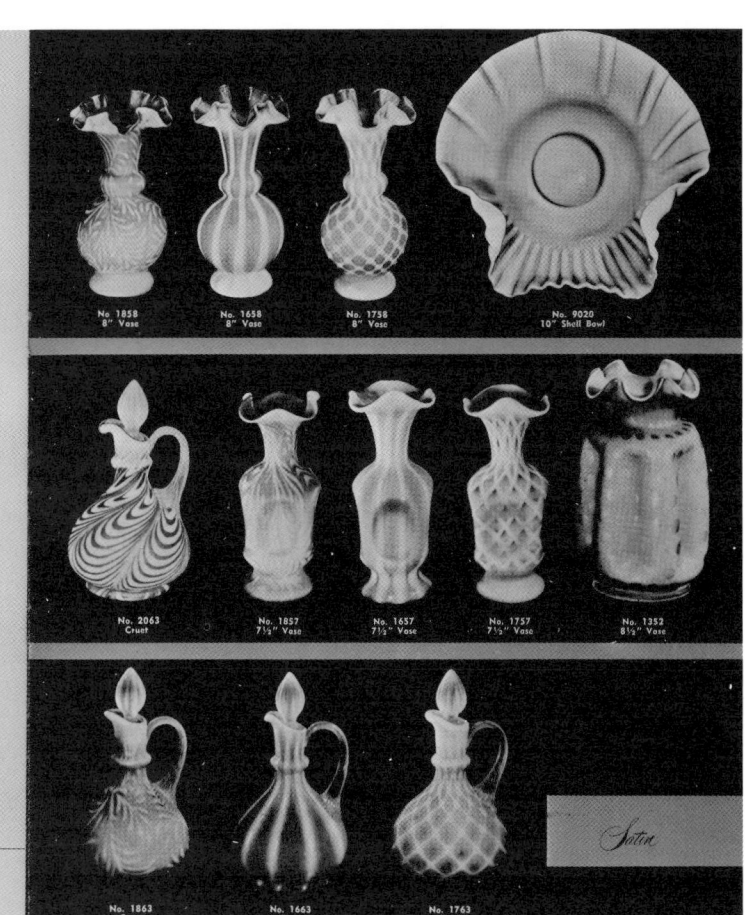

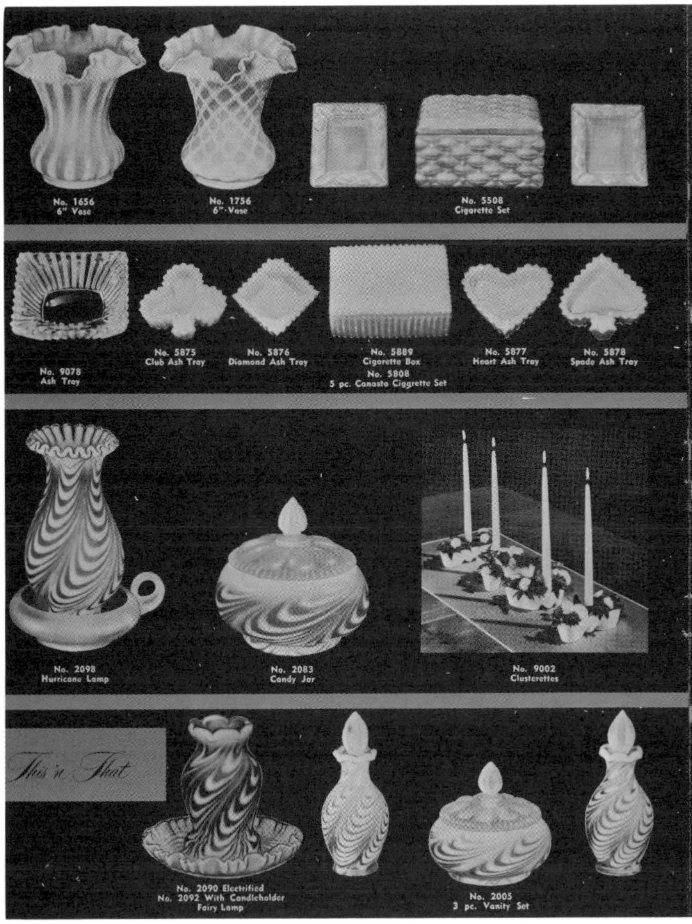

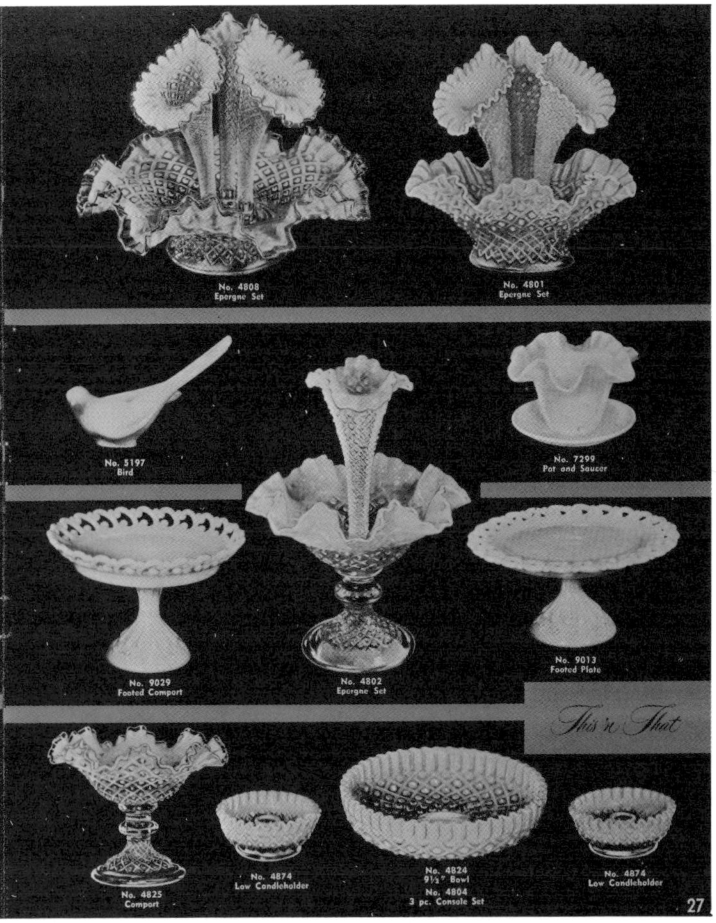

1953-54 Catalogue

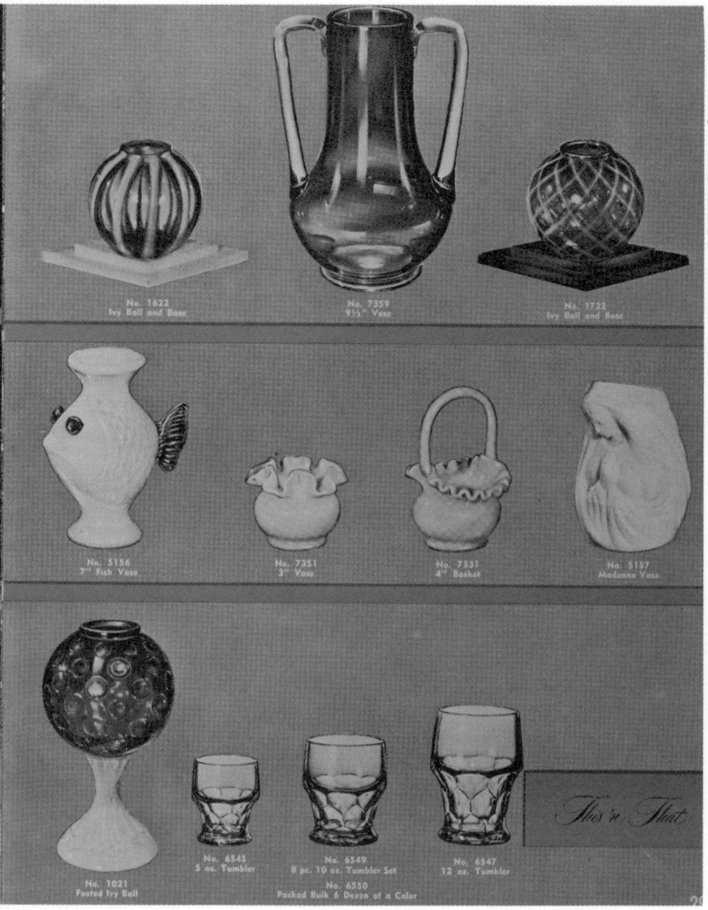

- No. 5595 Planter Bookend
- No. 9018 8" Plate
- No. 9019 9" "C" Plate
- No. 9099 "C" Plate Planter
- No. 5182 (White Body) / No. 5183 (White Head) Hen on Basket
- No. 9011 11" Plate
- No. 9028 Footed Comport

This 'n That

- No. 5185 Chick
- No. 5188 (White Body) / No. 5189 (White Head) Chickenserver

1955 Supplement

- No. 1622 Ivy Ball and Base
- No. 7359 9½" Vase
- No. 1725 Ivy Ball and Base
- No. 5156 7" Fish Vase
- No. 7351 3" Vase
- No. 7331 4" Basket
- No. 5157 Madonna Vase
- No. 1021 Footed Ivy Ball
- No. 6545 5 oz. Tumbler
- No. 6549 8 pc. 10 oz. Tumbler Set
- No. 6530
- No. 6547 12 oz. Tumbler

This 'n That

1953-54 Catalogue

- No. 1993 #3 Hat
- No. 1992 #2 Hat
- No. 1991 #1 Hat
- No. 1994 Bootee
- No. 1995 Slipper
- No. 1936 6" Basket
- No. 1934 4" Basket
- No. 1935 5" Basket
- No. 1937 5½" Bonbon
- No. 1956 6" Vase
- No. 1929 9" Bowl
- No. 1927 7" Bowl
- No. 1957 8" Cupped Vase
- No. 1958 8" Vase
- No. 1959 8" Fan Vase

Daisy and Button

- No. 1903 Sugar & Cream Set
- No. 1953 3" Vase
- No. 1954 4" Vase
- No. 1974 2-Lite Candleholder
- No. 1920 10½" Bowl
- No. 1904 3 Piece Console Set
- No. 1974 2-Lite Candleholder

Daisy and Button

130

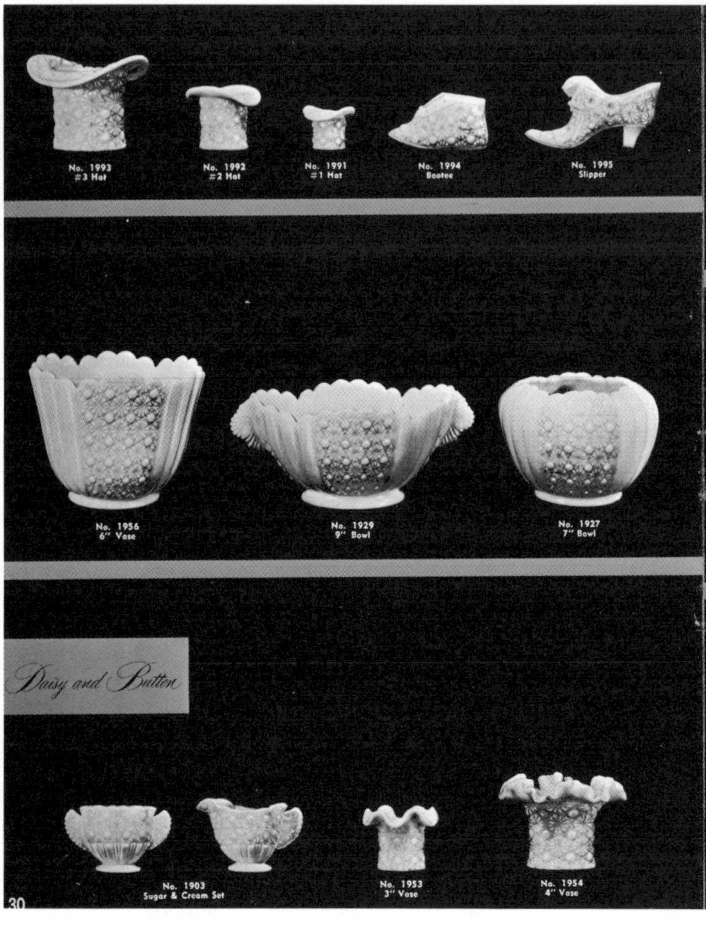

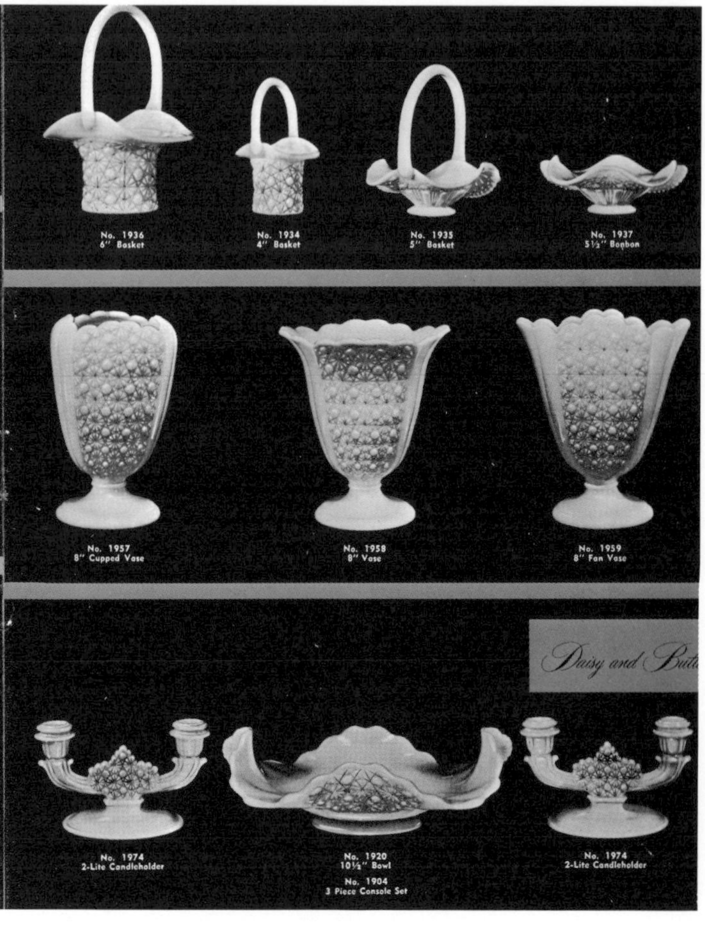

January 1954 Supplement

131

Circa 1951

No. 489
Hat

No. 489
Witch's Kettle

No. 489
Cup

No. 3003
6" Vase
Also in 7" Size

No. 3001
7" Vase

No. 3001
5" Vase

The Fenton Art Glass Company

30

July 1954 Supplement

No. 4381 Candy Jar
No. 4306 Salt and Pepper
No. 4301 Sugar & Cream Set
No. 4303 Mayonnaise Set
No. 3255 5" Vase
No. 4369 Oil Bottle

No. 7353 6" Vase
No. 7302 Bathroom Set
No. 3977 ½ lb. Covered Butter
No. 3253 6" Vase
No. 7348 6" Bud Vase

No. 4808 Epergne Set
No. 7295 3 Tier Tidbit Tray
No. 7294 2 Tier Tidbit Tray
No. 3252 8" Vase
No. 7349 6½" Bud Vase

SEE THE COMPLETE LINE OF FENTON HANDMADE GLASS AT THE SUMMER AND FALL GIFT SHOWS.

IN ATLANTA
 LES L. HOLLOWAY
 125 Ellis St. NE and
 Municipal Auditorium

IN CANADA
 A. W. DEWEY & SONS
 Brighton, Ontario

IN CHICAGO
 MARTIN M. SIMPSON & CO.
 1562 Merchandise Mart

IN DALLAS
 THOMAS AND MOORE
 322 Second Unit
 Santa Fe Building

IN LOS ANGELES
 MacLENNAN SALES CO.
 Room 308-712 South Olive

IN NEW YORK
 HORACE C. GRAY CO.
 200 Fifth Avenue

OTHER REPRESENTATIVES:

CARL VOIGT
 Henrietta, N. Y.

A. S. BELL
 1355 Market St.
 San Francisco, California

ALAN W. SYMMES
 Chelmsford, Massachusetts

L. R. WULF
 528 Hennepin Ave.
 507-13 Merchandise Bldg.
 Minneapolis 2, Minn.

HOWARD GIBB
 Riverton, New Jersey

E. R. WADLINGTON
 209 Terminal Sales Bldg.
 Seattle, Washington

HARRY HYMAN & SON (Export)
 254 W. 54th Street
 New York 9, N. Y.

M. G. VanAUKEN (Industrial)
 3040 Sunset Boulevard
 Los Angeles 26, Calif.

FACTORY SHOWROOM
Williamstown, W. Va.

THE FENTON ART GLASS COMPANY

Fenton Glass

RESENTS...

THE NEW HOBNAIL LAVABO, a useful and ornamental wall planter embodying old world charm in a new world setting, and made by craftsmen with over half a century's experience. This lovely piece of handmade ware will become your suggestion to a discriminating buyer who is looking for something unique and indicative of thoughtful selection.

Also shown are 14 new pieces designed from our experience of what has proved steadily salable. Our new cased Lilac is shown here for the first time.

July-1955
Catalogue Supplement

AD AND CATALOGUE REPRINTS

The reprints on this and the next page were found in an old design scrapbook kept by Frank L. Fenton, from which ideas for Fenton designs could be developed. This massive volume covered a period of over ten years, circa 1932 to 1945, and contained hundreds of clippings from magazine and newspaper advertisements. Among them were a few Fenton ads, unfortunately undated, which we are sharing with you here.

(Left) The punch bowl shown here appears to be a SHEFFIELD pattern set, but there is no record in the inventory to validate that such a set was ever made by Fenton. Perhaps Frank L. got his idea for the design from this set.

Early newspaper advertisement which featured Fenton's DAISY AND BUTTON vanity set in crystal, which retailed for $1.50. This ad dates around 1938.

Illustrated here are a number of items offered by Abels, Wasserburg and Co. of New York. It was called their Charleton line, hand decorated, and can be found today sometimes with original paper labels. The vase and vanity set are Fenton items, whereas the three jar "bathroom set" may or may not be Fenton. The remaining three items are definitely not Fenton, and appear to be made of china. This early advertisement apparently dates around 1942, based on the vase in CRYSTAL CREST.

(Left) Pictured here is an early Advertisement found in a 1940 issue of Ladies Home Journal, which pictures the original Wrisley Hobnail cologne, and offers suggestions for its use after the contents have been used. Note the original wooden stopper. This stopper was later replaced by a round milk glass stopper by the new manufacturers.

• Unusual in theme is the design of the bowl and double candlestick shown below. Just introduced by the Fenton Art Glass Co., this is a part of the "Viking" line, built on a figure-head motif. Other new Fenton designs are the "Pineapple" line of bon bons, console sets, candlesticks, candy boxes, and other items; the "Velvatone" etching, arbor decorations showing different tree motifs in bowls, covered jars, and vases; "Sung-ko," vases and bowls whose color effects are, like old Chinese pottery, as fire has made them with no two alike; the "Swan" console sets, bon bons, and other items, the body of the piece formed by the wings of the swan and the neck and head forming the handle.

(Above) If it wasn't for the Fenton scrapbook, we may never have known about the very rare VIKING line made around 1938. The ad is self-explanatory. Any collector can consider this console set a treasure. Production was undoubtedly limited, as it appears nowhere in the Fenton catalogues or inventory.

Miscellaneous Fenton

Historic America

In 1937 a representative from Macy's Department Store and its affiliates contacted Fenton about producing a line of glassware to accompany a line of dinnerware being promoted by Johnson Brothers (England). Fenton Glass Company complied with this request and created their HISTORIC AMERICA line of seven items, all illustrated here. This line was sold exclusively to Macy's and their affiliated stores, but did not sell well off the shelves, so the line was soon discontinued.

This quality line of glassware has the look and feel of much older glass and is sometimes found in antique shows at inflated prices. However the rarity and unique nature of this unusual table line gives HISTORIC AMERICA a special value all its own.

Pictured above is a close-up photo of the tiny cup plate depicting a scene of "MOUNT VERNON". It is quite rare and highly collectible. The other six items to this set, picture other historic scenes.

MISCELLANEOUS FENTON

Historic America

(Left) 5½" iced tea glass with scene of "BROADWAY, NEW YORK", complete with horse-drawn carriages and cobblestone streets; also 6" goblet depicting "CAPITOL AT WASHINGTON"

(Right) Almost 4½" tall wine or cocktail, with early scene of "FORT DEARBORN"; finger bowl with a covered wagon scene depicting "THE ROCKIES"; 4½" sherbert picturing "INDEPENDENCE HALL"

(Left) 8" plate picturing scene of "NIAGARA FALLS"

MISCELLANEOUS FENTON

Plymouth Pattern

(Left) 8 oz. PILSNER, 8" PLATE, 3 oz. WINE or COCKTAIL and GOBLET, all in quality crystal

(RIGHT) 7 oz. OLD FASHIONED, 2½ oz. WHISKY, and rare MUG, all in crystal

(Left) 8" PLATE, 8 oz. HIGHBALL, and 8 oz. PILSNER, all in French opalescent

MISCELLANEOUS FENTON

Fenton #1602 10¼" bowl with additional mold tooling to create a cluster of fruit at the front and back. Shown here in crystal—also known in Periwinkle blue (very rare). Dates circa 1935.

No. 1700 LINCOLN INN crystal match holder and salt shaker; No. 1800 SHEFFIELD jigger glass, also in crystal

No. 1935 whiskey and decanter in crystal; also made in a highball, a tumbler and a juice glass. Other colors made include amber, ruby and royal blue. Weatherman calls this FRANKLIN.

No. 1800 SHEFFIELD 6½" vase in stiegel blue, circa 1936

MISCELLANEOUS FENTON

(Left) Rare Fenton No. 6 Swan candlestick in blue opalescent, circa 1938. This item, and the other two shown on this page, are part of Fenton's limited Depression-era production of opalescent novelties.

(Right) Fenton #1533 dolphin-handled compote with crimped top in rare blue opalescent color. Probably dates from the depression era, when several molds originally used earlier were revived for limited production.

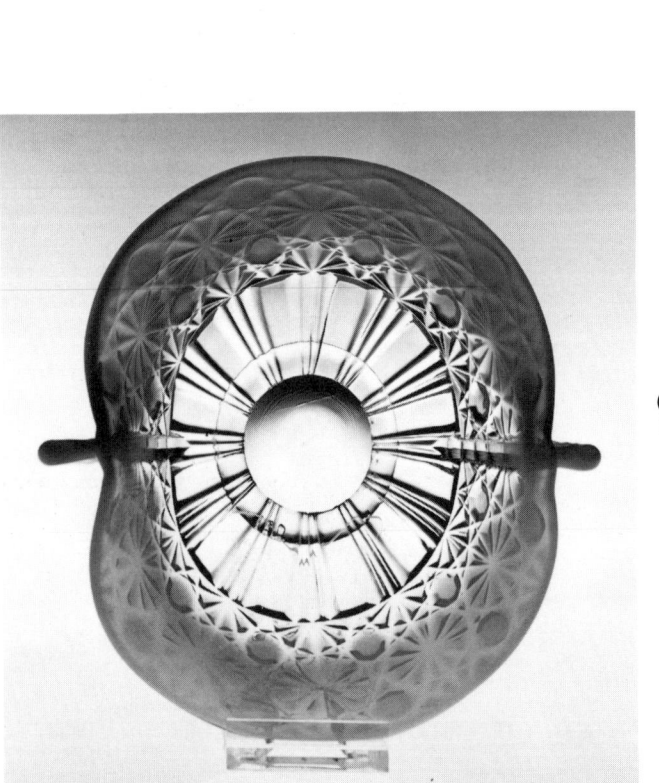

(Left) Fenton #1900 Daisy and Button handled bon-bon, circa 1938, in light blue opalescent.

(Left) Crystal Satin etched boudoir lamp, circa 1932. This same lamp can be found in other clear and opaque colors.

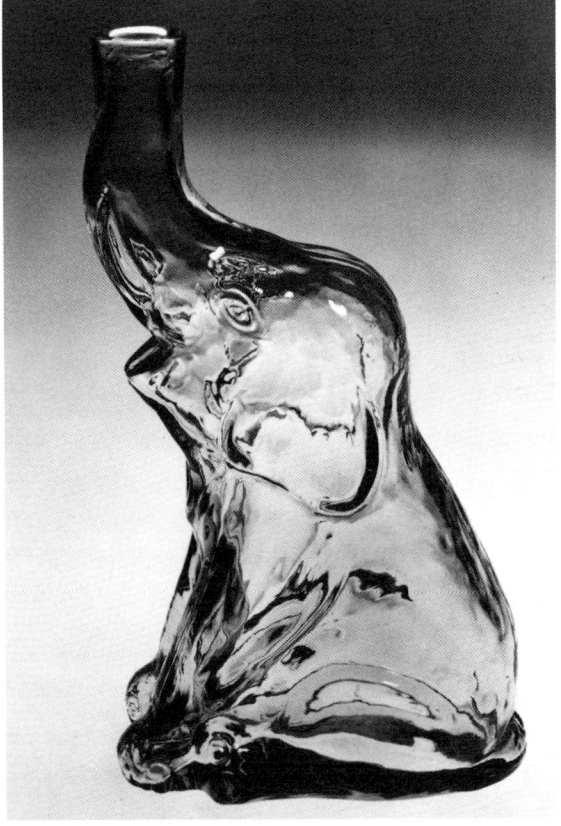

(Right) Rare crystal ELEPHANT bottle, made in Periwinkle blue in 1935. This whiskey bottle states on the base, "Federal Law prohibits the sale or reuse of this bottle"

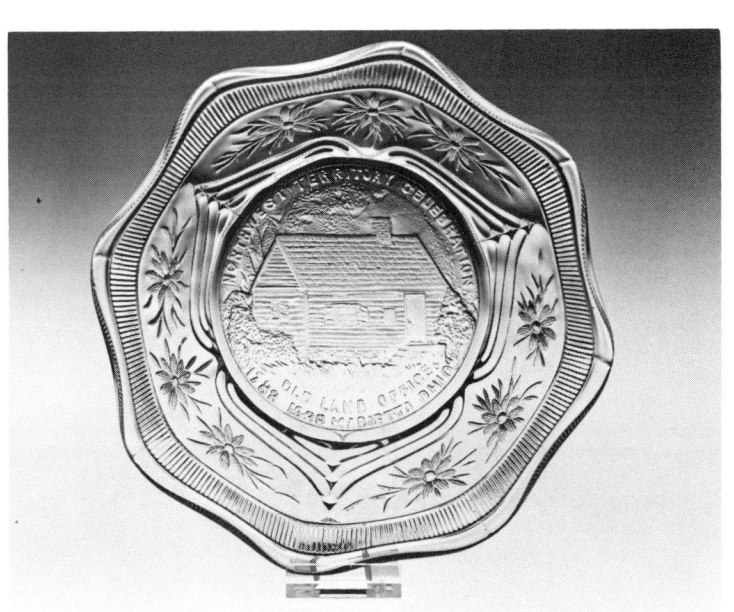

(Left) Rare commemorative 8" bowl depicting the old land office in Marietta, Ohio, as part of the "NORTHWEST TERRITORY CELEBRATION", 1788-1938. Obviously made in 1938.

(Left) No. 1043 one pound covered bonbon in Florentine green stretch. Not pictured in my first Fenton book, this same design comes in a half-pound size (No. 943) with a non-fluted stem. Also known in Velva Rose, this dates circa 1926.

(Right) Also not shown in Fenton 1, this small compote in Florentine Green stretch appeared on a catalogue page which had no numbers assigned to the items pictured. It appears to date circa 1925.

(Left) Fenton No. 250 Fern dish in Persian Pearl (white stretch), circa 1921. The Figures 362 and 388 bowls shown in the first book were actually Northwood. See next page for detailed photo which clearly shows the difference between the two.

Is it Fenton?

(Left) NO—This covered bon-bon is shown without the lid in my first Fenton book as the No. 250 fern dish, whereas it is actually Northwood's #706. See previous page for the real Fenton 250 fern dish.

(Right) MAYBE—We have no records to prove this divided ruby-amberina bowl was made by Fenton. The design at the edge of this bowl is almost identical to the SILVERTONE pressed line, and the deep ruby blending to a yellow-amber base is reminiscent of Fenton's color.

(Left) No—The GEORGIAN pattern was a popular design made by other companies other than Fenton, including Paden City and Cambridge. The Cambridge version is shown here for comparison, but it is easily identifiable by the C-in-a-Diamond trademark.

Is it Fenton?

(Above left) NOT CERTAIN—The tiny little Peacock is an almost perfect match in design to the No. 711 Peacock bookend. This "chick" is almost 2 ¾" tall. It is known in crystal (illustrated) and green satin. The mold design on the body and tail is identical to the known Fenton bookend. However, the heads and beaks are different. There are no records to indicate the smaller version is Fenton. Thus, attribution remains a mystery.

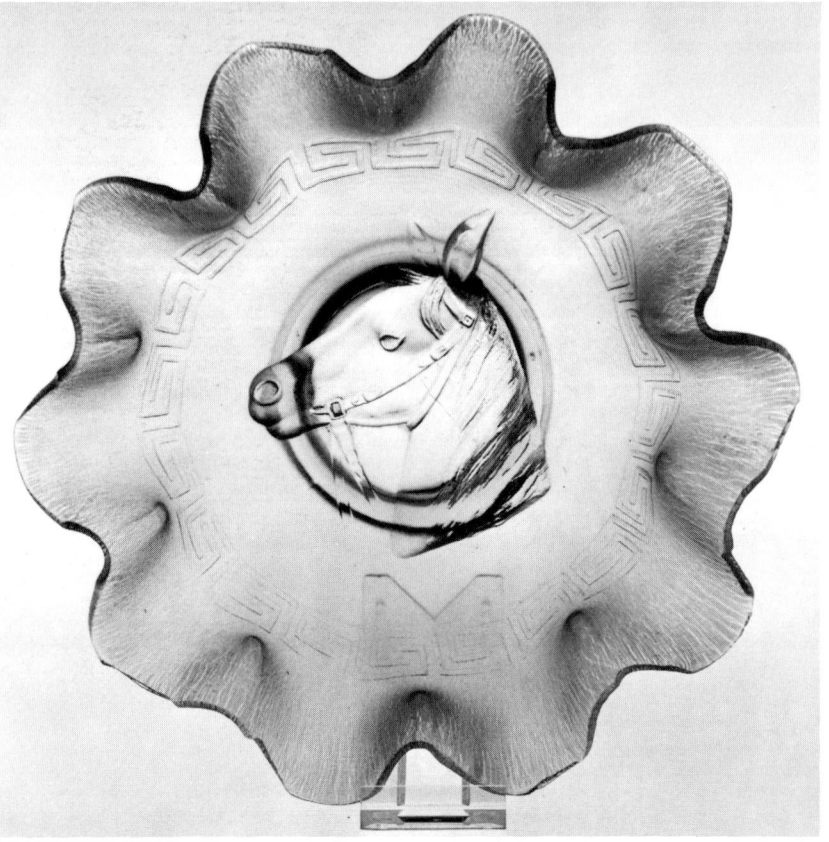

(Right) NO—We have a real mystery with the PONY bowl shown here. This bowl is known in carnival glass and stretch glass (illustrated). Note the unusual clipped edge on this bowl shown here, as if someone took shears and snipped off hunks of glass while it was still warm. The PLAID bowl, attributed to Fenton in my first book through Butler Brothers catalogues, is also known in stretch glass with this unique edge treatment. This Pony bowl would have been a possible Fenton design had I not found a shard in the pattern from the Diamond Glass-Ware Company dump site at Indiana, Pa. I had overlooked this shard in previous reports because it was so small. The color of the shard is pink stretch.

(continued from page 24)

advertising as far as the agencies were concerned, but it was a sizeable amount from the company's standpoint. After a year or so, a long look was taken at the results of the campaign. The books were checked and the salesmen consulted. It came out that there were now two choices: the company could either launch an all-out advertising program and forget about new design, or it could turn its attention to new design and postpone national advertising. The decision favored new design.

Design had been a problem for the young executives. It was an uncharted area since from the early days Frank L. and Robert C. had made all the decisions. Naturally in the changeover little new was offered in either design or color. In 1949 an apartment-sized epergne set in Coin Dot and Diamond Lace was added. A smaller Hobnail epergne set was made in French Opalescent, Blue Opalescent, and Milk. Coin Dot and Hobnail items in the familiar colors of French Opalescent, Blue Opalescent, and Cranberry were continued. Other colors used during the year were Silver Crest, Emerald Crest, Peach Crest, Aqua Crest, Ivy, and the Overlays—Blue, Green, and Yellow. A number of Milk glass items were in the line. The #192 melon-shaped items had a bead pattern worked into the design. The new number was 711, and the line was called Tiara, but it did not sell well. 1950 saw little change in production. The buyers' market remained and sales and earnings were at a low point.

In 1951 Frank M. and Bill made their first serious effort at new design. The new Priscilla pattern was in crystal, blue, and green, and the new Snow Crest pattern was in amber, green, and ruby overlay. The latter were transparent pieces with a spiral optic and a rim of opaque milk glass around the edges. Another newcomer was Square Hobnail tableware in French Opalescent. This consisted of 11 inch plates, small salad plates, and a cup squared off at the top. The line was a failure. While traditional Hobnail still sold well, the square product did not meet the public's fancy. The slump continued in 1952 as the industry remained in the doldrums. A four piece clusterette set was energetically promoted. Although it enjoyed some initial success, reorders were not numerous.

Bill Fenton (right) and the midwest sales force of FAGCO. The event was the 1948 Chicago gift show. This photo was taken at the Bismarck Hotel and pictures several buyers and sales representatives of Fenton glass at the time. Particularly important were Martin M. and Lew Simpson (second and third from left), Ted Figler (fifth from left) and Warren Hill (sixth from left), all associated with Martin N. Simpson Company.

Chapter Nine
A NEW BEGINNING

A troublesome problem facing the young Fenton brothers was that of labor relations. This stemmed from two sources: the general business decline and an industry-wide strike. Because of the business slowdown there was insufficient work to keep everyone fully occupied. Time was shared among skilled workers as in the Depression. The semi-skilled employees were furloughed by seniority. At length it became necessary to cut down the skilled work force, too, which the union contract permitted if economic conditions warranted it. Consequently, in September, 1951, Fenton permanently reduced the number of its hot metal workers, retaining only the best people and providing them with full-time work.

In the midst of these difficulties the one great industry-wide strike occurred. The union contract was negotiated annually between the AFGWU and the National Association of Manufacturers of Pressed and Blown Glassware at the joint Atlantic City conference. The union would convene in June, draw up its demands and present them to the manufacturers at its August meeting. As with most unions the AFGWU submitted an extravagant list of proposals which it never expected to be accepted, and then, as negotiations progressed, it would withdraw the more extreme ones. The Association usually countered with its minimal list, and then gradually a middle ground of compromise was reached.

But in 1950 it was different. For the only time in history there was no middle ground of compromise. The union's final demand included a ten cent hourly wage increase, two weeks' vacation instead of only one, and from three to six paid holidays. The Association's final offer called for a seven and one-quarter cent wage increase, two weeks' vacation only for employees with a minimum of five years on the job, and was silent on paid holidays. This offer was rejected by the union and orders were sent to the 9,000 members to pull out on Labor Day, Monday, September 4, 1950. Actually the strike affected only hand and combination plants in West Virginia, Pennsylvania, Indiana, Illinois, New York, and New Jersey. Combination plants were those which carried on both machine and hand operations. The straight machine plants did not strike because the companies involved acceded to the union's demands.

On September 4, the hand and combination plants closed down, which in Fenton's case meant the idling of 230 workers. Replying to a *Marietta Times* reporter, Frank M. Fenton said he had no idea what the outcome would be. He noted that pickets were parading around the plant, but that the attitude of the employees was friendly. In contrast to the 1936 dispute which led to a three-day walkout, this strike lasted 17 days. Moreover, it was industry-wide, not local. A majority of delegates from all the locals voted to strike, although the decision was by no means unanimous. There is some reason to think that many hand glassworkers favored accepting the Association's offer.

With no break in sight, the Federal Mediation and Conciliation Service induced union and Association officials to agree to another set of talks. Consequently, representatives of the two groups met in Cleveland on Tuesday, September 12. Frank Walsh, the federal mediator, urged a "general review of the situation," but the talks proved fruitless and everyone went home. It was reported that the Association was willing to accept the wage and vacation demands, but balked at paid holidays.

One reason for the union's intransigence was that its 90-man Executive Board was composed largely of machine plant men. Hand and combination plants were barely represented on the Executive Board. And since the union had already signed a profitable contract with the machine plants, it pushed aggressively for the same agreement with the hand and combination plants. Its spokesmen were cocky and bold and even insisted that if their demands could not be met, the whole hand glass industry should go out of business. It appeared to the Association's Executive Committee that the machine plant workers were trying to destroy the hand plant industry without even consulting the hand plant workers.

Playing into the hands of the union were sharp internal frictions among the Association's Executive Committee members. J. Raymond Price writes that "about half of them came from plants who foresaw increased business from their commercial customers and the other half faced a future darkened by increased competition from imports, plastics, and the Automatic Machine Plants." Even before the abortive talks in Cleveland, several companies, whose glass production was only incidental to their main operations; had pulled out of the Association, preferring local negotiations. After the Cleveland meeting, this secessionist trend became more pronounced. In all, 15 of the 42 hand plants in the Association exited at this time. Each withdrawal further weakened the Executive Committee's position, and the pressure to settle on the union's terms was soon overwhelming.

At length an Association meeting was held in Pittsburgh on September 19. The Indiana Glass Company, one of the major combination plants, withdrew from the group and acceded to the union demands. This broke the ranks of the manufacturers, as other companies in direct competition with Indiana abandoned the fight. The agreement was submitted to the union membership on the next day and accepted without debate. The strike was over. Telegrams were sent out to all the companies Thursday morning, September 21, and the first shifts reported for work later that day. FAGCO resumed operations on the second shift at noon. Furnace fires at the plant had been kept at low heat since September 4, but were turned on full blast Tuesday, shortly after the Pittsburgh meeting ended.

Ike Willard had been employed by Fentons for less than two months when the strike erupted. He recalled that during the 17-day shutdown two supervisors were on duty at the plant at all times. For example, he and Raymond Scott, a hot metal foreman, worked the midnight to seven a.m. shift. Their duties were primarily those of watchmen, to make sure that the temperatures of the pots and tanks were kept under control. The fires could not be put out because the pots and tanks would crack and be ruined. The temperatures could be lowered slightly — to 2200 degrees for the pots and 1400 for the tanks — but those were minimal points. Willard and Scott's chores were not exactly onerous, and there were many idle moments, but they enjoyed each other's company and for them the days and nights of the shutdown passed by rather quickly.

The 1950 strike had one important consequence for the Fenton company, namely, withdrawal from the National Association. Since World War II the machine and combination plants had gradually gained control of the industry and whatever they decided was binding on the hand companies. And frequently, as in the recent strike, what they decided was scarcely in the interests of the hand plants. The latter had been dragged into a two and one-half week strike which neither they nor their employees favored. As Frank M. Fenton said, "we were forced to give an increase which we felt was related strictly to the machine branch of the industry." Business was on the decline anyhow and this settlement was a further burden.

The 1950 contract was good for one year—that is until September, 1951—at which time another one year contract was negotiated. Scarred from the 1950 strike, the hand and combination plants this time accepted without a fight a settlement even more costly than that of 1950. But they had had enough. Fed up with machine worker domination of the union and weary of being forced into expensive agreements when their business was going down hill, the hand and combination plants began a general exodus from the Association. Fostoria Glass Company, whose president, Robert Hannum, had been a frequent target of union barbs as president of the Association, led the way. Hannum resigned his post of Association president on April 21, 1952, and pulled his company out. A number of other plants, including Fenton, soon followed Fostoria's lead and by June, 1952, only one hand plant—the Thatcher Glass Manufacturing Company— still belonged to the Association. It too would shortly quit.

What did withdrawal from the Association really mean? Its principal importance was that those companies which had withdrawn, rather than negotiating future contracts with the union's national officers on a collective basis, would deal with local union officials on an individual basis. In preparation for its separate negotiations, Fenton officials spent many hours devising a new wage contract, which would reflect their philosophy and yet meet union approval. Eventually, a document based on several excellent contracts then in force but modified to meet local needs, was drafted and submitted to union representatives. It was generally acceptable, but the union did insist on including the wage and move list drawn from the old contract. This was satisfactory to the company. It was also agreed that any other rule from the old book which either the union or the company might want included in any future contract, would be so included. In September, 1952, this new one-year contract went into effect.

Individual negotiations of union contracts proved a much better arrangement than the industry-wide talks of former times. One of several advantages, in Raymond Price's view, being that "hand employers are at least spared the humiliation and the contemptuous treatment they received from union negotiators in recent years." Still, a serious drawback remained.

The union did not like separate negotiations, being fearful that different rates might somehow be adopted in different plants. Wage uniformity throughout an industry always was a cardinal principle of unionism, but it was endangered where the negotiations were fragmented. On the other hand, the companies, while in no mood to placate the union in light of the latter's irritating behavior, were troubled because this apprehension in the union was an obstacle to smooth negotiations. The union did not necessarily want the hand plants to rejoin the Association, but they would like it much better if the hand plants could get together themselves and discuss contracts with the union as a unit.

Harry A. Cook, International President of the AFGWU, initiated discussions for a resumption of collective negotiations in a letter to all companies on May 6, 1953. His note, replete with protests of past cooperation and mutual devotion, argued that independent negotiations were more damaging to the companies than to the union. He pointed out that

> individual negotiations represent many disadvantages not only to us but, we believe, to the independent manufacturers as well. Certainly, there is a lot of lost motion and inefficiency which, if the independent manufacturers were organized for negotiation purposes, could be eliminated. It is our sincere belief that the disadvantages of separate negotiations are, in many ways, even more pronounced for the independent manufacturers than for the union.

The independent companies were cool to Cook's proposal, but he kept pushing it and by late summer the companies were willing to go along with it, with certain qualifications. Perhaps one reason for the companies' change of heart was that the union had peacefully negotiated a contract early in August, 1953, with a collection of independent companies engaged in manufacturing glass lamp globes and shades.

On August 11, 1953, 12 hand companies engaged in tableware manufacture, including Fenton, telegraphed Cook that they were ready to take part in group talks under the following conditions:

> ... that such [union] representation be limited to national officers of the AFGWU and workers directly and exclusively employed by the factories in attendance, that only financial matters and economic issues be discussed ... [and] that the various local contracts be continued except for changes negotiated and signed locally. The undersigned companies declare that they are not bound to attend any further meetings and that they do not consider or imply that their attendance at this proposed meeting is an agreement to meet in groups at any future time ...

Negotiations commenced at the Allerton Hotel in Cleveland on Monday, August 24, 1953, and an agreement was quickly arrived at, much similar to that agreed upon by the lamp and shade manufacturers earlier in the month. Since 1953 contract talks have been carried out in this way, with the tableware and lamp/globe companies each negotiating as a group with the AFGWU.

When the hand glass plants withdrew, they were greatly concerned over the fate of their contract records stored in the Association's Pittsburgh office. Reference to these documents was essential at wage talk time, and there was doubt whether they would have unrestricted access to them now that they had pulled out of the Association. Happily, the problem was quickly resolved. The key figure in the matter was J. Raymond Price, Secretary of the Association, who happened to be partial to the hand glass plants. With the approval of the Association, Price resigned his post as secretary in 1952, soon after the hand plant secession, and established his own corporation, the Industrial Service Bureau. He was allowed to take all the records of the hand factories with him, and he became, in effect, a consultant and adviser for those companies. Whenever contracts were discussed, or whenever problems over wage rates occurred, Price was brought in from his Pittsburgh office to supply his expert opinion. He performed a valuable service in this capacity for the hand plants.

* * * *

Perhaps more necessary than anything else at the time of the changeover was a fresh look at the Fenton business philosophy. The old order—Frank L. and Uncle Bob—built up the company in an unsophisticated age. Glassmaking skill was all important, while office management, bookkeeping procedures, and sales techniques were of secondary concern. But as the years passed by methods of business administration became highly developed, and some of the old casual practices no longer applied. The elder Fentons had put together a prosperous organization, but they were by nature conservative and wedded to the old way of doing things. After World War II when the European importers turned away, and when business conditions generally caused a slowdown in sales, certain changes became necessary. Many hand factories failed to adjust and went to the wall. Fentons' new leadership, however, recognized the need for a new departure and were ready to break with the past. In so doing they saved the company.

One example of this was the decision, described earlier, to drop the jobbers. This traditional sales machinery was no longer serving a real purpose, yet it is unlikely that the old order would have ever abandoned the system. So many close personal relationships were tied up with jobbing that Frank L. and Uncle Bob would have overlooked any financial disadvantages it might have created. But while the younger brothers had similar bonds with many of the old jobbers, they also understood the shortcomings of the system and the need to try something else.

Frank M. also came to the conclusion that the prices the company charged were not realistic. He had discussed with his father many times the methods used in determining the prices of the different products. He felt the prices were too low and did not properly reflect labor costs. Frank L. never agreed with Frank M. on this point, but after the former's death the new president decided to test his ideas on prices. Since sales were down and business declining in 1950-1951, it might have seemed a poor time to raise prices, but he went ahead anyhow. Gradual increases were instituted on those items thought to be most out of line, until in some cases the price was up 25 per cent. If the item stayed alive, good! If not, then it was better to drop it completely than to sell it for less than it cost. For example, milk glass, which had been selling at a loss, was pushed up drastically, but since its popularity was growing, it continued to move without interruption. In the end the price increases were justified. No catastrophic results followed and a much truer cost-price index was established.

An experiment with contemporary design in the early fifties proved unsuccessful. In 1952 Stan Fistick was employed by Fenton as the company's designer. There was much talk of contemporary glass at this time and FAGCO hired Fistick, a specialist in modern design, with the idea of entering the field. Modern cookie canisters were introduced that year, but they were difficult to produce and did not last long. The following year Fistick developed a number of contemporary items. These were delightful pieces and sold well at first, but then lost their appeal. After two or three years Fistick and the company became disillusioned at the poor sales of the contemporary items and dropped the experiment. Fistick entered the academic field while Fenton resumed its exclusive concentration on traditional lines.

Under the old regime, profit-and-loss statements were prepared only once a year. Occasionally, Frank L. was surprised to learn how well things had gone in the previous 12 months. This had to be changed and Frank M. went immediately to quarterly statements. This also proved inadequate and it was not long before the company had monthly profit-and-loss reports. It was found, further, that the plant's physical properties had not been appraised for almost 20 years. Regular appraisals were desirable on general principles, but one was needed at once for insurance purposes. The American Appraisal Company was hired to do the job, which gave rise to a flood of rumors that the new owners were going to sell out. Nothing was further from the truth, of course; the appraisal was simply long overdue.

A final consideration at the time of the change in control was the question of expansion. The older Fenton brothers had long contended that to expand was to invite disaster. Frank L. was firmly convinced that the only companies which survived the Depression were those that held the line on growth, while those which failed were the very ones which tried to grow. However, the younger brothers came to the conclusion that to stand still was to stagnate, and that if they hoped to continue in business in the highly competitive post-war years, they must expand.

* * * *

"We are sorry, but we simply cannot increase our wages, and we will not. If it becomes necessary for us to go along with this group and grant the increase, we will be forced to withdraw from the group and close our factory." W. L. Orme, president of the Cambridge Glass Company, was speaking before the joint company-union conference at Toledo, Ohio, in August, 1955. The proposed wage increase was granted and Cambridge Glass passed into history, another victim of the diverse economic and philosophical forces which struck hard at the hand glass industry after 1950. Richard Slavin, in his book "The Pressed and Blown

Glassware Industry," reports that some 16 hand plants went out of business in the fifties, and while perhaps a dozen companies were fighting their way through those difficult years, the future of the industry was not a promising one.

Why the bleak outlook? Various company executives blamed their troubles on the government's low tariff policies, but this was only part of the story. Slavin argued that some organizations simply dissolved when their owners died, while others—like Cambridge—were squeezed out under union pressures. A few more were victimized by natural disasters, and decided not to rebuild. An example of this was the United States Glass Company's plant at Glassport, Pennsylvania. A cyclone destroyed the structure and the company confined its future operations to its Tiffin, Ohio, factory. United States Glass then lost its Tiffin plant as a result of stock market manipulations. Consequently, death, labor disputes, and nature, as well as the tariff, all played a role in the high mortality rate of hand plants after World War II.

But the most important causes for failure were inadequate leadership and archaic business procedures. And nowhere was this more apparent than in the small, family-controlled plants. Slavin wrote that

> where families have been long in the industry, the leadership goes from father to son, the son serving his apprenticeship within the organization. While some scions have acquired the necessary managerial abilities, and have been quite successful in carrying on the business, others have failed to measure up to acceptable standards, usually at the expense of the enterprise.

The techniques of modern business management were more important than ever in the forties and fifties. Outmoded bookkeeping and accounting practices brought about the demise of more than one company. In 1959 one of the country's leading tableware producers went broke through an accounting blunder, wherein the inventory was listed at full market value. Another plant carried no depreciation allowances and following a minor fire, had no funds for repairs and was compelled to close. Other business shortcomings included the failure to develop new lines, obsolete pricing and distribution procedures, and the absence of glassworker training programs.

According to the Slavin formula for failure, FAGCO should have been one of the first hand glass companies to go. And the most appropriate moment for its leaving would have been right after the first generation died out. Business was declining, the new owners were young and inexperienced, and certain stockholders were losing faith. But Slavin also told us that a few family-controlled hand plants managed to survive by modernizing their outlooks and methods. The Fenton company is an outstanding example of an organization which broke with the past and pushed imaginatively ahead. The treacherous pitfalls which spelled the doom of so many other factories were scrupulously avoided. Skilled and professional administrators were hired to update business procedures, researchers went to work to develop new lines, skilled glassworkers were trained from within the company's own ranks, public relations were promoted through plant tours and a glamorous Gift Shop, new equipment and facilities were installed, and new buildings were built. FAGCO did not rest on its earlier reputation, good as that was, but it strove restlessly forward, testing every new idea, instrument, or procedure that might improve the company's product and administrative efficiency.

With respect to improving the product, the golden age of milk glass was at hand. Hobnail Milk began to develop in 1952, and the ivy balls of the twenties were re-introduced with Milk Glass bases and diamond optic, straight rib opalescent treatment. In 1953 the Daisy and Button items of the thirties were brought back in Milk Glass, accompanied by the new backward C plate and other open edge items which came into the line also in milk. Milk Glass sales were increasing as milk began to supercede the long established opalescent.

But patterns in other colors were also beginning to move well as the company's new leadership gained in knowledge and experience. Coin Dot remained a favorite. The #7110 shell bowl in satin finish was an attractive item, which remained in the line for a number of years. A new 13-inch footed cake plate in Silver Crest proved an excellent seller. In fact, during the trying years of 1951 and 1952 the Hobnail and Silver Crest lines helped significantly in keeping FAGCO in business. Another substantial source of business was in the supplying of private mold lamp parts, primarily in opalescent, to many lamp manufacturers.

The first fairy lamp, #2092RA in *Swirled Feather,* was introduced in 1953. It was made in a satin finish in Green Opalescent, Blue Opalescent, and Cranberry Opalescent. The #5197 bird in black and milk, made from a mold purchased in 1950 from the now defunct Paden City Glass Company, also entered the line at this time. A line of Georgian tumblers, popular in the thirties, was revived in 1953 in assorted colors. The Silver Crest line was expanded with the addition of a three tier tidbit tray. The new 1953 catalog advertised 45 different color combinations.

The product was becoming stronger and more varied. Although the industry as a whole was still having its problems, Fenton increased its sales and appeared to be doing better than most other companies. Only modest changes were made in 1954. The Swirl pattern in opaque pastel colors and Milk Glass was added, but was not well-received in those colors and discontinued. The Lamb's Tongue pattern entered the line in pastel colors, and the Cranberry Spiral treatment of the thirties was brought back in new vase shapes.

* * * *

While major renovations were not made until the late fifties and sixties, a number of minor improvements were undertaken in the early years of Frank M.'s presidency. The process by which raw materials were unloaded was overhauled in 1948-1949. Until this time the basic materials—sand and soda ash—were handled in a cumbersome fashion. Sand was stored in a large pit under the floor near the Number 2 lehr, about 35 to 40 feet from the railroad siding. When the boxcar came up to the unloading dock, a man would climb into it, shovel a wheelbarrow full of the stuff, roll the wheelbarrow over to the sand pit opening and dump the sand into the pit. When the area directly beneath the opening was full, the workman had to crawl down into the sand and shovel it into the pit area away from the opening to allow more room to dump in more sand. "A very inefficient, ineffective way of handling it," Frank M. Fenton reflected. Soda ash was stored in open bins above the floor level, so it was easier to handle than sand, but other factors made it more unpleasant to work with. Dust from the soda ash irritated the nasal passages and made breathing difficult, so it was never easy to obtain workmen to unload it. Occasionally, the company would use some of its own people, but generally it hired outsiders.

The new system utilized a track hopper, a bucket elevator, and silo storage, which eliminated all manual handling of the sand and soda ash. The hopper now permitted direct unloading through an opening in the bottom of the boxcar into a conveyor which took the material over to a bucket elevator and deposited it into the elevator. Two new silos were built, one for sand and one for soda ash, and the bucket elevator carried the sand or ash up to the top of the silos and deposited them into the appropriate one. Robert Armstrong of the Armstrong Tank Company of Williamstown designed and built the hopper and elevator, the first of a number of jobs he would do for Fenton. A new rotary-type mixer was installed at the same time and while it satisfied the company's immediate needs, it proved to have too small a capacity and was difficult to clean. It was replaced by a larger and better machine in 1963.

The "Rubel Room" was built probably in 1949 or 1950. A small concrete block structure on the west side of the factory along 4½ Street, it was originally designed to provide additional storage space. Just at the time it was completed, however, representatives from Rubel and Company of New York approached Fentons with an unusual proposition. Rubel had been buying a number of items from the Paden City Glass Company and "drop-shipping" them to their customers. But Paden City had just gone out of business and Rubel wanted to know if FAGCO would make for them the items which Paden City had formerly produced. "We'll bring our men down," the Rubel agent explained, "and if you will make the merchandise and give us some warehouse room, you can bill us as soon as you put it in the warehouse; it will be our responsibility to sell it." Fentons accepted the offer—"we were hungry for business"—and turned the new little warehouse building over to Rubel and it was henceforth known as the "Rubel Room." The Rubel connection continued for several years until rising prices made it no longer profitable for either party. The business had proved helpful to FAGCO, however, at a time when the hand glass industry was in the doldrums.

Little new construction or renovation was carried out after 1950 until 1957. The intervening years were difficult ones due to the passing of the old order and the industry-wide economic decline. These were the days when so many companies ceased operating. As Frank M. put it, "we were trying to make sure we didn't spend anymore money than we had to." All that the records show is the construction of the "Rubel Room" and a refractory shed, the opening of the Gift Shop, which remained quite primitive until its 1957 remodeling, and the erection of a wire fence around the property.

As the Fenton company entered its golden anniversary year, 1955, three new colors were added, Rose Pastel, Turquoise, and Cased Lilac. More and more items were switched to Hobnail Milk Glass, an increasing number of open edge pieces were coming out, and Silver Crest, Emerald Crest, and Peach Crest continued to do well. The major new piece of the year, Hobnail Lavabo, was introduced in the summer. The Block and Star pattern, a reproduction of the Hobbs, Brockunier, and Company pattern with elaborations by Fenton, was added to the line in Milk Glass and Turquoise.

By 1955 few pieces remained from the earlier years. Only one water pitcher, the two leaf plates, and the Georgian tumbler assortment were still retained from the thirties. From inauspicious beginnings during the Depression, Milk Glass had become Fenton's top product. Up until 1955 the company had been the number two supplier in Milk Glass and number one supplier in Opalescent Glass. It was on the threshold of becoming number one in both for dealers throughout the country.

* * * *

Fifty years had seen the Fenton Company grow from a two-man decorating shop in Martins Ferry into one of the finest art glass plants in the country. It had survived two world wars, one worldwide Depression, and a sharp decline in the hand glass industry itself. There had been changes in the product, the philosophy, and the leadership. A new start had been made and 1955 was the best year the younger Fentons had yet known. Now as the company faced the second half century of its history it was prepared to write an even more successful chapter than those which have gone before.

CORRECTIONS AND ADDITIONS

Research of **any** type is an ever-changing endeavor, especially in the case of glass. Listed below are a number of corrections and additions to the text of FENTON GLASS—THE FIRST TWENTY-FIVE YEARS. Some were light typographical errors, others were brought to light by continued research efforts, and a few are unexplainable mistakes. But most are simply additions to the text which we feel are important to the truly informed collector of early Fenton glass.

FIGURE 46	There is a difference between the BUTTONS AND BRAIDS water pitchers made by Fenton and Jefferson. See the catalogue reprint on page 103 for better detail. There are five "C's" or leaves on the vine-like scroll at the center of the pattern. On the Jefferson variant of this pattern there are seven of those "C's". Fenton did not make this pitcher in cranberry.
FIGURE 55	This FENTON BASKET nappy was also made as late as 1937
FIGURE 100	I failed to mention this same bowl was made with a plain interior. Thus the BUTTERFLY AND BERRY master berry bowl can be found with five different interiors.
FIGURE 123-124	APPLE TREE is Fenton's #1561 pattern—this is a misprint
FIGURE 136-137	The "Cannonball" pitcher is Fenton's #821 mold, not #1576
FIGURE 214	WATER LILY is Fenton's #1804, not #1807
FIGURE 318	There is a distinct possibility that this mystery bowl was made by Dugan or Diamond Glass Company, Indiana, Pa. We now know that this firm copied many of Northwoods best-selling patterns, including **Grape and Cable** and **Peacock at the Fountain.**
FIGURE 323	The color of this set is Celeste Blue, not Wisteria
FIGURE 362	This is not Fenton. It is the base to Northwood's #706 covered bon-bon. Notice the difference from the actual #250 Fern dish shown at the top of page 86.
FIGURE 388	The same is true of this bowl—it is Northwood's #706
FIGURE 408	This may be the color Fenton called AZURE BLUE
FIGURE 418	This should be Fenton's #1608—a misprint
FIGURE 437	This is definitely Fenton—the archives include a mold drawing and a statement from the mold maker that Fenton sampled it
FIGURE 490	Misspelled the word coasters
FIGURE 491	This color may be what Fenton called VICTORIA GREEN
FIGURE 496	This color may be what Fenton called VICTORIA TOPAZ

INDEX

Listed below are major Fenton patterns, colors and specialty items (i.e., lamps) and corresponding page numbers where illustrations can be found. I have not listed vague categories, such as vases, or lengthy production colors like blue opalescent. Pattern names are listed in italics.

Apple Tree, 50, 59
Aqua Crest, 47, 61, 100, 112-113
Azure Blue, 86

Beaded Melon, 42, 51, 59, 61, 115
Beatty Rib (repro), 50
Beatty Waffle (repro), 50, 57, 61
Black Rose, 48, 61, 123, 126
Blackberry Banded, 64
Block and Star, 50, 51, 58, 77
Blue Overlay, 41, 5, 112-113
Blue Ridge, 53, 71
Boggy Bayou, (vase) 64

Chinese Yellow, 29, 59
Clusterettes, 64, 121
Coin Dot, 25, 53, 55, 56-5, 77, 80, 104-106, 122, 128
Crystal Crest, 49, 134

Daisy and Button, 34-36, 50-51, 57-58, 60, 6, 81, 89, 96, 130, 134, 140
Dancing Ladies, 29, 31, 40, 86, 96
Diamond Lace, 46, 110-111, 129, 132
Diamond Optic, 25, 30, 32, 34, 36, 59, 74, 80, 120, 122, 129-130
Dot Optic, 55-56, 64, 97
Drapery, Fenton, 62, 63

Ebony, 28, 62
Elephant (Bottle), 27, 141
Elephant (Flower Bowl), 28-29
Emerald Crest, 47, 61, 80, 133

Fern (Opalescent), 122
Fish Vase, 50, 61, 123, 130
Fenton Basket, 28, 96
Flame, 26
Franklin, 139
French Opalescent, 53

Georgian, 30, 32-34-35, 50, 77, 82, 130, 143
Gold Crest, 49
Gold Overlay, 59, 75
Grape and Cable, 63, 86
Green Overlay, 42, 75
Green Pastel, 58

Halo (etched), 39
Hand vase, 53, 64, 102, 127
Historic America, 136-137
Hobnail, 25, 43-46, 51, 58, 73-74, 76-80, 101-102, 107-110, 114, 120-121, 123-125, 131-132, 135

Idyll (vase), 64
Ivory Crest, 49, 71, 103
Ivy, 42, 116

Jade Green, 29, 59, 66, 87

Lamb's Tongue, 58, 61, 132
Lattice and Grape, 40
Lavabo, 133
Leaf Tiers, 50, 86
Leaf Tray, 31, 57, 77, 102, 133

Lilac, 58, 61, 129
Lincoln Inn, 29-30, 34, 40, 42, 60, 139

Mandarin Red, 26
Mikado, 28
Milk Glass, 50, 76-78, 96, 119, 121, 129, 133
Ming, 33, 38, 93
Mongolian Green, 27, 68
Moonstone, 50, 59
Mulberry, 36, 74

New England Pineapple, 116
New World, 123, 126

Orange Tree, 34, 63, 64

Panther, 62
Peach Blow, 48, 2, 99
Peach Crest, 48, 72, 74-75, 103, 113, 126
Peacock Bookend, 42, 144
Peacock vase, 26-27, 50
Pekin Blue, 41
Periwinkle Blue, 27
Persian Medallion, 64
Persian Pearl, 86
Pineapple, Fenton, 31, 40, 91, 95
Planter bookend, 35, 121, 130
Plymouth, 30, 35, 53, 83, 138
Poinsettia, 37, 91, 94
Polka Dot, 55, 78
Priscilla, 60, 118

Rib Optic, 53-54, 56-64-122-123, 126, 129
Ring (Opalescent), 53, 97
Rose Crest, 49, 61
Royal Blue, 32, 65
Ruby, 30-31, 87
Ruby Overlay, 52, 74, 113

San Toy (etched), 39, 92
Sheffield, 30, 35-37, 53, 90, 134, 139
Silver Crest, 49, 75, 112-113, 116-117, 126-127, 132
Silvertone (etched), 37, 91, 97
Silvertone (pressed), 35, 36, 88, 143
Snow Crest, 42, 60, 75, 80, 120, 127
Snow Fern, 93
Spiral Optic, 53-56, 57, 70, 91, 98-99, 127, 132
Swan line, 34-36, 40, 140
Swirled Feather, 25, 56, 61, 123, 129

Teardrop, 50, 58, 77, 133
Turquoise, 58, 78
Turtle (bowl), 60
Twin Ivy, 98

Velvatone (etched), 39, 94
Viking line, 135
Vintage, 64

Water Lily and Cattails, 64
Wide Rib (Opalescent), 97
Wistaria (etched), 38, 91-92

NOTES